Scalable Internet Architectures

Scalable Internet Architectures

Theo Schlossnagle

DEVELOPER'S
LIBRARY

Sams Publishing, 800 East 96th Street, Indianapolis, Indiana 46240 USA

Scalable Internet Architectures

Copyright © 2007 by Sams Publishing

All rights reserved. No part of this book shall be reproduced, stored in a retrieval system, or transmitted by any means, electronic, mechanical, photocopying, recording, or otherwise, without written permission from the publisher. No patent liability is assumed with respect to the use of the information contained herein. Although every precaution has been taken in the preparation of this book, the publisher and author assume no responsibility for errors or omissions. Nor is any liability assumed for damages resulting from the use of the information contained herein.

International Standard Book Number: 0-672-32699-X

Library of Congress Catalog Card Number: 2004092644

Printed in the United States of America

First Printing: July 2006

09 08 07 06   4 3 2 1

Trademarks

All terms mentioned in this book that are known to be trademarks or service marks have been appropriately capitalized. Sams Publishing cannot attest to the accuracy of this information. Use of a term in this book should not be regarded as affecting the validity of any trademark or service mark.

Warning and Disclaimer

Every effort has been made to make this book as complete and as accurate as possible, but no warranty or fitness is implied. The information provided is on an "as is" basis. The author and the publisher shall have neither liability nor responsibility to any person or entity with respect to any loss or damages arising from the information contained in this book.

Bulk Sales

Sams Publishing offers excellent discounts on this book when ordered in quantity for bulk purchases or special sales. For more information, please contact

U.S. Corporate and Government Sales
1-800-382-3419
corpsales@pearsontechgroup.com

For sales outside of the United States, please contact

International Sales
international@pearsoned.com

Acquisitions Editor	Shelley Johnston
Development Editor	Damon Jordan
Managing Editor	Gina Kanouse
Project Editor	Andy Beaster
Copy Editor	Geneil Breeze
Indexer	Larry Sweazy
Proofreader	Kathy Bidwell
Technical Editors	Alec Peterson, Kevin Murphy
Publishing Coordinator	Vanessa Evans
Book Designer	Gary Adair
Page Layout	Gloria Schurick

 The Safari® Enabled icon on the cover of your favorite technology book means the book is available through Safari Bookshelf. When you buy this book, you get free access to the online edition for 45 days. Safari Bookshelf is an electronic reference library that lets you easily search thousands of technical books, find code samples, download chapters, and access technical information whenever and wherever you need it.

To gain 45-day Safari Enabled access to this book:

- Go to http://www.samspublishing.com/safarienabled
- Complete the brief registration form
- Enter the coupon code CPA9-NUSB-2JMG-ZYCT-DM8Q

If you have difficulty registering on Safari Bookshelf or accessing the online edition, please email customer-service@safaribooksonline.com.

❖

This book was made possible by the endless devotion and encouragement from my wife, Lisa, and the intoxicating cheer and innocence of my children, Zoe and Gianna.

❖

Contents at a Glance

Table of Contents

About the Author

Theo Schlossnagle is a principal at OmniTI Computer Consulting, where he provides expert consulting services related to scalable internet architectures, database replication, and email infrastructure. He is the creator of the Backhand Project and the Ecelerity MTA, and spends most of his time solving the scalability problems that arise in high-performance and highly distributed systems.

Acknowledgments

Like all books, the efforts that created this text are not solely from the author listed on the cover. Help comes in a variety of forms, from adversity to editing.

I'd like to thank my family for being so supportive throughout the writing process; without them I would have been lost. My mother, Sherry, spent countless hours tearing apart my text and putting it back together again in an effort to make my rambling thoughts and run-on sentences coherent and correct; this book would not be half of what it is without her.

Ciprian Tutu, an expert in distributed systems, provided the Spread appendix on a very short deadline and with extreme quality.

I would also like to thank all of the brilliant minds that make up OmniTI, specifically my brother George. Every day I am challenged to meet a standard of quality that far exceeds any other environment I have ever had the privilege of working in. Everyone at OmniTI constantly challenges each other's ideas and solutions, resulting in truly amazing things.

Finally, I would like to warmly thank all of our clients: past, current, and future. Without your problems to solve, there would be no purpose to any of this.

We Want to Hear from You!

As the reader of this book, *you* are our most important critic and commentator. We value your opinion and want to know what we're doing right, what we could do better, what areas you'd like to see us publish in, and any other words of wisdom you're willing to pass our way.

You can email or write me directly to let me know what you did or didn't like about this book—as well as what we can do to make our books stronger.

Please note that I cannot help you with technical problems related to the topic of this book, and that due to the high volume of mail I receive, I might not be able to reply to every message.

When you write, please be sure to include this book's title and author as well as your name and phone or email address. I will carefully review your comments and share them with the author and editors who worked on the book.

Email: devlib@samspublishing.com
Mail: Mark Taber
           Associate Publisher
           Sams Publishing
           800 East 96th Street
           Indianapolis, IN 46240 USA

Reader Services

Visit our website and register this book at **www.samspublishing.com/register** for convenient access to any updates, downloads, or errata that might be available for this book.

Introduction

T HE INTERNET IS A BIG PLACE, and its population gets bigger every day. If you have something popular to say or sell, all those people might come knocking on your door— at the same time! If this doesn't scare you, it should.

In this book we cover several approaches to building solutions that can grow (and grow big), which will keep you sleeping soundly at night and your chair dry in the event of catastrophic disasters.

I spend my days (and nights) looking at big systems—sites with tens of millions of users, terabytes upon terabytes of information. They all have one thing in common: They aren't working. My area of expertise is troubleshooting systems and talking clients down off the ledge because someone, somewhere, didn't design with scale in mind.

I wrote this text because I haven't found any books out there that help people think big. Most books are focused on performance or scaling extremely specific technologies. A good architect must understand the problems at hand, understand the scale of those problems, and have a thorough understanding of a great many technologies. Scalable solution design is a frame of mind. I hope to take you there.

What You'll Find Inside

The most important thing about understanding how to build big systems is realizing that you should respect them. You need to understand the terminology, the teams, the business, and the responsibility. The second most important thing to learn is how *not* to build big systems.

This book falls into two sections. In the first section we look at big picture issues, mostly in the realm of management and operations of mission-critical systems. In the second section, we jump feet first into some serious engineering discussions.

Management and Operations

The first three chapters discuss what it truly means to work with big systems. Although many books have a thousand pages of technical details and examples, this book is terse and to the point. The first three chapters will satisfy both the technical and nontechnical person who wants insight into why working in large, mission-critical environments is challenging. If you hit something technical that you don't understand, just barrel on through it, or ask your engineering staff, perhaps a systems administrator—they just love that.

Knowledge you'll gain:

- **Defining scalability**—You will gain an understanding that scalability and performance are indeed different.

- **Avoiding failure**—Perhaps the most intimidating aspect of big systems is the old saying, "the bigger they are, the harder they fall." You will learn a variety of methods for mitigating risk.

- **Developing**—On the technical side, the only differentiator between your business and other businesses is that which you have developed. This book guides you through sane development practices that will help carefully control agility and risk.

- **Monitoring**—Are your servers up? Is your business functioning? Oddly, it is rare that the same person asks both of those questions. I will show you that it is vital to monitor both technical and business-level metrics.

- **Managing costs**—Cost management is an art. Although this book does not delve deeply here, we will discuss how bad choices can explode the ongoing costs of your architecture.

Engineering

The second part of this book becomes more technical with each chapter as we discuss engineering solutions to real-world problems. Chapters 4 and 5 are a testament to the confusion surrounding high availability (making sure things are...you guessed it, available) and load balancing (which has nothing to do with availability). Too often these terms are used interchangeably and without a care; that should stop.

The rest of the book is a mixture of case studies and discussions of design approaches. It varies from conceptual and light on the technical details to extremely deep exploration of a problem and its solution.

We will focus on presenting solutions to problems rather than implementations of solutions to problems. Focusing on the implementation in a specific language is a good way to lose the attention of a programmer of a different language. The language is mostly irrelevant. I can't count the number of times I've heard people say "Java doesn't scale" or "PHP doesn't scale." No language scales; solutions scale. By mixing up the examples to use a variety of operating systems, languages, and other technologies, I hope to have you thinking about the nature of the solution instead of the details.

Knowledge you'll gain:

- **HA/LB**—High availability and load balancing are different terms and mean different things. We'll discuss decoupling their roles to allow for better architecture decisions. At the very least, I guarantee you will no longer mix up the terms.

- **Static caching**—By building a content distribution network, you will have the tools to improve performance and user experience.

- **Dynamic caching**—Although the benefits of dynamic caching are similar to those of static caching, the concepts are drastically different. You will learn about the various types of dynamic caching and how they can help your architecture.

- **Database replication**—This is perhaps the most misunderstood technology today. Different vendors mean different things. I will guide you through this maze of nuance, and you will learn to do replication on your own terms.

- **Clustered logging**—Logging is simply ignored by most people. I will illustrate how useful logging can be with compelling examples. You will certainly want to rework your logging infrastructure after reading this book.

The Challenge

I challenge you, the reader, and everyone you can influence, to step up and understand your problems before you attempt to solve them. This applies to management, operations, programming, and architectural design (and quite frankly, life as well). You must understand how what you are building will be used and, *from the beginning*, design for scalability those parts that need to scale. Too often it involves no more effort to design and implement a solution that scales than it does to build something that will not—if this is the case, respect yourself and build it right.

## 1

Scaling Up (and Down)

WHEN BUILDING A SOLID WEB infrastructure, the most important aspect is to maintain a strategy for growing and shrinking the system in a way that is both timely and economically conservative. By making intelligent decisions throughout the evolution of an architecture, scalability will be a matter of engineering rather than redesign, large purchasing, or black magic.

Defining Scalability

What does it mean to *scale*? Essentially, it means how well a particular solution fits a problem as the scope of that problem increases. One of the original approaches to this book was to present a few illustrative case studies demonstrating epic and catastrophic business-collapsing mistakes. The dot-com bubble popping provides ample material for such horror stories. Instead, specific common problems will be presented, as well as progressive solutions that scale well. It is hoped that this approach to refining the solutions will provide insight into sound approaches to solving difficult (and easy) problems and result in improved architecting skills.

Some solutions are defined as scalable simply because the capacity of a system can be increased by adding more of the same hardware or software. This approach is called *horizontal scalability* and is the best (and only true) type of scalability. However, simply having a solution that scales horizontally doesn't mean that you are safe.

Solutions that do not scale horizontally (rarely called vertically) can be scaled up by adding more horsepower. This is typically done by adding storage, processors, and/or RAM to build a bigger, faster, better machine. This is an expensive strategy and should be used only to solve problems that are difficult to solve with a horizontal scaling paradigm. Difficult does not mean inconvenient. Difficult problems are those that are considered academically difficult—problems for which no legitimate solutions are available on the market.

One such academically difficult problem are large ACID-compliant databases. *ACID* stands for *Atomicity, Consistency, Isolation, and Durability.* Chapter 8, "Distributed Databases Are Easy," delves into why this is such a difficult problem, and why solving it in a horizontally scalable way requires tremendous compromise. In the world today, databases are one such architecture component typically scaled by placing the service on a mammoth machine. With the introduction of grid computing and truly distributed database architectures maturing, I foresee this changing in the immediate future.

On the other hand, problems such as serving DNS, FTP, and static web content are well understood and horizontally scalable by nature. This does not mean that building such a system is idiot-proof; great care must still be taken when building this "scalable" system.

Why Do We Need to Scale?

Although I did say that the approach to this book would not be a collection of Stephen King short stories, perhaps that approach is best employed to answer the question of why we need to scale. The need to scale can be easily demonstrated by a story or two of "scaling gone wrong."

The inherent need for scalability is due to changes in business that can cause the size of a problem to dramatically ebb or swell. Obviously, building an architecture that can serve millions of users when your current user base is only 10,000 is a waste of money. The goal is to build a system for 10,000 users but to architect it in such a fashion that scaling it up to serve millions will not require application or architectural redesign.

Scaling Up Gone Wrong

I once encountered an architecture used to service online shopping malls. The site's purpose was to be a cookie-cutter shopping center portal service with strong online editing (Wiki) for stores, shopping center managers, and corporate managers. Users (mall shoppers) could visit online to register and learn of new sales, events, and online coupons from their favorite stores; use an online, dynamic gift guide; and subscribe to weekly email bulletins that contained information about their personally selected stores and special email-only offers.

It sounds simple enough. However, when I arrived at the architecture, the site was offline regularly due to capacity issues that occurred often, and the weekly email, which was supposed to be delivered all in one morning, was taking more than 24 hours to get out the door. Why? Very bad design issues both on an application level and a system level.

What was so bad about this design? Well, the one requirement was for 24x7 uptime, and that was not being achieved. The system was built on commodity hardware, and that hardware occasionally failed. The application was designed with no caching infrastructure and a data model not suited for the online transaction processing required to drive the website or the bulk querying required to construct the weekly emails.

The site originally started with only a few tens of thousands of users and infrequent visits. The ill effects of the poor design were not made immediately apparent due to the minimal stress on the architecture initially. However, when more traffic was driven to the site through marketing and advertising, the site capsized. The ramifications of shoddy development, design, and construction were clear.

Fortunately, we were able to take over the architecture and were given free reign to perform a complete reimplementation. As the foundation of the architecture was quite small, it was rebuilt in about a month, coming in at 30,000 lines of Perl code for application business logic and presentation. As always, the code change was the most profound but the least noticeable by the owner because software and development are such abstract things. Also, during the process of a normal application reimplementation, the presentation, creative and copy, does not change, so the only visible effects of the work are performance and reduction of long-term maintenance costs.

The architecture itself changed as well. The site was and still is run on commodity hardware, but the preexisting environment was riddled with single points of failure. The new hardware architecture was marginally more expensive, doubling up on specific devices in the content delivery pipeline to address both performance and availability demands.

Although it sounded easy enough to do, and from a technical point of view it was, it took a month of labor (and costs) to reengineer an architecture that had a considerable (and wasted) capital investment. In addition to the sunk and unrecoverable costs of the first failed attempt at developing the site, and the costs of reengineering the entire solution from scratch, a month was lost as well.

During the month in which reimplementation and deployment took place, all Internet-based business initiatives that required "new development" were drastically slowed and often completely derailed. Time is money—usually much more than any techie will ever realize.

What Goes Up Should Go Down

When the term *scalable* is tossed around, nearly 100% of the time it is used with respect to scaling systems up. There is a concern that the architecture will not work well or cease to function entirely if the scope of the problem it solves increases. This concern is twofold. First, the architecture will break and thus will not fulfill the purpose as intended. Second, time and money must be spent to redesign and rebuild the system to handle such a load.

Although a decrease in the scope of a specific problem would unlikely stress the solution in a way that would lead to breakage, some serious financial issues make scaling down efficiently a must.

The inability to scale usually has much more visible effects. When a site wants to scale up, it is from demand. Demand and the demonstration of customer growth are powerful factors in raising money and legitimizing investment in new technologies. So, when things need to scale up and they are implemented poorly, more often than not the organization will find the money to solve the problem—even if it is with brute force.

Scaling down is an entirely different matter. If the solution needs to scale back, an organization is doing so to respond to a decreased demand and usually wants to dramatically lower operating costs. Essentially, if there is nothing to be saved by scaling a solution back, there is no reason to do so.

Fundamentally, it is more difficult to scale an architecture up than it is to scale it down. Over-utilizing the infrastructure in an architecture has glaring usability effects, whereas under-utilizing it has only subtle financial effects.

Generally, it is much easier to scale back if you have gone through the process of scaling up (you can basically retrace the steps of your architecture's evolution). However, if you start big and need to scale down from there, it can be less apparent.

I know two companies that collapsed due to the inability to reduce operating costs when the utilization of their sites diminished. The dot-com user base (of intangible monetary value based on registered users) did not grow and generate revenue as expected. There was a substantial number of loyal users, and both companies were able to redefine their business plans to turn a profit by catering solely to their loyal user base. However, the business plans required reducing operational costs, and due to countless bad application design decisions, the applications would not operate on architectures substantially smaller than the large-scale originals.

Although the traffic and utilization of their architectures dropped to about 10% of the original goal, they were only able to realize a 20% reduction in operational costs. If the applications were redesigned from scratch, they could have scaled back, but an investment in redesign was not in their budgets. Both companies capsized.

Scaling down is good to keep in mind from an engineering point of view. Most online businesses faced with a 50% or more reduction in customers end up closing shop, so scaling down isn't often an important consideration. From an engineering perspective, it is a valuable exercise because engineers build solutions and the components that comprise them. Business goals change, and although the size of the overall solution may not change dramatically in scope, specific components may be sized up, sized down, or even become unnecessary.

One important rule of thumb is that adding independent components to an architecture complicates it linearly. Adding components on which other components depend to an architecture complicates it exponentially.

Real-World Considerations

When scaling any system, four things are guaranteed:

- Capital investment will be made.
- The system will become more complex.
- Maintenance costs will increase.
- Time will be required to act.

Architectural design is not simply understanding a technical challenge and devising a blueprint. Both the approach and the final design will be influenced dramatically by the four factors listed previously.

Every business will take its stance on the actual price of these four happenings. Dot-com companies and small-to-medium Internet-based businesses tend to place emphasis on reducing up-front investment and time to implementation. Large companies like to minimize risk and thus concentrate on maximizing the simplicity and maintainability of their systems.

The real world is a different environment from that of academic institutions, online courses, textbooks, and white papers. The latter tell a story or demonstrate a concept but seldom in a rapidly changing environment.

The real world changes, and it changes quickly. My team of system administrators (SAs) and I constantly find ourselves posed with architectural challenges. Customers come in with seemingly simple requests that often require substantial planning and engineering. Combine that with a tight deadline, and you have a recipe for disaster.

Understanding the scope of the problem and being able to step outside the current solution is essential to building efficient systems. The initial solution to a problem may be the entirely wrong approach to the problem as it evolves. Chapter 10, "The Right Tool for the Job," discusses the process of rethinking and reengineering a solution to meet new demands.

Being a Good Architect

Scaling architectures up is often not a great challenge. I have seen several companies simply double, triple, or more their existing large architecture to solve an acute scaling need. That genre of scaling is not the goal of this book. Here we want to devise solutions to specific problems that operate as efficiently as possible.

Because our goal is to build Internet architectures that scale well, we need to look under the covers a bit. Architectures are comprised of components, and our mission is to make those components as autonomous and cost-effectively scalable as possible. By doing so, we can approach a doubling of demand as a stress on the components of the overall architecture. In most cases, these stresses are not uniform, and handling the new demand requires only scaling one or two of the architecture's internal components.

An architecture with efficient and maintainable components can scale much better than an efficient and maintainable monolithic architecture.

At the end of the day, managing large systems requires good engineering. An architect should be able to see above and beyond a set of business requirements and their corresponding engineering plans. Analysis of the business goals, an eye on the competition, surveillance of the market in which the solution plays, and a good bit of luck will result in a relatively accurate forecasting of future architectural requirements. Aside from plain, good old engineering, anticipating change is what makes a good Internet architect.

Scaling systems is a balance between cost, complexity, maintainability, and implementation latency. I honestly believe that there is no "right" proportion of each. Experience is the ultimate weapon. I am a big fan of learning from one's own mistakes. I have countless stories of stupid decisions in my early years, and although documenting them in a book would be amusing to some, it would serve little purpose. Truly learning from one's mistakes requires making them, and the ramifications of those mistakes ensure that you don't forget.

2

Principles for Avoiding Failure

AVOIDING FAILURE IS A GOAL SHARED BY every operations, business, and development team. Although I am more of a manager and software engineer now, my roots are in systems administration. During the dot-com bubble, I managed the systems and network administration for several large dot com infrastructures.

I may be biased (though I think I'm right) in saying that avoiding failure is more fundamental to systems administrators than many other disciplines. Why is this so? Because systems administrators are the ones awake at 3 a.m. when disaster strikes and who spend the next 36 consecutive bleary-eyed hours trying to fix the problem.

People on the business side want things desperately, but the want is incomplete because they do not have the skills to execute those wants personally. Instead they collaborate with two teams of people: the development group and the operations group. Because the development group works so closely with the business group to satisfy their demands, both groups tend to lose the valuable insights offered by the operations group. At the end of the day, things have to run. The sole purpose of an operations group is to make sure that things run smoothly. Having the operations group available and participating regularly in the goal-oriented business meetings and technical development meetings can be enormously valuable.

Systems administrators like things automated. Ideally, everything would run itself, and all our time would be spent reading our favorite websites and RSS feeds. In some environments this is possible. Large web architectures have a tendency to deviate from this utopia. Many sites still have break-neck development schedules and are constantly adapting business needs that demand newly developed technology to drive them. This means that the business demands the development team to relentlessly launch new code into production.

In my experience, developers have no qualms about pushing code live to satisfy urgent business needs without regard to the fact that it may capsize an entire production environment at the most inopportune time. This happens repeatedly. My assumption is that a developer feels that refusing to meet a demand from the business side is more likely to result in termination than the huge finger-pointing that will ensue post-launch.

It is not, however, a lost cause. By understanding the dynamics of the business you can formulate policies and procedures to prevent these things from happening. Regardless of whether formal procedures are even feasible in your company or whether fully written procedures for developing and writing procedures already exist, a set of principles for avoiding failure can be adopted. First and foremost is the education of the development team and the operations team regarding the ramifications of failure.

Working in Production Environments

There are so many different levels of production environments that it is difficult to speak to them all. The principles in this chapter can be applied to any important computing environment. Because this book is about Internet architectures, we won't address anything but the infrastructure used to directly service customers over the Internet.

Because most large architectures are run by multidisciplinary teams, there tend to be more than one set of guidelines for avoiding failure.

In the end it comes down to "don't be stupid." Although this is a simple and an intuitive expectation, what is clearly "stupid" on a small architecture is often subtle on large architectures run by multiple teams. There are three reasons that teams are used to manage projects:

- The work to be done on large systems exceeds what is humanly possible for a single individual to accomplish.
- It is less expensive and easier to find individuals with a deep, focused expertise in one of the technologies that powers the system than to find individuals with deep and broad expertise across every technology in the system.
- The "key man problem"—if your key man is hit by a bus (or simply quits), you must have business continuity.

All are obvious reasons, all are important, and all contribute a bit of chaos to the overall system. Through the application of good practices and the use of established tools, the chaos can be kept in check. Without the appropriate approach, working in a fast-moving production architecture is like working on a construction site without OSHA compliance and no hard hat—stupid.

Although it may not seem an obvious application at first, in the end it boils down to Murphy's Law—more specifically how to avoid it. Finagle's Law (a more generalized version of Murphy's Law) says: "Anything that can go wrong, will." However, more formally, Finagle's Law looks something like this:

$$((U+C+I) \times (10-S))/20 \times A \times 1/(1-\sin(F/10))$$

urgency (U): $1 <= U <= 9$,

complexity (C): $1 <= C <= 9$,

importance (I): $1 <= I <= 9$,

skill (S): $1 <= S <= 9$,

frequency (F): $1 <= F <= 9$

This equation illustrates Finagle's Law (a.k.a. Sod's Law) more formally. Although this equation, commissioned by British Gas, may seem a bit contrived despite it regressing well for British Gas's dataset, it still provides an excellent insight into the nature of the problems architects face.

The Dot Bomb and Its Effect on Building Large Systems

No one likes to lose data. No one likes to have the services they provide be inaccessible. No one likes to clean up messes. No one likes to spend money.

The last point is a real kicker, and although it may be absolutely ridiculous, the fact remains that companies of all shapes and sizes have a fear of investing in technology infrastructure.

Specifically, at this time in computing we are all just now beginning to recover from the dot-com bubble popping. Inside the bubble, online users had an unrealistic value to companies, business plans weren't sound, and a rough Internet-related idea was enough to get millions in funding.

Many times, in such initiatives, the architecture is brute-forced—a huge investment in hardware and services to compensate for poor or understaffed engineering combined with too-short timelines. This, of course, was good for hardware vendors (Sun, EMC, Hitachi, Cisco, F5, the list is long). I'll be the last one to tell you to go buy cheap hardware. However, I also know that there are many unnecessarily powerful components driving today's architectures.

In economics, there is a law of diminishing returns. The basic concept is that when workers are added to the wheat field, at some point, each additional worker will contribute less than his predecessor. This was first thought to apply only to agriculture but was later adopted as a universal economic law applicable to all productive enterprises. As with most laws in unrelated fields, we see parallels in the field of computer science.

Computers get faster every year. Moore's Law says they double in speed/capacity/performance every 18 months. That sounds great, but when a purchase is made and an architecture is designed, there is a single "market offering." In other words, at the time of the purchase you have a snapshot of a rapidly changing landscape. This means that what you buy today will be obsolete tomorrow and that you should count on your architecture running on yesterday's technology. Combine this with the law of diminishing returns, and you can see something more profound.

The "best" technology that can be bought today is expensive. Effectively, at the top end of the performance curve, more and more buys you less and less. So, you can blow your budget on the fastest, biggest, shiniest thing out there knowing that it will be inexpensive tomorrow and obsolete the next day, or you can leverage a better return on investment by buying today's (or even yesterday's) commodity hardware.

Why is this so? During the dot-com era (and even today) companies tended to buy the fastest hardware they can afford in order to "scale." Perhaps by now you can see the fundamental flaw in that mentality. If the intention is to accomplish seamless scalability by purchasing a large "fast" monolithic machine, you will inevitably saturate its capabilities and learn the difference between scalability and performance the hard way. Scale out, not up—horizontal, not vertical.

Scalability is the goal, but there are some other commonly overlooked challenges when working with big architectures. The dot com era taught us something that no businessperson would have ever believed before. It taught us that it is possible to take a concept at 8 a.m.; translate that into a business initiative; proceed through design, implementation, testing, and launch; and have millions of customers for that idea by the close of business. That fact that this is possible means that if the business can capitalize on such efficiencies, it will.

Many techniques attempt to handle the issues of rapid development. One such popular approach is that of extreme programming. Regardless of the technique involved, the fact that the solution not only has to work, but it also has to scale dramatically changes the playing field and complicates the rules of the game.

The rest of this book attempts to get you "thinking scalable." We will spend some time first on tried-and-true techniques that can help prevent disaster and speed recovery of mistakes due to rushed timelines or lapses in judgment.

Stability and Control

Stability and control sound like obvious requirements in a mission-critical system—and indeed they are. However, it should be no surprise that the demands that business places on information technology infrastructure can easily destabilize a large production system. Data systems, web servers, mail servers, and the like are all tools to accomplish some greater business goal. It is absolutely crucial to remember that, and by doing so you can avoid pursuing the wrong technology challenges and protect the infrastructure from uncontrolled change.

Uncontrolled change is perhaps the most fearsome monster in the dungeons of technology. It is a monster that takes many shapes: feature creep, milestone hopping (pulling features from future product milestones into the current), sloppy version control, and even premature implementation. Because it comes in many forms, uncontrolled change can be difficult to recognize and as such often goes unnoticed, until…there is an infestation of uncontrolled change in a variety of shapes and forms in various components and the architecture simply implodes. I've seen such glorious failures, and they carry heavy casualties—often entire businesses.

There is no final ultimate solution to stability and control that will please everyone. However, it is important to satisfy each business unit's needs as completely as possible. (From a pessimist's standpoint, this means not dissatisfying anyone to the point of rebellion.) Effectively, the business side should want technical innovation and deployment "on-demand." Although horsepower is pretty much available in that fashion, architectural design, business logic adaptation, and the overall application development process are not.

On the flip side, the technology side of the house wants complete specifications for projects so that the design investment occurs once, and maintenance is truly maintenance (bug fixes and minor revisions). However, the truth of business is that business changes and with that comes the need to reinvent the business processes and technologies that power it. The two organizational units are at odds.

You can spend a lifetime and invest a fortune devising and implementing a strategy where everyone wins. Honestly, I don't think you'll succeed (if you do, somebody could have been pushing harder and accomplishing more). I have found, however, that by exercising the proper amount of resistance with respect to uncontrolled change, you can ensure no losers—and that's a darn good outcome. This "resistance" is simply using the right tools and techniques to manage and maintain your technology.

Rapid Development

Although this may not apply to everyone, I'll wager it applies to the vast majority of readers. Where I work, rapid development is about 95% of what we do. For many of the systems I touch, project deadlines are measured in hours or tens of hours. In the rapid development model, the luxuries of clearly delineated development, testing, and quality assurance phases are replaced by an amorphous development cycle that splits testing responsibilities across all participants. Although traditional development and testing cycles measure in weeks or months, these cycles spin so fast I can only sit back and say "Oh, neat. A pinwheel." If this sounds familiar, stability may seem like something beyond the horizon, but control is certainly possible.

How do you control such a beast? There isn't one solution—no silver bullet. But like any self-respecting engineer, we can grab the low-hanging fruit. The heaviest fruit on this tree is version control. Version control is simple, safe, reliable, and, quite frankly, you would be out of your mind not to use it. Simply sticking all your code in version control is the baseline, but by truly leveraging its power you can put in place a peace of mind that is invaluable.

The next step in controlling the beast is planning—good planning. What is a plan? Simply put, a plan is the steps taken to perform a change from configuration A to configuration B. Realistically, those steps are planned *before* you perform them. A change in configuration is anything that affects the production environment: code pushes, database schema changes, vendor software fixes and upgrades, OS patches and upgrades, hardware changes, network changes, and so on. Where I work, all these things are given a single name: *push.* A push is a controlled and planned action that changes the production architecture.

So, if you think up what you want to do and then do it, you had a plan, right? Yes, but this lack of diligence leads to catastrophic failures. Planning is time consuming and challenging, but it isn't rocket science. A successful push plan has four parts: a plan to get from A to B, a plan to get from B to A, a plan to restore A from bare metal, and a successful test of the first two. (Testing a bare metal restore for every push would be suicide, or at least leave you constantly contemplating it.) Although it is always a good idea to have a tested plan for reverting a change (backing out a push), in a rapid development environment it is fundamental. Rapid development often leads to less testing and quality assurance, which means that changes are pushed, and bad things happen.

In a general sense, it just makes sense. From the technical side, however, there is more than just the safety of the IT infrastructure. With a thorough, documented plan, you can look a peer, boss, or customer in the eye and explain that pushes can and do go wrong, but you were prepared. You had a 100% confidence that you could recover, a reasonable ETA for rectifying the situation (because you had tested it), and the unexpected downtime was kept to a minimum because the recovery efforts were preplanned and executed with confidence.

Although there are many a fruit on this tree of solutions, the last one I'll mention is unit testing. Rapid development suffers from rapid changes. Rapid changes can lead to breakage that goes unnoticed. Unit testing is one solution to that problem, and, although it is not nearly as "low hanging" as version control and proper planning, it is so powerful that I would be remiss not to give it a chance to tell its story.

Unit Testing

When a topic is presented, you can tell whether someone likes the concept. If the person presents the disadvantages last, it allows them to elucidate on them as they see fit, and it leaves you with the disadvantages fresh on your mind. On the other hand, if the presenter goes over the disadvantages first, he is merely qualifying them and then moves on to the merits.

Unit testing is difficult and has some serious disadvantages, but it *can* prevent disaster. Although many of the customers, clients, colleagues, and open projects I have worked with did not subscribe to the unit testing philosophy, I will pointedly discuss its disadvantages first so that the power and purpose of unit testing is the message that concludes my mere lip service to this philosophy.

Unit testing plays on the concept that most information systems are built in a modular manner. Although these modules aren't entirely autonomous (they often sport a vast number of interconnects and dependencies), they are self-contained from the standpoint of code base and maintenance.

The reason unit testing is so difficult is because its challenges are deceptive. As with any test, you control the inputs, so the test is limited to the input sets you provide. In no way will any form of testing ever ensure that your architecture will work under every possible condition. Period. With that said, testing is designed to ensure that a system will arrive at an expected outcome given a prescribed input. This is immensely valuable, but if you can understand that this is *all* that testing provides, you can manage your (and other's) expectations.

Writing a full, start-to-finish business testing infrastructure can be (and usually is) much more work than writing the systems that will be tested. This is why the vast majority of systems out there do not have business-cycle testing.

Unit testing, on the other hand, is designed to keep tests small, easy to manufacture, and easy to maintain. An example of business-cycle testing is a test that attempts to simulate a web client to access the pages and post the form data, walk through the site and place an order resulting in a account creation, credit card data insertion, and successful billing. An example of unit testing is a test that takes the credit card 4444333322221111, performs a mod10 validation test, and arrives at the expected result—pretty different.

Unit testing does not ensure that the various infrastructure modules will be used correctly, but it does ensure that if they are used correctly that they function as they should.

The tests are small and can easily be written by the same party who writes the code to be tested; so why is this hard? Well, for starters, it takes a bit of practice and experience to learn to write good, thorough unit tests. Bad unit tests don't end up testing much and are a complete waste of time.

Next, it is dramatically more useful if you unit test everything (over unit testing only bits and pieces). Having 10 unit tests across two modules in a system with 500 modules doesn't buy you much at all, and I argue that it gives you a false sense of confidence. Because the unit tests are not actually required for the corresponding module to function, you can be delinquent and not write unit tests as thoroughly as you should—or even omit them entirely. When you slip, you slide, and your unit testing framework is compromised. Unit testing is a religion: You need to live it, breathe it, preach it, and evangelize it. Often, if you want it to succeed in your enterprise you might need to pull an old religion trick and just simply force it on everyone else.

I am not trying to say that it is bad to subscribe to unit testing for a specific module when other modules in your architecture do not. That is good, but the value add is dramatically less than a complete unit testing picture. This, of course, makes unit testing difficult to adopt completely in systems with large legacy code bases.

Because unit testing development must go hand-in-hand with existing development, it means that projects will take longer (marginally). This change can be difficult to swallow in work environments that have hectic schedules and do not want to compromise productivity. And although I can tell you and provide case studies that demonstrate that unit testing will save you both development time and downtime in the future, that didn't seem to work well for extreme programming—a programming technique that is powerful but not widely adopted.

Now that you know why unit testing is difficult, let's see what it buys you. This is best done by example, and no example serves like a real-world example.

In one of the systems I regularly work on, there is a database layer. The system talks to Oracle, and we manage that through an abstracted database layer so that we can control how queries are made and log how often queries are made, what bind values are most commonly used, and how they perform (wall clock time during query preparation, execution, and data retrieval). Generally, it is useful, and every other part of the system that interacts with the database leverages this module to do so.

One night assume the story goes: We changed the database abstraction layer, and the unit test failed; therefore the unit test was successful. That would be a fairly lame test case example. In fact, the change set and problem set were wildly obtuse and complicated. We needed to take advantage of cached queries using Perl DBI/DBD::Oracle's `prepare_cached` method. This was all well and good and solved the acute issue we were having (with a frequently invoked data insertion query). However, this change was made on a global level, and all queries now used `prepare_cached`. This did not cause the database abstraction unit test to fail, nor did it cause the transaction processing system unit test to fail. Instead, an administrative data manipulation module had its unit test fail. It turns out that there was a problem with the use of some stale cursors that would be triggered if the database connection was lost and reestablished. This error was subtle with a rather obtuse outcome in that certain processes here or there would suddenly begin to malfunction seemingly out of the blue.

Because I regularly troubleshoot obtuse bugs, I'd have to say that the subtle ones are the worst. Things malfunction infrequently and even self-correct. Nevertheless, each malfunction could cause a user-visible error that could cause the user not to retry a failed financial transaction or could lower the user's confidence level in such a fashion that you could lose a customer forever. These kinds of errors are simply unacceptable. Although unit testing is not a silver bullet, any reasonable means of reducing the amount of failures and increasing the overall product quality should be seriously considered for inclusion in an organization's standard operating practices.

Version Control

As mentioned previously, version control is likely the heaviest fruit on the tree of stability and control. Version control systems (VCSs) are designed to manage bits of data, tracking when, why, and by whom the changes to those bits were made. It sounds simple enough, and any good development team will tell you they already use version control, but using it well is the key.

Several version control systems are available today. Arguing over which is better and which is worse gets you nowhere. However, each has a set of highly overlapping features, and by ranking the importance of those features in your architecture, you can quickly arrive at the right tool for the job.

One of the first mistakes made by organizations choosing version control solutions is vendor bias. Many of the more popular systems are used by the open source community. This places an interesting angle on vendor bias.

I submit that the concept of version control is simply not that complicated. That is not to say that building a reliable, robust VCS is a trivial exercise, but it is well within the realm of open source technologies. In fact, commercial version control systems simply don't offer that many advantages in the realm of systems and development. (They do have some good advantages still with respect to managing version control on files with proprietary formats such as Microsoft Word documents—this simply doesn't apply to us.)

Online debates between world-renowned open source developers show that developers tend to harp on features such as distributed, disconnected operation, managing vast numbers of changesets, and the suitability of the system to allow the easy application of vast numbers of external patches. I argue that this is biased toward a genre of development that is dramatically different from the needs of the typical lone Internet architecture.

The typical commercial architecture places tremendous value on the code and configuration that drives it. There is a desire to keep it unified, authoritative, protected, and private—*keep it secret, keep it safe.* This means that the importance of good distributed and disconnected operation is mostly irrelevant. Instead, availability is the remaining feature requirement in that realm.

Additionally, individual components of the architecture typically have small teams that work closely together to handle development and maintenance. This means that the management of changesets and patches is vital, but vast quantities of outstanding changesets and patches are unlikely to occur.

So, now that I've disqualified the typical concerns of the average open source developer, what is important?

- Stability, durability, consistency, and restorability—This system will hold all that is dear to the architecture. You must be able to have complete confidence that it will work as documented. In VCS systems, the term *check in* has been replaced by *commit* over time. As in database systems, if a commit succeeds, it must completely succeed, and if it fails, it must be as if it never happened—there is no room for error. It is also vital that there are clean, effective ways of consistently backing up the data to allow for complete and safe disaster recovery.

- Branching and tagging—It is vital that the system be capable of managing several concurrent copies of the intellectual assets. Development branches, production branches, personal branches, product version branches, and so on. Tagging or at least the ability to understand and repeat a "snapshot" of the tree is vital for production change control.

- Usability—A VCS system is utterly useless if its supposed users are not educated on how to use it best. Users must be comfortable enough with the system that it is a productivity tool and not a hindrance. Additionally, it is crucial that the tool run seamlessly everywhere in your architecture. It must run on every hardware platform, architecture, and operating system you run. If it does not run on some of your production systems, it is highly likely that things pertaining to that system will not embrace version control as extensively everything else. (This is a great vote for open source systems.)

- Changesets—Although integrated changeset support is not fundamental in these systems, the capability to understand that the changes to several indirectly related bits can be correlated together as a single high-level change is important. This makes it much easier to determine what changes were necessary across the architecture to effect a desired change. It also dramatically simplifies reverting the change or applying just that change to another branch.

Each of these features is fundamental. Given the size of your architecture, how much you will manage in the VCS, and the number of users interacting with it, you can weight the preceding features in each VCS product and choose the one right for your architecture.

In our environment, we have between 10 and 20 people regularly touching the VCS. The code and configuration information therein is deployed on approximately 150 machines. Our developers are most familiar with Concurrent Versioning System (CVS). Our managed assets come in rather small at about two gigabytes.

Originally we used CVS for all asset management. However, over time, the need to branch and merge efficiently on large repositories and the desire to have changesets began to surpass the importance of developer usability. The inability to tag large trees often (an inherent problem in the implementation of CVS) started to make the tool a hindrance instead of a productivity booster. After a few large commits failing halfway through and leaving the CVS trees in an inconsistent state, we decided to reevaluate which features were most important.

As we are a consultancy, we are paid to be productive. The idea of retraining our entire CVS user base on a new technology (let alone a new VCS paradigm) was something we wanted to avoid. Capitalizing on existing knowledge and introducing a minimal interruption to overall productivity was paramount. In the end, we did a vast amount of experimentation and evaluation of different systems and found that the features provided by Subversion and the low barrier to entry was the best choice for us.

At the end of the day, the actual VCS you implement is of no consequence so long as it sports the features that are important in your architecture and is adopted religiously by the all the parties involved. One crucial step of selecting a VCS is to engage its user community and ask for positive and negative experiences on architectures that are most similar to yours. If you can't find a user of a specific VCS with an architecture that resembles yours, ask yourself if you want to be the first.

So, you have a robust, reliable version control system, what do you do with it? How does it aid the overall management of your architecture?

Version Control in Action

Version control allows you to understand how your code changes, by whom, and for what reason. As such, almost all development work that takes place today is done in a VCS. However, more often than not, that VCS is not leveraged for deployment.

Let's poke around in a Subversion repository a bit and demonstrate how you can use Subversion to manage deployment.

Because this book really isn't about installing and administrating Subversion, we'll assume that you have a working Subversion install hosting your "superapp" repository at https://svn/superapp/. You can find more information about Subversion at http://subversion.tigris.org/.

In Subversion you lay out your repository in three main sections:

- /trunk/ is used for mainline development. All new features start here.
- /production/ holds only production-ready code. Code placed in this location has been developed and tested in /trunk/, and basic quality assurance has been performed. Only severe, critical bugs are fixed directly in this section and from there moved back into /trunk/.
- /tags/ holds copies of the /production/ branch that are suitable for a push.

The concepts of software management are well out of the scope of this book, so we won't delve into the policies and procedures for committing code in /trunk/ or moving that to /production/. However, we can use the /tags/ section for launching code. Typically in a software engineering environment, the /tags/ section of a Subversion repository is for product releases. For example, version 1.3.2 of your superapp would be placed on /tags/1.3.2/ and from https://svn/superapp/tags /1.3.2/ you would roll your "release."

In a fast moving web architecture, it is not uncommon to have more than one production release per day. Additionally, the "application" tends not to be a shrink-wrapped software product—it isn't installed but rather patched. The "application" is an entire architecture with a huge number of subproducts, configurations, and dependencies, and often has multimachine deployments that are not identical. We actually have one client who has performed 10 production code pushes in a single day.

One of the most fundamental rules of science is that you must have controls in your experiments. In many ways a production push is like an experiment. You expect everything to go as planned; you expect your hypothesis (success) to be met. Occasionally, however, the experiment yields an unexpected outcome. When things go wrong, we immediately look at our controls to ensure that the environment for the experiment was the environment we expected. With a daily production push schedule, the environment you push in was not the environment that the application was developed in.

Subtle bugs in systems sometimes take days or weeks to manifest effects large enough or acute enough to notice. This, in itself, poses a quandary. What caused the problem?

In a production troubleshooting situation, religious use of version control is a lifesaver. It allows for both systems administrators and developers to review the concise logs about what has changed, when it changed, and why it changed. Additionally, by pushing tags into production, reversion to a previous "system state" is easier. "Easier" is not to be confused with "easy." There are still many things to take into account.

New application code is often accompanied by changes to database schema, scheduled maintenance jobs, and systems and network configuration changes. Although reverting the system to a previous state is not always as easy as simply checking out that previous tag and pushing it into production, but, as discussed already, it is critical to accompany all substantial production changes with a plan, and that plan has a reversion plan that has been tested.

What a good VCS can provide is a simple, consistent implementation of a plan for reverting the simpler production pushes. A vast majority of the production pushes I see on a daily basis are minor feature or maintenance related. As such, they can all be reverted by checking out a previous "stable" tag. Beyond that, most are unrelated changes and fixes, so instead of reverting to an older tag, we can just back out the changeset that caused the problem.

When used right, a good VCS can allow you to "roll back the clock" in your production and development environments. This sort of flexibility and immediately available change history is invaluable.

A Different Approach to Disaster Recovery

Nothing will ever replace the need for a bare-metal recovery. When a machine dies and must be replaced and reinstalled, it is a relatively simple step-by-step approach: bootstrap, restore configuration from tape, apply configuration, restore data from tape, test, make live. However, there are a variety of other failures that, although disastrous, do not require a bare-metal recovery.

Imagine a reboot where your interfaces have the wrong configuration (wrong IPs), or a missing software configuration file. A web server restarts and some of the virtual hosts are "missing" or otherwise malfunctioning. Perhaps it is brought to your attention that some critical recurrent job hasn't been running and though it should be in the crontab on the machine it isn't.

Although mysterious things tend to happen less in strict production environments, they happen in development often. And the more aggressive your production push schedule is, the more likely oddities will arise in the production environment. One of the most coveted skill sets in any large, fast-paced architecture is keen production troubleshooting skills. Things are changed during the investigation and problem-solving process, and the solutions to these acute problems often lead to online production reconfiguration. This can make managing the overall production configuration challenging to say the least.

How do you solve this challenge induced by untracked, poorly documented, "emergency response" style configuration changes? Well, simply put, track it and document it—using your VCS.

On your version control server, set up a process that will back up the important files from all your production servers. This includes configuration files, custom kernels, and package applications installed after the full OS install (such as your installations of Apache, Oracle, Postgres, MySQL, and so on). The bulk of this data should range between 10 megabytes and 500 megabytes, entirely reasonable for a version control system. From these backups you will commit changes. Using a protocol such as rsync for synchronization of these data sources, they can be inexpensively replicated allowing for short sync/commit cycles.

Alternatively, the approach can be embraced more completely by placing important files on a system directly under version control and making each system responsible for applying changes directly to the VCS. This eliminates a step in the process but requires a bit more finesse in the configuration to ensure that all appropriate files are backed up. In our systems, we rsync /etc/ and other important configuration directories to a central control box and apply the changes to the repository; when new files are added on a production machine, they are automatically placed under revision control—it has been a life-saver.

The nice thing about this approach is that by looking only at core configuration information and static applications, the file sets are unlikely to change with any frequency. This also means that the changeset notification messages (the emails sent to the team on every commit) are infrequent and useful for keeping the whole operations team both up-to-date on intended changes and aware of unintentional reconfigurations—such as those that occur during hectic troubleshooting sessions.

The advantage of backups cannot be replaced. However, the ability to restore the configuration of a server to a specific point in time is much less valuable than the ability to understand how it has changed over that time. It will give you far better insight into the cause and effect of changes.

Good Design

In the end, no amount of careful planning and precisely followed procedure will make up for a poorly designed architecture. The root of the problem is that poorly designed architectures are prone to failures under stress and additionally lack the infrastructure for real-time analysis and modification.

Although I certainly can't describe all aspects of good design in this section, or even in this book, I intend to challenge some of the traditional approaches to Internet application development and, at the very least, motivate you to always prove to yourself that a technology is the right fit before you use it as a building block in a large architecture.

Time and again, I hear statements such as "Perl is slow" and "Java doesn't scale." These are dangerous statements, because when knowledgeable people say them, they are stating that a particular design and implementation in Perl or Java is slow or not scalable. However, when people hear these things and repeat them as gospel they breed ignorance. Languages aren't slow; implementations of languages are. Language selection and scalability have little to do with each other; architectural design and implementation strategy dictate how scalable a final product will be. I beg of everyone, stop making blanket generalizations—say what you mean.

The most important rule to abide by when implementing a large system is that you design it first. The challenge of this rule is that implementation in most environments is organic and continually evolving, and a master architect will not be involved in every aspect of ongoing development. So, what to do? Hold coders to a higher standard; they must be architecturally savvy.

Don't think like a coder; think like an architect. I have the utmost respect for coders—I am one—but a coder who cannot step back and see the big picture is effectively a hammer-wielder, not a carpenter. It is essential that you can see the overall architectural plans and understand the purpose of the overall system. When you get the 30-inch-wide doorway at the top of the handicap accessibility ramp, everyone (not just the foreman) should be asking "how will a wheelchair fit through this?"

Good design is essential, but a good initial design is merely a foundation for success. The structures built on those foundations can be neglected and crumble to the ground unless good design principles are continually applied.

The reality is that it is challenging to find a project leader, coder, or systems administrator who has enough breadth of knowledge to make generally excellent design decisions on an ongoing basis. This is why it is so essential that regular collaboration take place between the business, development, and operations teams—it is, perhaps, the most fundamental ingredient in good design.

3

Mission-Critical Environments

*M*ISSION-CRITICAL IS A COMMONLY ABUSED term. Some think it describes any architecture that they run; others believe it is a term for "systems that launch spacecraft." For the purpose of further discussion, we will equate mission-critical systems with business-critical systems. *Business-critical* is easy to define: Each business can simply choose what it believes to be vital to its operations.

Perhaps the most important issue to address from a technical perspective is to determine what aspects of a technical infrastructure are critical to the mission. Note the word is *aspects* and not *components*. This isn't solely about equipment and software; it is also about policies and procedures. Without going into painful detail, we will touch on five key aspects of mission-critical environments:

- High availability (HA)
- Monitoring
- Software management
- Overcomplication
- Optimization

To effectively manage and maintain any sizable mission-critical environment, these aspects must be mastered. Mission-critical architectures are typically managed by either a few focused teams or a few multidisciplinary teams. I prefer the latter because knowledge and standards tend to be contagious, and all five aspects are easy to master when aggregating the expertise of all individuals on a multidisciplinary team. Although it is not essential that every participant be an expert in any or all of these areas, it is essential that they be wholly competent in at least one area and always cognizant of the others.

Being mindful of the overall architecture is important. As an application developer, if you habitually ignore the monitoring systems, you are likely to make invalid assumptions resulting in decisions that negatively impact the business.

High Availability

Because high availability was the first item in the previous list, the first thing in your mind might be: "What about load balancing?" The criticality of an environment has absolutely nothing to do with its scale. Load balancing attempts to effectively combine multiple resources to handle higher loads—and therefore is completely related to scale. Throughout this book, we will continue to unlearn the misunderstood relationship between high availability and load balancing.

When discussing mission-critical systems, the first thing that comes to mind should be high availability. Without it, a simple system failure could cause a service interruption, and a service interruption isn't acceptable in a mission-critical environment. Perhaps it is the first thing that comes to mind due to the rate things seem to break in many production environments. The point of this discussion is to understand that although high availability is a necessity, it certainly won't save you from ignorance or idiocy.

High availability from a technical perspective is simply taking a single "service" and ensuring that a failure of one of its components will not result in an outage. So often high availability is considered only on the machinery level—one machine is *failover* for another. However, that is not the business goal.

The business goal is to ensure the services provided by the business are functional and accessible 100% of the time. Goals are nice, and it is always good to have a few unachievable goals in life to keep your accomplishments in perspective. Building a system that guarantees 100% uptime is an impossibility. A relatively useful but deceptive measurement that was widely popular during the dot-com era was the *n nines* measurement. Everyone wanted an architecture with *five nines availability*, which meant functioning and accessible 99.999% of the time.

Let's do a little math to see what this really means and why a healthy bit of perspective can make an unreasonable technical goal reasonable. Five nines availability means that of the (60 seconds/minute * 60 minutes/hour * 24 hours/day * 365 days/year =) 31,536,000 seconds in a year you must be up (99.999% * 31,536,000 seconds =) 31,535,684.64 seconds. This leaves an allowable (31,536,000 - 31,535,684.64 =) 315.36 seconds of unavailability. That's just slightly more than 5 minutes of downtime in an entire year.

Now, in all fairness, there are different perspectives on what it means to be *available*. Take online banking for example. It is absolutely vital that I be able to access my account online and transfer money to pay bills. However, being the night owl that I am, I constantly try to access my bank account at 3 a.m., and at least twice per month it is unavailable with a message regarding "planned maintenance." I believe that my bank has a maintenance window between 2 a.m. and 5 a.m. daily that it uses every so often. Although this may seem like cheating, most large production environments define high availability to be the lack of *unplanned* outages. So, what may be considered cheating could also be viewed as smart, responsible, and controlled. Planned maintenance windows (regardless of whether they go unused) provide an opportunity to perform proactive maintenance that reduces the risk of unexpected outages during non-maintenance windows.

Monitoring

High availability is necessary in mission-critical systems, but blind faith that the high availability solution is working and the architecture is always available (no matter how fault tolerant) is just crazy! Monitoring the architecture from top to bottom is necessary in a mission-critical system to ensure that failed pieces are caught early and dealt with swiftly before their effects propagate and cause the facing services to malfunction.

The typical approach to monitoring services is from the bottom up. Most monitoring services are managed by the operations group and as such tend to address their immediate needs and grow perpetually as needed. This methodology is in no way wrong; however, it is incomplete.

In my early years as a novice systems administrator, I was working on a client's systems after an unplanned outage and was asked why the problem wasn't caught earlier. The architecture in question was large and relatively complex (500,000 lines of custom perl web application code, 3 Oracle databases, and about 250 unique and unrelated daily jobs). The problem was that cron (the daemon responsible for dispatching daily jobs) got stuck writing to /var/log/ocron (its log file) and simply stopped running jobs. I won't explain in more detail, not because it is outside the scope of this book, but rather because I don't really understand *why* it malfunctioned. We had no idea that this could happen, and no bottom-up monitoring we had in place alerted us to this problem.

Where is this going? Bear with me a bit longer. I explained to the client that we monitor disk space, disk performance metrics, Oracle availability and performance, and a billion other things, but we weren't monitoring cron. He told me something extremely valuable that I have never forgotten: "I don't care if cron is running. I don't care if the disks are full or if Oracle has crashed. I don't care if the @#$% machine is on fire. All that matters is that my business is running."

I submit that top-down monitoring is as valuable as bottom-up monitoring. If your business is to sell widgets through your website, it doesn't really matter whether your machine is always on fire if you are smoothly selling widgets. Obviously, this statement is the other extreme, but you get the picture.

A solid and comprehensive monitoring infrastructure monitors systems from the bottom up (the systems and services), as well as from the top down (the business level). From this point on, we will call them *systems monitors* and *business monitors*, respectively.

Monitoring Implementations

Saying that you are going to monitor a web server is one thing; actually doing it is another. Even systems monitors are multifaceted. It is important to ensure that the machine is healthy by monitoring system load, memory-use metrics, network interface errors, disk space, and so on. On top of this, a web server is running, so you must monitor the number of hits it is receiving and the type and number of each type of response code (200 "OK," 302 "Redirect," 404 "Not Found," 500 "Internal Error," and so on). And, regardless of the metrics you get from the server itself, you should monitor the ability to contact the service over HTTP and HTTPS to ensure that you can load pages. These are the most basic systems monitors.

Aside from checking the actual service using the protocols it speaks (in this case web-specific protocols), how do you get all the metrics you want to monitor? There isn't one single answer to this, but a standard protocol is deployed throughout the industry called *SNMP (simple network management protocol)*. Almost every commercially sold product comes instrumented with an SNMP agent. This means that by using the same protocol, you can ask every device on your network metric questions such as "How much disk space is used?" and "How many packets have you received?"

SNMP pretty much rules the monitoring landscape. Not only do most vendors implement SNMP in the architectural components they sell, all monitoring implementations (both commercial and free) support querying SNMP-capable devices. You'll notice that I said "most commercial components" and didn't mention free/open components. Sadly, many of the good open-source tools and free tools available are not instrumented with SNMP agents.

Probably the largest offender of this exclusion practice is the *Mail Transport Agent (MTA)*. Most MTAs completely ignore the fact that there are standardized SNMP mechanisms called *Management Information Bases (MIBs)*. The point here is not to complain about MTAs not implementing SNMP (although they should), but rather to illustrate that you will inevitably run into something you need to monitor on the systems level that doesn't speak SNMP. What happens then?

There are two ways to handle components that do not expose the needed information over SNMP. The first method is to fetch this metric via some unrelated network mechanism, such as SSH or HTTP, which has the tremendous advantage of simplicity. The second is to take this metric and export it over SNMP, making it both efficient and trivial to integrate into any monitoring system. Both methods require you first to develop an external means of determining the information you need (via a hand-written script or using a proprietary vendor-supplied tool).

Although the second choice may sound like the "right way," it certainly has a high overhead. SNMP is based on a complicated hierarchy of MIBs defined by a large and scattered set of documents. Without a very good MIB tool, it is difficult to decipher the information and an unbelievable pain to author a new MIB. To export the custom metrics you've determined over SNMP, you must extend or author a new MIB specifically for this and then either integrate an agent into the product or find an agent flexible enough to publish your MIB for you.

When is this worth it? That is a question that can only be answered by looking at the size of your architecture, the rate of product replacement, and the rate of change of your monitoring requirements. Remember, the monitoring system needs to monitor all these system metrics, as well as handle the business metrics. Business metrics, in my experience, are rarely exported over SNMP.

Some services are distributed in nature. Spread is one such example that cannot be effectively monitored with SNMP. The purpose of Spread is to allow separate nodes to publish data to other nodes in a specific fashion. Ultimately, the health of a single Spread daemon is not all that important. Instead, what you really want to monitor is the service that Spread provides, and you can only do so by using the service to accomplish a simple task and reporting whether the task completed as expected.

Criteria for a Capable Monitoring System

What makes a monitoring system good? First and foremost, it is the time invested in it and winning, or at least fighting, the constant battles brought on by architecture, application, and business changes. Components are added and removed on an ongoing basis. Application changes happen. Business metrics are augmented or deprecated. If the monitoring infrastructure does not adapt hand-in-hand with these changes, it is useless and even dangerous. Monitoring things no longer of importance while failing to monitor newly introduced metrics can result in a false sense of security that acts like blinders.

The second crucial criterion is a reliable and extensible monitoring infrastructure. A plethora of commercial, free, proprietary, and open monitoring frameworks are available. Rather than do a product review, we'll look at the most basic capabilities required of a monitoring solution:

- SNMP support—This is not difficult to find and will support most of the systems monitoring requirements.

- Extensibility—The ability to plug in ad hoc monitors. This is needed for many custom systems monitors and virtually all business monitors. Suppose that a business sells widgets and decides that (based on regressing last week's data) it should sell at least 3 widgets every 15 minutes and at least 20 widgets every hour between 6 a.m. and 10 p.m. and at least 10 widgets every hour between 10 p.m. and 6 a.m. If, at any point in time, those goals aren't met, it is likely that something technical is wrong. A good monitoring system allows an operator to place arbitrary rules such as this one alongside the other systems monitors.

- Flexible notifications—The system must be able to react to failures by alerting the operator responsible for the service. Not only should an operator be notified, but the infrastructure should also support automatic escalation of failures if they are not resolved in a given time period.

- Custom reaction—Some events that occur can be rectified or further investigated by an intelligent agent. If expected website traffic falls below a reasonable lower bound, the system should notify the operator. The operator is likely to perform several basic diagnostic techniques as the first phase of troubleshooting. Instead of wasting valuable time, the monitoring system could have performed the diagnostics and placed the output in the payload of the failure notification.

- Complex scheduling—Each individual monitor should have a period that can be modified. Metrics that are expensive to evaluate and/or are slow to change can be queried less frequently than those that are cheap and/or volatile.

- Maintenance scheduling—Monitors should never be taken offline. The system should support input from an administrator that some service or set of services is expected to be down during a certain time window in the future. During these windows, the services will be monitored, but noticed failures will not be escalated.

- Event acknowledgment—When things break that do not affect the overall availability and quality of service, they often do not need to be addressed until the next business day. Disabling notifications manually is dangerous. Instead, the system should acknowledge the failure and suspend notifications for a certain period of time or until a certain fixed point in time.

- Service dependencies—Each monitor that is put in place is not an automaton. On any given web server there will be 10 or more individual system checks (connectivity, remote access, HTTP, HTTPS, time skew, disk space, system load, network metrics, and various HTTP response code rates, just to name a few). That web server is plugged into a switch, which is plugged into a load balancer, which is plugged into a firewall, and so on. If your monitoring infrastructure exists outside your architecture, there is a clear service dependency graph. There is no sense in alerting an operator that there is a time skew on a web server if the web server has crashed. Likewise, there is no sense in alerting that there is a time skew or a machine crash if there is a failure of the switch to which the machine in question is attached. A hierarchy allows one event to be a superset of another. System alerts that go to a person's pager should be clear, be concise, and articulate the problem. Defining clear service dependencies and incorporating those relationships into the notification logic is a must for a complete monitoring system.

Coping with Release Cycles

Most architectures, even the small and simple ones, are much more complicated than they first appear. For truly mission-critical applications, every piece must be thoroughly tested and retested before it is deployed in production. Even the simplest of architectures has hardware, operating systems, and server software. More complicated architectures include core switches and routers (which have software upgrade requirements), databases, load balancers, firewalls, email servers, and so on.

Managing the release cycles of external software, operating systems, and hardware is a challenge in mission-critical environments. Flawless upgrades are a testament to a good operations group.

Managing internal release cycles for all custom-built applications and the application infrastructure that powers a large website is a slightly different beast because the burden is no longer solely on the operations group. Development teams must have established practices and procedures, and, more importantly, they must follow them.

Internal Release Cycles

The typical production environment, mission-critical or not, has three vital components: development, staging, and production.

Development

Development is where things break regularly, and experiments take place. New architectural strategies are developed and tested here, as well as all application implementation.

In particularly large and well-funded organizations, research and development are split into two entities. In this scenario, things do not regularly break in development, and no experimentation takes place. Development is for the creation of new code to implement new business requirements.

The research architecture is truly a playground for implementing new ideas. If a substantial amount of experimentation takes place, splitting these architectures is important. After all, having a team of developers sitting by idly watching others clean up the mess of an experiment "gone wrong" is not a good financial investment.

Why research at all? If your business isn't technology, there is a good argument not to do any experimentation. However, staying ahead of competitors often means trying new things and adopting different ideas before they do. This applies equally to technology and business. A close relationship with vendors sometimes satisfies this, but ultimately, the people who live and breathe the business (your team) are likely to have a more successful hand in creating innovative solutions that address your needs.

Staging

Applications and services are built in development, and as a part of their construction, they are tested. Yet staging is the real infrastructure for testing. It is not testing to *see* whether it works because that was done in development. Instead, here it is testing to *make sure* that it works.

This environment should be as close to the production environment as possible (usually an exact replica) down to the hardware and software versions. Why? Complex systems are, by their very definition, complex. This means that things can and will go wrong in entirely unexpected ways.

The other big advantage that comes with an identical staging and production environment is that new releases need not be *pushed* (moved from staging to production). Because the environments are identical, when a new release has been staged, tested, and approved, the production traffic is simply *pointed* to the staging environment, and their roles simply switch.

Staging new releases of internal (and external) components provides a proving ground where true production loads can be tested. The interaction of changed pieces and the vast number of other components can be witnessed, debugged, and optimized. Often, the problems that arise in staging result in destaging and redeveloping.

The architecture must allow operations and development teams to watch things break, spiral out of control, and otherwise croak. Watching these things happen leads to understanding the cause and in turn leads to solutions.

Most architectures are forced to cope with two different types of internal releases. The first is the obvious next feature release of the application. This contains all the business requirements specified, built, tested, and integrated since the last release. The other type of internal release is the bug fix. These are incremental and necessary fixes to the current release running in production.

Bug fixes are usually staged in an environment that is much smaller than the current production environment. Because they are minor changes, the likelihood that they will cause an unexpected impact on another part of the architecture is small. The true mission-critical environments have three identical production environments: one for production, one for staging revisions, and another for staging releases.

Production

Production is where it all happens. But in reality, it is where nothing should happen from the perspective of developers and administrators. Things should be quiet, uneventful, and routine in a production environment. Money and time are invested in development environments and staging environments to ensure this peace of mind.

A Small Dose of Reality

Few businesses can afford to invest in both a complete development and a deployment environment. This is not necessarily a horrible thing. Business, like economics, is based on the principle of cost versus benefit (cost-benefit), and success relies on making good decisions based on cost-benefit information to increase return on investment. The introduction of technology into a business does not necessarily change this. This is perhaps one of the most difficult lessons for a technically oriented person to learn: The best solution technically is not always the right solution for the business.

Over the years, I have consulted for many a client who wanted to avoid the infrastructure costs of a solid development and staging environment. Ultimately, this is a decision that every business must make. Because it is impossible to say what *will* happen if you don't have an adequate staging environment, I'll place some numbers from my experience on the potential costs of not having good procedures and policies and maintaining the appropriate infrastructure to support them.

I worked on an architecture that had about a million dollars invested in hardware and software for the production environment, but the owner was only willing to invest $10,000 in the development and staging environment combined. With resources limited that way, proper staging and thorough developmental testing were impossible. Given that, about 1 in 5 pushes into production had a mild negative impact due to unexpected bugs, and about 1 in 500 pushes failed catastrophically. Before we judge this to be an ideological error, understand that all these decisions simply come down to business sense.

The mild mistakes were fixed either by reverting the bad fragments or with a second push of corrected code, and the catastrophic errors were handled by reverting to a previous known-good copy of the production code. And it turns out that the nature of these failures generally did not cost the business anything and produced only marginal unrealized profits.

A fully fledged staging and development environment could have cost an additional two or three million dollars. The cost of regular small mistakes and the rare catastrophic error were found to be less than the initial investment and maintenance of an architecture that could reduce the likelihood of such mistakes.

But, all businesses are not the same. If a bank took this approach…well, I wouldn't have an account there.

External Release Cycles

External release cycles are the art of upgrading software and hardware products deployed throughout an architecture that are not maintained internally. This typically constitutes 99% of most architectures and usually includes things such as machinery, operating systems, databases, and web server software just for starters.

External releases are typically easier to handle on an individual basis because they come as neatly wrapped packages from the vendor (even the open-source products). However, because 99% of the architecture consists of external products from different vendors, each with its own release cycle, the problem is compounded into an almost unmanageable mess.

On top of the complications of attempting to roll many unrelated external releases into one controlled release to be performed on the architecture, you have emergency releases that complicate the whole matter.

Emergency releases are releases that must be applied with extreme haste to solve an issue that could expose the architecture from a security standpoint or to resolve a sudden and acute issue (related to performance or function) that is crippling the business.

Examples of emergency releases are abundant in the real world:

- An exploit in the OpenSSL library is found, which sits under mod_ssl, which sits inside Apache to provide secure web access to your customers. Simply put, all your servers running that code are vulnerable to being compromised, and it is essential that you upgrade them as quickly as is safely possible.

- A bug is found in the version of Oracle used in your architecture. Some much-needed performance tuning was done, and the bug is manifesting itself acutely. You open a ticket with Oracle, and they quickly track down the bug and provide you with a patch to apply. That patch must be applied immediately because the problem is crippling the applications that are using Oracle.

The preceding examples are two of a countless number of real-life emergency rollouts that I have encountered.

The truth is that managing external releases is the core responsibility of the operations group. It is not a simple task, and an entire book (or series of books) could be written explaining best practices for this management feat.

The Cost of Complexity
Shackled to Large Architectures

It has long since been established that, in the world of technology, having even the smallest gadget grants certain bragging rights. However, for one reason or another, when it comes to the technology architecture, everyone likes to brag that he has bigger toys than the next guy.

I can't count the number of times I've overheard developers and engineers at conferences arguing about who has the larger and more complicated architecture. Since when did this become a goal? The point of building scalable systems is that they scale easily and *cost effectively*. One aspect of being cost effective is minimizing the required infrastructure, and another is minimizing the cost of maintaining that architecture. Two people arguing over who has the more complicated architecture sounds like two people arguing over who can burn money in a hotter furnace—I hope they both win.

Of course, architectures can be necessarily complicated. But a good architect should always be battling to *KISS (keep it simple, stupid)*. Two fundamental truths about complex architectures are as follows:

- Independent architectural components added to a system complicate it linearly. Dependent architectural components added complicate it exponentially.

- Complex systems of any type are complicated.

The first means that when one component relies on another component in the architecture, it compounds the complexity. An example of an independent component is a transparent web proxy-cache. The device sits out front and simply attempts to speed viewing of the site by caching content. It can be removed without affecting the function of the architecture. On the other hand, the complexity of a core database server is compounded because the web application depends on it.

Although the second truth may sound overly obvious, it is often ignored or overlooked. A complex system is more difficult to operate, develop, extend, troubleshoot, and simply be around. Inevitably, business requirements will change, and modifications will need to be made. Complex systems have a tendency to become more complex when they are modified to accomplish new tasks.

Looking for Speed

From a fundamental perspective, performance and scalability are orthogonal. Scalability in the realm of technical infrastructure simply means that it can grow and shrink without fundamental change. Growing, of course, means serving more traffic and/or more users, and that directly relates to the performance of the system as a whole.

If you have two load-balanced web servers that serve static HTML pages only, this is an inherently scalable architecture. More web servers can be added, and capacity can be increased without redesigning the system or changing dependent components (because no dependent components are in the system).

Even if your web servers can serve only one hit per second, the system scales. If you need to serve 10,000 hits per second, you can simply deploy 10,000 servers to solve your performance needs. This scales, but by no means scales well.

It may be obvious that one hit per second is terribly low. If you had used 500 hits per second as the performance of a single web server, you would only have needed 20 machines. Herein lies the painful relativity of the term *scales well*—serving 500 hits per second of static content is still an underachievement, and thus 20 machines is an unacceptably large number of machines for this task.

It should be clear from the preceding example that the performance of an individual component in the architecture can drastically affect how efficiently a system can scale. It is imperative that the performance of every introduced architectural component is scrutinized and judged. If a component performs the needed task but does not scale and scale well, using it will damage the scalability of the entire architecture.

Why be concerned with the performance of individual components? The only way to increase the performance of a complex system is to reduce the resource consumption of one or more of its individual components. Contrapositively, if an individual component of a complex system performs slowly, it is likely to capsize the entire architecture. It is fundamental that solid performance-tuning strategies be employed through the *entire* architecture.

Every architecture has components; every component runs software of some type. If your architecture has performance problems, it is usually obvious in which component the problems are manifesting themselves. From that point, you look at the code running on that component to find the problem. A few common scenarios contribute to the production of slow code:

- Many developers who are good at meeting design and function requirements are not as skilled in performance tuning. This needs to change.

- It is often easier to detect performance problems after the system has been built and is in use.

- People believe that performance can be increased by throwing more hardware at the problem.

Given that there is no magical solution, how does one go about writing high-performance code? This is an important question, and there is a tremendous amount of literature on the market about how to optimize code under just about every circumstance imaginable. Because this book doesn't focus on how to write high-performance code, we will jump to how to diagnose poorly performing code.

Gene Ahdmal stated that speeding up code inside a bottleneck has a larger impact on software performance than does speeding up code outside a bottleneck. This combined with classic 90/10 principle of code (90% of execution time is spent in 10% of the code) results in a good target.

Do *not* choose the slowest architectural component or piece of code to focus on. Start with the most common execution path and evaluate its impact on the system. The thing to keep in mind is that a 50% speedup of code that executes 0.1% of the time results in an overall speedup of 0.05%, which is small. On the other hand, a 50% speedup of code that executes 5% of the time results in an overall speedup of 2.5%, which is significant.

At the end of the day, week, month, or year, there will be code that is bad. Even the best developers write bad code at times. It is important that all infrastructure code and application code be open to review and revision and that performance review and tuning is a perpetual cycle.

I honestly believe the most valuable lessons in performance tuning, whether it be on the systems level or in application development, come from building things wrong. Reading about or being shown by example how to do a task "correctly" lacks the problem-solving skills that lead to its "correctness." It also does not present in its full form the contrast between the original and the new.

By working directly on an application that had performance issues, you can work toward improvement. Realizing performance gains due to minor modifications or large refactoring has tremendous personal gratification, but there is more to it than that. The process teaches the analytical thought processes required to anticipate future problems before they manifest themselves.

Sometimes performance tuning must be "out of the box." Analysis on the microscopic level should regularly be retired to more macroscopic views. This multiresolutioned problem analysis can turn a question such as "How can I merge all these log files faster?" into "Why do I have all these log files to merge and is there a better way?" Or a question such as "How can I make this set of problematic database queries faster?" becomes "Why am I putting this information in a database?"

Changing the scope of the question allows problems to be tackled from different angles, and regular reassessment provides an opportunity to use the right tool for the job.

It's Not a One-Man Mission

If the mission is critical, trusting it to one man is folly. To meet the objective, time, effort, and money have been spent to make an architecture with no single point of failure, so having a single person managing it violates the objective. Personnel are part of the architecture.

This leaves us with more than one man and in all fairness a decent-sized multidisciplinary team. Although in large teams, it isn't cost effective to educate every person involved on every aspect of running the system—that is, after all, why it is called a multidisciplinary team—it is vital that the lines of communication be kept open so that responsibilities and knowledge are not strictly isolated.

As soon as you lose respect for any one of these key aspects you will be bitten.

4

High Availability.
HA! No Downtime?!

OFTEN, PEOPLE REFER TO HIGH availability (HA) and load balancing (LB) interchangeably and incorrectly, using high availability when they mean load balancing alone and/or when they mean high availability and load balancing together. High availability has become a part of high availability/load balancing because product brochures and promotional material combine high availability and load balancing in a way that implies that they are one and the same thing. This is simply wrong. High availability is an orthogonal concept to load balancing, and, if approached as such, a better understanding can be achieved.

High availability means that things are always available. Even in the event of an unexpected failure, the services being provided should remain available. This is known as *fault tolerant*.

> **Fault tolerance:**
> The capability of a system or component to continue normal operation despite the presence of hardware or software faults. Also, the number of faults a system or component can withstand before normal operation is impaired.

Simply put, actors may die, but the show must go on. But before you say "Great! Let's do that!" take a look at costs and benefits. Figure 4.1 depicts a classic network diagram with no fault tolerance. Figure 4.2 depicts the same architecture with fault tolerance networking infrastructure. Basically, this network architecture eliminates any single point of failure in the egress point to our network provider.

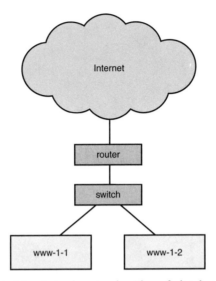

Figure 4.1   A simple network with no fault tolerance.

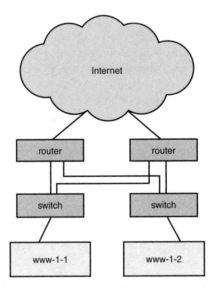

Figure 4.2   A simple, fault-tolerant network.

Obviously, if all the components fail, there is no way the service can survive. But how many components can fail? If an architecture allows for a single component failure without the underlying service being jeopardized, it is considered *1 fault tolerant*. On the other hand, if every component but one can fail (the strongest guarantee possible) while maintaining the availability of the service, the system is called *N-1 fault tolerant*.

Because making a system highly available adds cost, what can you hope to gain for your pains? The following are some advantages of investing time, money, and effort in building and maintaining a highly available architecture:

- Taking down components of your architecture for maintenance and upgrades is simple. When an architecture has been designed to transparently cope with the unexpected loss of a system or component, it is often trivial to intentionally remove that system or components for testing, upgrades, or anything else your heart desires.

  A simple example of this outside the web world is the operation of mail exchanges. SMTP, albeit an ancient protocol, has an intrinsic requirement of responsibility and reliability. A mail server *must* hold onto a message until it has decidedly handed that message to the responsible party. In the case of Internet email, a Message Transfer Agent (MTA) will try all the listed mail exchanges in ascending order of preference until one succeeds. Although this may sound obvious, the intrinsic fault tolerance of the system may not be so obvious.

  This means that, at any time, you can intentionally or accidentally disable an advertised mail exchange, and all inbound emails will simply use the other mail exchanges that are still accessible. SMTP's simple and elegant design allows for this basic fault tolerance without the need for extraneous (and often expensive) hardware or software solutions to provide high availability. HTTP provides no such intrinsic fault tolerance, and that forces us to architect an appropriate highly available solution.

- Well-designed highly available architectures often lend themselves to higher capacity. The rest of this book details how to approach the issues of highly scalable architectural design. Although you can always take "the wrong path" and build a large highly available system that scales poorly, we will concentrate on the fact that it *can* be done "right" and afford the architect, maintainers, and users the luxury of a system that scales without the need for fundamental engineering changes.

  It is important to keep in mind that any hardware required for the architecture to run cannot be considered redundant. If you rely on your redundant hardware for the purposes of handling routine load, it isn't really redundant hardware at all.

  Well-designed distributed systems offer the benefits of controlled and understood horizontal scalability. One example of this "good design" is some of today's peer-to-peer (P2P) systems. A key feature of their success is that as the networks grow to arbitrarily large sizes, and the number of machines on the network increases, that growth neither requires the individual machines to be more powerful nor sacrifices the quality of service.

- After tackling the three-node cluster, scaling to *n* nodes is a process not an experiment. When building a cluster of machines to serve a single purpose, one of the most common problems encountered is getting those machines to cooperate toward the common goal. This is the most tremendous challenge of distributed systems design. For some services, such as DNS, this exercise is simple and easy. For other systems, specifically databases, this challenge poses a problem that we can consider academically difficult.

Database replication is a controversial topic. Many claim that the problem is solved; others claim the solutions are inadequate. The simpler two-node solution has been used for many years in the financial industry. This *replication* is usually employed to ensure high availability on two systems using a protocol such as two-phase commit (2PC) or three-phase commit (3PC). Unfortunately, these commonly deployed solutions do not handle the expansion to three nodes in an elegant way due to the limitations of the protocols they use. In short, there are no good enterprise-ready, horizontally scalable, N-1 failure tolerant database systems in existence. This problem is expensive to solve correctly, so instead of solving the three-node problem, the accepted approach is to engineer around it.

We won't delve into this subject too deeply here because Chapter 8, "Distributed Databases Are Easy, Just Read the Fine Print," is dedicated to the exploration of distributed, fault-tolerant databases both from a theoretical aspect and in the real world.

Now that we know what we've bought, let's take a look at the bill. The disadvantages of building and maintaining a highly available architecture are both serious and unavoidable:

- Implementing a high-availability solution means more equipment and services to maintain. By their very nature, highly available systems have multiple working components. Multiple components allow for survivability in light of failures. Assuming that the system is N-1 fault tolerant, you may find yourself building a service with a multitude of components and should truly understand the technical, financial, and emotional cost of maintaining them. As illustrated in previous chapters, solid policies and procedures can help minimize these costs.

- Troubleshooting distributed systems is dramatically more difficult than their single-node counterparts. Web services are built on top of HTTP, so a long single transaction from the end-user's perspective is actually composed of a series of simple and short transactions. Because a single conceptual transaction is actually individual POST and GET requests over HTTP, each one could conceivably arrive at a different machine in a cluster. One solution to this is to force the entire conceptual transaction to visit the same machine for each incremental web transaction. Chapter 5, "Load Balancing and the Utter Confusion Surrounding It," discusses the numerous pitfalls to this approach. We are left with tightly coupled events occurring on separate machines. This vastly complicates identifying cause and effect, which is the most fundamental of troubleshooting concepts. Chapter 9, "Juggling Logs and Other Circus Tricks," discusses approaches to unifying the logging across all the machines in a web cluster to provide a single-instance perspective. This in turn provides an environment where traditional troubleshooting techniques can be applied to solve problems.

- Application programmers must be aware of content synchronization issues. When running a web service on a single machine, it is intrinsically impossible to have content synchronization or consistency issues. However, when applications are deployed across a cluster of machines, there is a risk of a difference in content between two servers affecting the integrity of the service being provided to the end-user.

  Code consistency is generally a simpler issue to solve. At first glance, the problem would seem to manifest itself as one user seeing one thing, and a second user seeing something different; however, the problem is more severe. As subsequent requests in the same user's session arrive at different machines, a variety of complicated problems can arise.

  Content synchronization is a much more complicated issue because it can manifest itself in a wide variety of scenarios ranging from dynamic content in web pages to synchronizing user session states. Several techniques can be used to distribute content and user data across a cluster of machines, but most are foreign concepts to classic application design.

- The mere fact that you need a highly available solution speaks to the attention required to properly manage the overall architecture. Managing production systems is an art. More than that, it is the responsibility of a group of multidisciplinary artisans who always have their hand in changing the artwork. As availability demands increase, the margin for error decreases. Developers, systems administrators, database administrators, and the rest of the crew are required to work more closely to ensure that availability requirements can be met.

Why High Availability and Load Balancing Are Different

One of the keys to successful systems is to clearly define the requirements before embarking on the implementation path. Determining whether a system needs high availability or load balancing or both is essential. So, what is the difference between high availability and load balancing? Well, aside from fundamentally different definitions, nothing.

High availability:

Remaining available despite the failure of one's components; usually used to describe a system or a service; above and beyond fault tolerant.

Load balancing:

Providing a service from multiple separate systems where resources are effectively combined by distributing requests across these systems.

Almost all load-balancing hardware vendors in existence advertise their devices as providing high availability and load balancing. They take a single device and magically make a set of 10 servers work together for a tenfold performance increase. Pay the price, buy the product, and all your pain will disappear. Yeah. Right.

Aside from the fundamental foresight that statement lacks, this is an absolute falsehood. The idea that a web cluster of 10 machines can use each box to its optimal capacity is a misconception. That would require knowing all the requests that will come in the future, how long they will take, what resources they will occupy, and exactly what the available resources are on every machine in the cluster at the time that a request arrives to be load balanced. That information isn't available, so obviously you cannot build an optimal system. In fact, most solutions don't even use best-of-breed performance metrics in their decision making, which makes them more a simple "load distributor" than a "load balancer."

Keep in mind that the goal is not to build an optimal system (that is impossible), but rather to run the business well. A system that meets the business needs is efficient and has a total cost of ownership that is reasonable over the short and long term.

Load Balancing Is Not High Availability

Load balancing has the effect of unifying separate systems to accomplish a common goal. Available resources from each machine contribute to a virtual resource pool, and that pool is drawn upon to accomplish a computing task (for example, serving a web page). Each contributing machine can have a different amount of available resources. Here is where it starts to touch on high availability.

If a machine in that pool suddenly has no resources to provide, tasks can still be completed using the resources available from other machines. So in effect, if a machine crashes, a valid load-balancing configuration will refrain from allocating tasks to that machine (or using its resources) until it becomes available once again.

This is not a solution to high availability. In fact, it doesn't solve the problem at all; rather, it moves the problem into a different tier of components. Often, this just shifts the responsibility from systems administrator (SA) to network administrator (NA). Although this is good for the SA and bad for the NA (from a responsibility perspective), the business has not gained or lost any availability assurances—though it has likely lost a good chunk of money on building the solution.

High Availability Is Not Load Balancing

High availability simply means resilience in light of failures. Nowhere in its definition does it imply efficient resource usage or increased capacity. Specifically in hot-standby systems, one system is performing all the work while the other waits idle for the active system to crash. In these configurations, one system is contributing 100% of its resources, whereas all others are contributing 0%.

Although some two-node failover and peer-based, highly available systems offer the flexibility of using both components at the same time, this should not be considered a load-balancing solution. A legitimate load-balancing scheme must have some intelligent mechanism of allocating the available resources. These systems—although capable of providing concurrent service on more than one component—do not incorporate any intelligence into the process of allocating their resources.

It is possible to build a system that so tightly couples high availability and load balancing that they are indistinguishable, but, armed with the previous information, I challenge you to find a web-centric high availability/load balancing device where you can't partition the feature sets as clearly as the concepts of high availability and load balancing are presented here.

Traditional High Availability—The Whitepaper Approach

A wide variety of products are on the market today that provide high availability. Most of these utterly confuse the load balancing they provide with the notion of high availability. It is important to understand both heads of this beast (high availability and load balancing), so that you aren't duped into buying a safety blanket that won't keep you warm.

A traditional hardware high availability device provides a mechanism for advertising a virtual service (either UDP/IP or TCP/IP) to end-users and distributes the requests to that service to a set of machines providing that service (shown in Figure 4.3). In the case of web services, the device listens on an advertised IP address on port 80, and any web requests that arrive on that IP address are distributed over a set of locally configured web servers.

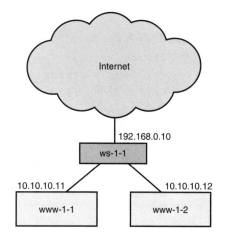

Figure 4.3 A load balancer advertising a virtual IP for real servers.

The device here has the capability to run service checks against the web servers to determine whether they are available to service requests. The service checks on these devices can range from simple ICMP pings to full HTTP requests with content validation. This means that if a machine fails, the device will eliminate that machine from the eligible set of machines over which it distributes requests. As long as a single machine is alive and well in the pool of servers, the service will survive. Sounds perfect, right? Not really.

Let's investigate the positive and negative aspects of using a dedicated high availability/ load balancing device. In Figure 4.3, you'll notice that the high availability/load balancing device is clearly a single point of failure.

The fact that almost every large architecture has hardware load balancers deployed should tell you that they have powerful selling points. It is important to keep in mind that selling points aren't buying points and that some of the positive aspects listed may simply not apply to your architecture.

- These devices are widely used and relied on at some of the largest Internet deployments in existence. This means that they work. They are tried, true, and tested. It is also unlikely that they will fail.

- As hardware devices specifically designed for load balancing web (among other) services, they are high performance and scale well. Some devices boast being capable of managing 15 million concurrent connections and more than 50 gigabits/ second sustained throughput.

- Application servers are no longer a single point of failure. In other words, the service can survive N-1 application server failures. If one remains up, things keep on ticking.

- Services distributed across multiple machines can still be advertised as a single IP address to the world. The ramifications of not behaving this way are discussed in detail in the later section of this chapter called, "High Availability Rethought (Peer-Based)."

Of course, with the good comes the bad. Hardware high availability/load balancing devices have some glaring disadvantages:

- The device here costs money and often a substantial amount of it. Its mere existence introduces architectural complexities. Consider first the ongoing maintenance and support costs. Second, to have a truly sound development and staging environment, it must match your production environment as closely as possible. This results in duplicating this architectural component in those environments.

- By deploying a single high availability/load balancing device in your architecture, have you made the system fault tolerant? The service will survive the failure of any one or N-1 of the web servers in the architecture. However, we now have a new component (the high availability/load balancing device), and the singular failure of that component will clearly cause a service outage. The solution? Buy two. However, it is still disturbing to implement a solution only to find that your high availability/load balancing device needs its own highly available solution!

Surveying the Site

Two main protocols are used for high availability and failover, and all use the concept of heartbeats. *Virtual Router Redundancy Protocol (VRRP)* is a protocol under draft by the IETF to be the standard protocol for device failover between routers on the Internet. Cisco has a proprietary implementation of the same concepts called *Hot Standby Routing Protocol (HSRP)* that has been deployed on thousands of routers and switches across the Internet and in corporate environments.

For classic computing systems, vendors and implementers have chosen a different path with the same ultimate goal of transparently migrating a service from a machine that has failed to another available machine. There are several open and closed solutions to server failover:

- Veritas Cluster Server
- SGI's Linux Failsafe
- LinuxHA
- CARP (OpenBSD's Common Address Redundancy Protocol)

All these products purport to offer solutions to the single point of failure. Saying that one is better than the other would be unfaithful to their intentions.

There are a slew of issues to deal with when tackling high availability, including shared storage, application awareness of system failures, and responsibility migration. Some of these products attempt to do everything for you, whereas others provide the fundamental tools to grow the solution that is right for you.

In the narrow world of the World Wide Web, shared storage isn't a common need. Typically, web services are horizontally scalable and work as well as separated distributed systems. This alleviates the need for shared storage and the need for application failover because the application is already running on all other nodes. Web systems that do rely on shared storage often find network attached storage (such as NFS) to be more than sufficient. Routers are in a similar position; routers route and post-failure, there isn't a tremendous amount of logic or procedure involved in enabling services on a router aside from assigning it IP addresses and making it participate in whatever routing negotiations are needed.

Databases, on the other hand, are much more complicated beasts. The classic path-of-least-resistance approach to making databases highly available is through shared attached storage and a heartbeat between two machines. We will go into this in Chapter 8. Each product has its place.

Pouring Concrete—Foundry ServerIron

Instead of referring to *the device* and *the service*, let's look at a concrete example. To focus narrowly on high availability, we will investigate a static website with no complicated content synchronization or session issues. This short example is not a "guide to the Foundry ServerIron"; for that, you should download the product documentation from the vendor. Here we intend only to demonstrate purpose and placement as well as overall simplicity.

www.example.com is a site that serves web pages over port 80 from the IP address 192.168.0.10. Our goal is to ensure that if any single architecture component we control fails, the service will survive.

Let's first look at a simple picture of two machines (www-1-1, www-1-2) running Apache with IP addresses 10.10.10.11 and 10.10.10.12, respectively. Out front, we have a Foundry Networks ServerIron web switch (ws-1-1) providing high availability. The ServerIron has a clean and simple configuration for "balancing" the load across these two machines while remaining aware of their availability:

```
server predictor round-robin

server port 80
  tcp

server real www-1-1 10.10.10.1
  port http url "HEAD /"

server real www-1-1 10.10.10.2
  port http url "HEAD /"

server virtual www.example.com 192.168.0.10
  port http
  bind http www-1-1 http www-1-2 http
```

This configuration tells the ServerIron that two real web servers are providing service over HTTP and that they should be considered available if they respond successfully to a HEAD / request. A virtual server listening at 192.168.0.10 on port 80 should send requests in a round-robin fashion back to those two configured real servers. This configuration can be seen with the additional fault-tolerant switching infrastructure shown in Figure 4.4. (This is a costly evolution from Figure 4.3.)

> **Note**
>
> In practice, this routing configuration is somewhat involved and is well outside the scope of this book. The configuration of adjacent networking devices and the overall network topology can drastically affect the actual implementation. Refer to the appropriate vendor-provided configuration guide.

However, although we have solved the issue of service vulnerability due to the loss of www-1-1 or www-1-2, we have introduced a new single point of failure ws-1-1. We are no better off. You might argue that a black-box networking device is less prone to failure than a commodity web server. That may be true, or it may not. You can run it in production and find out, or you can work the single point of failure out of the architecture; it's up to you.

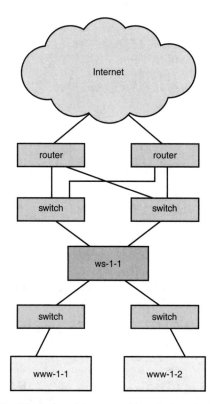

Figure 4.4   Network architecture with a single point of failure.

So, let's take the next step and build some fault tolerance into the web switch layer. Foundry, as do all other vendors, provides a built-in failover solution to accompany its product.

We add another identical ServerIron named, suitably, ws-1-2. We have Ethernet port 1 on each switch plugged in to our egress point to the outside world, and we have the switches cross-connected on Ethernet port 2. We configure them for hot-standby as follows.

On ws-1-1 and ws-1-2:

```
vlan 2
untag ethernet 2
no spanning-tree
exit

server router-ports 1
server backup ethernet 2 00e0.5201.0c72 2

write memory
end
reload
```

In a play-by-play recap, the first stanza places the second Ethernet port on the switch into a private VLAN, so the switches can chat together in private. The second stanza points out the Ethernet port connected to the router and configures hot-standby on the Ethernet port 2. The last stanza simply saves and reboots.

Presto! We now have failover on the web switch level, but how does the architecture change? Figure 4.5 shows the architecture recommended by many appliance vendors in their respective product documentation.

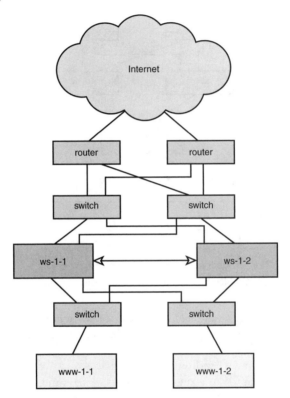

Figure 4.5 Network architecture with no single point of failure.

Now the web service can survive any single component failure—but at what cost? The architecture here has just grown dramatically; there is now more equipment to provide high availability than is presently providing the actual service. We have grown from the architecture depicted in Figure 4.4 to the one illustrated in Figure 4.5, effectively doubling the network infrastructure—all to make two web servers highly available.

Additionally, these hardware high availability/load balancing devices carry a substantial sticker price and add to that the ongoing support and maintenance costs.

Although this solution may make more financial sense when placed in front of 100 or 1,000 servers, the fact that it makes little sense in the scaled-down environment should be duly noted. Part of scalability is seamlessly scaling down as well as scaling up.

Remember that the focus of this chapter is high availability, not load balancing. This architecture needs only high availability but is paying for both. This example isn't to discredit ServerIrons or hardware high availability/load balancing devices, but rather to illustrate that they aren't always the right tool for the job. In the end, most of these devices are more useful in the load-balancing realm, but we'll talk about that in Chapter 5.

If the architecture looks sound, but the price tag does not, several commercial and noncommercial alternatives to the Foundry products described in the previous example are available. Freevrrpd is a free VRRP implementation, and linux-ha.org has several projects to perform pairwise failover. Due to concerns that VRRP is encumbered by intellectual property claims (and for the sake of building a better mousetrap), the OpenBSD team has developed a similar protocol called *Common Address Redundancy Protocol (CARP)*. These are all reasonable solutions because load balancing was never the goal—only high availability.

Additionally, some cost cuts can be made by collapsing the front-end and back-end switches onto the same hardware. However, this switch reuse often isn't applicable in large architectures because of the different demands placed on the front-end and back-end switches. Front-end switches are often inexpensive because they are simply used for connectedness of routers to high availability/load balancing devices and firewalls, whereas the back-end switches are core infrastructure switches with heavy utilization (and a hefty price tag).

High Availability Rethought (Peer-Based)

Why a new approach? It is clear that traditional pairwise failover approaches are sound because they are well understood and widely deployed.

Just because it will work does not mean that it is the right tool for the job. Trains are a fabulous method of mass transportation; however, bus lines still exist. Why? There is a market for them. The analogy is fitting when we consider the dynamic business needs of websites.

Trains are great if you know your waypoints, and you know they will not be changing. You can invest in laying the tracks and building the infrastructure. On the other hand, if you foresee the traffic patterns changing, and waypoints and routes coming and going, then buses are a more flexible and a more fitting solution.

Traditional high availability systems take the classic failover approach. System A is responsible for a task, but should it fail, System B can seamlessly take over its responsibilities. This leads to a lot of system pairs out in the world where one machine is completely idle.

Let's look at the high availability between the two web switches in the previous example. The roles and responsibilities of those switches are clear. The switches work together to ensure that a service is provided. The devices must work together to accomplish a task of load balancing requests across two back-end web servers. Should the active one fail, the backup assumes the responsibilities and obligations of the active role.

If we glance back at the two-machine www.example.com example, we notice that the goal was simply to achieve high availability. The two machines were not needed to increase capacity, rather just to provide failover. Why can't we employ the same logic used by the ServerIron pairs on the web servers themselves and have one web server assume the responsibilities of the other should it fail?

This is simple to accomplish with two machines where one is active. In fact, it is fairly easy, algorithmically, to solve with N machines when one is active. We can use a protocol such as VRRP or CARP to detect failures and promote a passive server into the role of the active server.

However, this approach is not commonly used. As soon as the website exceeds the capacity limits of a single server, multiple servers must be active to concurrently service clients for demand to be met. This leads to the obvious question: Why can't more than one of them be active?

The issues with multiple active machines in a high availability setup are responsibility and agreement. How can you be sure that all the responsibilities are being satisfied, while at the same time ensuring that no single responsibility is being handled by two machines concurrently? Some systems accomplish this by chaining master-slave so that every machine is a master of one service and a slave of another. This is overly complicated, prone to failure, and I submit to you that this answer is simply wrong. The answer is peer-based high availability.

Now that we are speaking of more than a pair of machines, we introduce the concept of a *cluster*. Although the concept may be obvious, let's put a clear definition on it anyway.

Cluster:

A bunch; a number of things of the same kind gathered together. In computers, a set of like machines providing a particular service united to increase robustness and/or performance.

Additionally, we will refer to a cluster as a set of machines working in unison to accomplish a specific goal or set of goals. These goals are services that are the responsibility of that cluster to keep running continuously and efficiently.

In a peer-based approach, the cluster is responsible for providing a set of services, but each available machine will negotiate and agree to assume responsibility over a subset of those services.

Let's take the two-node web cluster as an example. We have two machines with the IP addresses 10.10.10.1 and 10.10.10.2, respectively. Now, if machine one fails, one of those IP addresses will become inaccessible, and the cluster will have defaulted on its responsibility to serve traffic over that IP address. In the peer-based approach, the cluster of two machines is responsible for providing service over those two IP addresses. To which machine those IP addresses are assigned is irrelevant. More so, we don't care whether each has one or whether one has two and the other none—it matters not to the task at hand. Rather, you simply want a guarantee that if at least one machine is still standing the cluster will not default on its responsibilities.

So far, all the examples have been N services (web service from a particular IP address) and M machines (web servers) where N and M are equal. So, it makes sense that in a zero failure environment, each machine assumes the responsibility for providing service over a single IP address. If one machine were to fail, another machine would assume its responsibility, and it really does not matter which machine steps up to that challenge.

However, 1:1 is not the only way peer-based high availability can work. N:M is possible as well N < M and N > M, though it certainly makes sense that M is greater than one or you fail to accomplish the whole high availability goal!

This new paradigm for high availability is interesting, but what does it really buy us? The following lists a few advantages:

- No expensive hardware—Instead of implementing high availability with a solution that needs failover itself, the failover techniques that those products use can be enhanced and deployed on the machines providing the actual service.

- Free, open source implementations—This allows the process and logic to be modified if any unique features or decisions were required due to some unforeseen business need.

- Simplicity—No new network device or set of network devices is introduced in front of the existing service. Never underestimate the obscure problems that can occur in any complex system. The introduction of new components requires new monitoring, increased maintenance issues, and more complicated upgrade procedures, not to mention the fact that management of those devices often requires specialized skill sets. This means troubleshooting problems becomes more complicated and more expensive. Often, this is inevitable when a load-balancing system is needed.

Unfortunately, there is a negative aspect of pure peer-based high availability for services such as the web. Peer-based highly available systems really require multiple IP addresses for more than a single machine in the cluster to be used simultaneously. This type of IP address consumption does not meld well with IP unfriendly services such as SSL. Although it works fine with a few SSL sites, more than a handful becomes unwieldy.

Services such as HTTP over secure socket layer (SSL) (also known as https://) do not allow distinct services to be provided from the same IP address. The reason is because when a client connects, it immediately negotiates with the server a secure, authenticated connection by reviewing the server's certificate and possibly handing over a client certificate of its own. The catch is that the client doesn't have the capability to ask for a specific certificate; it is simply handed *the* certificate.

This SSL certificate has the common name of the site www.example.com encoded in it, and the client will check, among other things, that the name inside the certificate matches exactly the name of the service it was attempting to contact. This prevents spoofing of identities.

Directly, this means that a single IP address can serve at most one common name over SSL. So, unlike plain HTTP, which can serve virtually unlimited distinctly named websites from a single IP address, 1,000 SSL-capable unique websites would require at least 1,000 unique IP addresses.

This clashes strongly with idea of publishing several IP addresses for each public service. This is not a shortcoming of peer-based high availability, but rather a shortcoming of this *use* of peer-based high availability.

Peer-Based High Availability in the Real World

Wackamole is a software product from the Johns Hopkins University's Center for Networking and Distributed Systems. It is a simple, yet powerful, open source implementation of peer-based high availability. We won't dig in too deeply (that is, the configuration snippets here are incomplete) because this is intended only to illustrate the concept of peer-based configurations. Chapter 6, "Static Content Serving for Speed and Glory," delves into the gory details of installing and configuring Wackamole for a highly available, high-throughput image-serving cluster.

Wackamole sits atop Spread—a group communication toolkit that is rapidly gaining popularity. Through Spread, it coordinates with other peer machines in the cluster to determine safely (deterministically) who will take responsibility for the virtual IP addresses advertised by that cluster.

To better demonstrate peer-based advantages, let's turn once again to the www.example.com example. We can easily adapt the previous example to use the peer-based paradigm. Instead of exposing the web service over a single publicly accessible IP address, we now advertise six IP addresses: 192.168.0.11 through 192.168.0.16.

The relevant portion of the example.com Bind zone file follows:

```
www.example.com. 5M IN A 192.168.0.11
                 5M IN A 192.168.0.12
                 5M IN A 192.168.0.13
                 5M IN A 192.168.0.14
                 5M IN A 192.168.0.15
                 5M IN A 192.168.0.16
```

To better illustrate the setup, we deploy three physical web servers responsible for making the www.example.com service available.

```
    wackamole.conf:
VirtualInterfaces {
  { eth0:192.168.0.11/32 }
  { eth0:192.168.0.12/32 }
  { eth0:192.168.0.13/32 }
  { eth0:192.168.0.14/32 }
  { eth0:192.168.0.15/32 }
  { eth0:192.168.0.16/32 }
}
```

A configuration file is provided to the Wackamole daemon that describes the full set of six virtual IP addresses for which the cluster is responsible. The daemon connects to Spread and joins a group unique to that cluster. By joining this group, each Wackamole instance has visibility to the other instances running Wackamole in the cluster. Those that are visible are considered *up and running*, and those that are not are considered *down and out*. Using the strong group membership semantics of Spread, the set of running Wackamole daemons can quickly and deterministically decide which machines will assume which IP addresses.

During normal operation, when all machines are functioning properly, each machine has two IP addresses as shown in Figure 4.6. When a Wackamole instance stops participating in the group (for any reason, be it a node failure or an administrative decision), a new membership is established, and steps are automatically taken to juggle IP addresses, as necessary, to ensure all configured IP addresses are spoken for. Figure 4.7 illustrates this "juggling" effect.

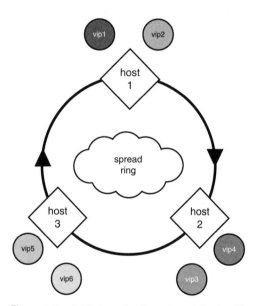

Figure 4.6   A Wackamole cluster in perfect health.

If a single IP address is being managed by a cluster of two machines, at most one machine will be responsible for that IP, and you will have a similar configuration to the hot-standby setup discussed earlier. What's new and different is the ability to add a handful more machines to the cluster and have seamless failover and N-1 fault tolerance. *And yes, 1 fault tolerant and N-1 fault tolerant are the same with two machines, but trying to make that argument is a good way to look stupid.*

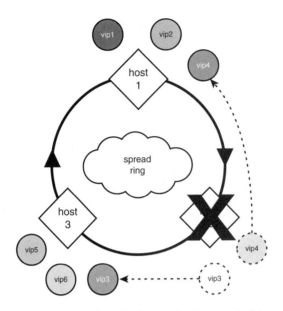

Figure 4.7   A Wackamole cluster following a node failure.

The new concept introduced by peer-based high availability is that more than one machine may be actively working at any given time. Although it is possible to architect a solution using traditional hot-standby failover that will exercise multiple machines, it is atypical and not the intention of the technology. In the peer-based approach, it is intrinsic—occurring any time the number of managed IP addresses exceeds one. To operate in this type of environment, the services must be provided by each machine authoritatively, and their concurrent use must not cause malfunctions. A perfect example of a service that always does well in this paradigm is DNS. Web services are usually conducive to concurrent operations (the same is required when load balancing across a cluster), whereas database services often pose challenges so tremendous that fundamental sacrifices must be made in their use or their performance.

It is important to keep in mind that although some services are not easily benefited by peer-based high availability with more than one IP address offered, they are still benefited by simple N-way hot-standby. Many databases, for example, work well out-of-the-box so long as only one is active. When a failure occurs, a new master is chosen or elected, and it assumes the responsibility of providing the database service over the single advertised IP address, and life continues on normally.

Wackamole can be programmed to elect a new master and perform whatever database administration is necessary to place the newly appointed database server in master mode.

We will delve deeper into distributed multimaster databases in Chapter 8 and gain a better understanding of the tremendous challenges previously mentioned.

Growing Seamlessly

As mentioned earlier, peer-based systems provide N services from M machines, where N and M could be both larger and smaller than each other. We have not touched on providing more services than machines.

If we expose 10 virtual IP addresses from a cluster of 10 machines, what must be done to increase the cluster size by 1 machine? If we simply add another machine, it acts as a global spare. There are no virtual IP addresses to juggle around because they are all spoken for.

If we were to expose 50 virtual IP addresses from a cluster of 10 machines, each machine would be responsible for 5 of them. If we were to add an 11th machine, each machine would relinquish responsibility over some of their 5 IPs to help even out the responsibility. Wackamole, in its default configuration, would cause 5 of the machines to relinquish control of 1 of their 5 IP addresses to result in 6 machines with 5 virtual IPs and 5 machines with 4 virtual IPs.

Diverging from the Web: High Availability for Email, DNS, and So On

High availability has many uses outside the Web. Any mission-critical system benefits by having fault-tolerant components. The most commonly ignored system components are networking equipment such as firewalls, switches, and routers. The reason for this is the term and the roles the various architects and engineers play in designing, building, and maintaining the overall architecture.

Consider the design of a modern automobile. Several multidisciplinary teams contribute to the final product. If the safety team, the engineering team, and the aesthetic design team all work together on the first draft, and then all further revisions leading to the final design are performed by the safety team, you will end up with one ugly car.

Think of the network engineering team as designing the suspension for the car. Often, systems engineers (the performance and engine mechanics) and developers (design and functionality specialists) are the two teams that work closely together to accomplish business goals, adding cup holders, adding automatic locks and windows, and upgrading the engine and exhaust systems.

After several additions and subtractions to the car's functionality and upgrading or downgrading a few core components, the car is going to act differently. There are no guarantees that the old suspension is adequate for the car. In fact, the old suspension system may be unsafe!

It is unfortunate that network engineers don't play a larger role in ongoing maintenance of production architectures. However, it is understandable. After you build a networking infrastructure, the people who conduct business over it rarely think about it so long as it is functioning correctly. Basically, it has to break to get attention.

This stems from the underlying reliability of networking equipment. If you install a switch in your environment, it will likely require zero administration for at least a year after the initial setup. It will continue to function. This leads to the misconception that it would not benefit from maintenance. As soon as another device is plugged in to that switch, it may no longer be optimally configured.

Artisans of different crafts have different focuses. A systems engineer looks at making sure that the system continues to work in light of a failure. However, many SAs are not cognizant that if the single switch they are plugged in to fails, all their work is for naught. It is immensely valuable for SAs to learn enough network engineering to know when they need review or assistance.

Network administrators likely will have never heard of peer-based high availability. The network world is a hardware one, full of black box products and proprietary solutions. Only recently has it become acceptable to perform routing on general-purpose server hardware—and it certainly isn't commonplace.

Given that, protocols such as HSRP and VRRP are understood and deployed throughout almost every production IP network environment in the world. The world is a different place now that you can deploy a $1,000 Intel-based commodity server running Linux or FreeBSD as a corporate or stub router attached to several 100Mbps and Gigabit networks with features such as multicast, IPSEC, IP tunneling, VoIP gateways, and more advanced IP network service in addition to a full set of standard routing protocols. Implementing smarter application level protocols is now possible because deploying those applications on these routers is easy: they run widely popular, free, open source operating systems. But in another respect, it is much easier to write an application for FreeBSD or Linux than it is for Cisco IOS.

So, why not use commodity routers in production? The vendor argument is that they are not proven or enterprise ready. Because a slew of companies are on the market ready and willing to support these systems in production, the only remaining argument is high availability. Free implementations of the VRRP protocol are available, but there is no good reason not to apply peer-based high availability to this problem as well.

Pouring Concrete

At one of our installations, we have a production environment that sits in a class C network (256 IP addresses). This environment must monitor thousands of services around the world for availability and functional correctness.

The services that it monitors are local and distributed across a handful of sites on networks far away. So, connectedness is a necessity.

Monitoring service availability for publicly accessible services is easy: making web requests, performing DNS lookups, sending mail, checking mailboxes, and so on.

Monitoring more private information requires more private channels. In this environment, our router is responsible for routing between three physically attached subnets and six different private IP networks over IPSEC VPNs, several of which require considerable bandwidth.

Purchasing a router from a leading network vendor such as Cisco, Juniper, or Foundry that supports routing three 100Mbps networks and six IPSEC connections would be rather expensive. Consider that we manage the installations at the other end of those VPNs as well. All need to be fault-tolerant. So, although the math is simple, things just don't add up. I need two routers at the primary location and, at the minimum, two VPN devices at the five other locations.

Let's take a look at a cost-effective solution. We buy two inexpensive 1U commodity servers with three Ethernet controllers. We install FreeBSD 4 on both boxes, configure IPSEC using Kame/Racoon, and set up our routing.

Our three subnets are

- Private—10.77.52.0/23
- Local—192.168.52.0/24
- External—172.16.0.0/29

Our hosting provider has the router at 172.16.0.1, and we route all Internet-bound traffic through that IP. The hosting provider routes all traffic to 192.168.52.0/24 through 172.16.0.4 (our router's IP).

Because our router must provide routing to all the machines on the private and local networks, it must have an IP address (for those machines to use as a default route). We keep it simple and standard by using 10.77.52.1 and 192.168.52.1, respectively.

Each box has three network interfaces to attach it to the three physical networks we plan to route. We have two FreeBSD boxes to apply to this problem, so we will give them each their own IP address on each network. This first box receives 10.77.52.2, 192.168.52.2, and 172.16.0.5, and the second box is assigned 10.77.52.3, 192.168.52.3, and 172.16.0.6, as shown in Figure 4.8.

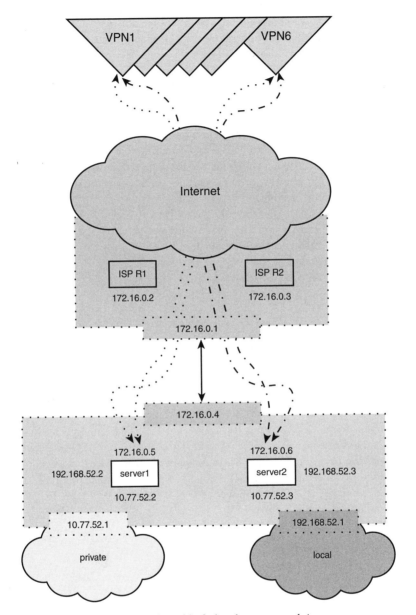

Figure 4.8   A real-world, fault-tolerant network ingress.

Using Wackamole, we can tell these two machines that they share the responsibility for being the router residing at 10.77.52.1, 192.168.52.1, and 172.16.0.4.

wackamole.conf snippet:

```
# We don't care who is the master
Prefer None
# We are responsible for a single virtual interface composed of set
# of three IP addresses.  It is important that if a machine takes
# responsibility then it must acquire ALL three IPs.
VirtualInterfaces {
  { fxp2:10.77.52.1/32 fxp1:192.168.52.1/32 fxp0:172.16.0.4/32 }
}
```

With Wackamole started on both machines, we see the following:

```
root@server1 # uptime
11:06PM  up 157 days, 18:07, 1 user, load averages: 0.00, 0.00, 0.00

root@server1 # ifconfig -a
fxp0: flags=8943<UP,BROADCAST,RUNNING,PROMISC,SIMPLEX,MULTICAST> mtu 1500
        inet 172.16.0.5 netmask 0xfffffff0 broadcast 63.236.106.111
        inet6 fe80::2d0:a8ff:fe00:518b%fxp0 prefixlen 64 scopeid 0x1
        ether 00:d0:a8:00:51:8b
        media: Ethernet autoselect (100baseTX <full-duplex>)
        status: active
fxp1: flags=8843<UP,BROADCAST,RUNNING,SIMPLEX,MULTICAST> mtu 1500
        inet 192.168.52.2 netmask 0xffffff00 broadcast 66.77.52.255
        inet6 fe80::2d0:a8ff:fe00:518c%fxp1 prefixlen 64 scopeid 0x2
        ether 00:d0:a8:00:51:8c
        media: Ethernet autoselect (100baseTX <full-duplex>)
        status: active
fxp2: flags=8843<UP,BROADCAST,RUNNING,SIMPLEX,MULTICAST> mtu 1500
        inet 10.77.52.2 netmask 0xfffffe00 broadcast 10.77.53.255
        inet6 fe80::202:b3ff:fe5f:c68f%fxp2 prefixlen 64 scopeid 0x3
        ether 00:02:b3:5f:c6:8f
        media: Ethernet autoselect (100baseTX <full-duplex>)
        status: active


root@server2 # uptime
11:07PM  up 338 days, 13:59, 2 users, load averages: 0.46, 0.39, 0.34

root@server2 # ifconfig -a
fxp0: flags=8843<UP,BROADCAST,RUNNING,SIMPLEX,MULTICAST> mtu 1500
        inet 172.16.0.6 netmask 0xfffffff0 broadcast 63.236.106.111
        inet6 fe80::2d0:a8ff:fe00:61e8%fxp0 prefixlen 64 scopeid 0x1
        inet 172.16.0.4 netmask 0xffffffff broadcast 63.236.106.102
        ether 00:d0:a8:00:61:e8
        media: Ethernet autoselect (100baseTX <full-duplex>)
        status: active
```

```
fxp1: flags=8843<UP,BROADCAST,RUNNING,SIMPLEX,MULTICAST> mtu 1500
        inet 192.168.52.3 netmask 0xffffff00 broadcast 66.77.52.255
        inet6 fe80::2d0:a8ff:fe00:61e9%fxp1 prefixlen 64 scopeid 0x2
        inet 192.168.52.1 netmask 0xffffffff broadcast 66.77.52.1
        ether 00:d0:a8:00:61:e9
        media: Ethernet autoselect (100baseTX <full-duplex>)
        status: active
fxp2: flags=8843<UP,BROADCAST,RUNNING,SIMPLEX,MULTICAST> mtu 1500
        inet 10.77.52.3 netmask 0xfffffe00 broadcast 10.255.255.255
        inet6 fe80::202:b3ff:fe5f:bf0c%fxp2 prefixlen 64 scopeid 0x3
        inet 10.77.52.1 netmask 0xffffffff broadcast 10.77.52.1
        ether 00:02:b3:5f:bf:0c
        media: Ethernet autoselect (100baseTX <full-duplex>)
        status: active
```

The preceding `ifconfig` outputs show that `server2` currently has all three IP addresses that are acting as the default route. If `server2` were to crash now, `server1` would acquire the three IP addresses specified in the `wackamole.conf` file within a second or two, and routing would continue as if nothing had happened at all.

The `uptime` was run to illustrate the stability of the systems despite running on commodity hardware.

The IPSEC VPNs are orchestrated with FreeBSD gif IP-IP tunneling and KAME and Racoon. After the IP tunnels are configured, they are utilized by routing traffic over them via FreeBSD's routing table. Because no additional physical IP addresses are added, the `wackamole.conf` file remains untouched. The specifics of the IPSEC implementation are outside the scope of this book.

This example demonstrates how peer-based high availability can provide what current networking failover protocols provide. However, two things are important to note:

- Wackamole can provide true N-1 fault tolerance to the previous setup simply by adding an additional router.

- If more than one virtual interface were exposed through Wackamole, more than one machine would be available for use. Although this is complicated to take advantage of in a stub router, if the same solution were applied to several machines running IP load balancing software (such as LVS), we would have a viable high availability/load balancing setup that has more scalability than a similar commercial solution (for example, a pair BIG/ip).

## 5

Load Balancing
and the Utter Confusion
Surrounding It

WE DISCUSSED THE DIFFERENCES between load balancing and high availability in Chapter 4, "High Availability. HA! No Downtime?!" so we will pursue that topic by seeking a better understanding of load balancing.

First, let's reflect on the term *load balancing.* Although it is obvious what it means—to balance a load—it is often misunderstood to mean balance the system load. *System load* is defined as the average length of the run queue (processes in a runnable state waiting for the system processor) over the last 1 minute, 5 minutes, and 15 minutes; typically updated on 5-second intervals.

When you type **uptime** on your Unix or Linux system, you should see something like what I see on one of our production web servers:

```
9:38pm  up 292 days, 23:35,  0 users,  load average: 0.94, 0.75, 0.70
```

The numbers seen at the end are the 1-, 5-, and 15-minute load averages, respectively. So, what is wrong with thinking of load balancing as an attempt to even the load average of the machines in a cluster? In short, everything.

Load Balancing Basics

Load balancing is intended to mean evenly balancing the workload across the machines in a cluster. Specifically, in a web-based environment, work is short—very short. Typical requests can take as little as a few milliseconds to complete, and a server can handle thousands of static page requests per second and almost as many dynamic pages per second. The nature of these transactions makes the concept of system load inappropriate.

Imagine a cluster of servers equally utilized. A new server is brought online and initially has a system load of 0. Balancing on system load alone would cause all subsequent requests to be directed to this new machine. Thousands will arrive in the first second, and the load will be zero. Thousands more will arrive in the next second, and the load will be…that's right…zero. The system load won't update for another 5 seconds, and, even when it does, it will be the 1-minute average. This in no way reflects the current workload of the machine because web requests are too short and too fast to measure in this way. By the time the load changes to reflect the current workload, the machine will have been thrashed, and it will be far too late to correct. This problem is called *staleness*. The metrics are so stale, decisions on them are nonsensical.

So what is the right approach to load balancing? The answer to that is academically difficult, but it is based on a simple concept: effective resource utilization.

Some practical approaches taken by available load-balancing products (both hardware and software) are

- Round robin—One request per server in a uniform rotation. This suffers from a classic queueing-theory problem where servers that become overworked don't have the reprieve they require to settle down again.

- Least connections—Assuming that the implementation is good, this is a relatively sound algorithm. Although no guarantees are given that resources are used optimally, the faster a machine can service connections (accept, satisfy, and disconnect), the more work they will receive. Conversely, if a machine is slow, the connections will backlog, and the server will not be dealt more requests. This technique has serious problems if several load balancers are used, and each is making decisions in parallel.

- Predictive—Usually based on either round robin or least connections with some added ad-hoc expressions to compensate in the information staleness issues induced in rapid transaction environments. However, vendors rarely publish the actual details of the algorithms they use, so your mileage may vary.

- Available resources—Although this is an ideal concept, the staleness issue is severe, and good results can rarely be extracted from this model.

- Random—Randomized algorithms have taken computer science by storm over the last 10 years, posing elegant solutions to complicated problems that yield good probabilistic outcomes. Although a purely random assignment of requests across machines in a cluster sounds silly (because it completely disregards available resources), combining this methodology with resource-based algorithms as a probabilistically decent solution to the staleness problem is an excellent approach.

- Weighted random—Weighting anything administratively is a kooky concept. Is a dual processor system twice as fast as a single processor system? The answer is "it depends." Assigning some arbitrary constant (such as 2) to the faster machines in a clustered environment is making an assumption that should make any self-respecting engineer cry. Although this technique can work well, it requires a lot of manual tweaking, and when servers are added or upgraded, the tweaking process begins all over again. Load balancing is about effectively allocating available resources, not total resources.

In addition to the problem of choosing a method to decide which server is the best, multiple parallel load balancers also must work in unison. If two (or more) load balancers are deployed side-by-side (as peers), and both are active and balancing traffic, the game plan has changed substantially. As has been mentioned, the only way to make perfect decisions is to know the future. This is not possible, so algorithms that estimate current conditions and/or attempt to predict the effects of decisions are employed in an attempt to make "good" decisions.

The situation is greatly complicated when another system attempts to make decisions based on the same information without cooperation. If two machines make the same decisions in concert, the effects of naive decisions will be twice that which was intended by the algorithm designer. Cooperative algorithms limit the solution space considerably. You might find a random distribution beating out the smartest uncooperative algorithms.

A tremendous amount of academic and industry research has taken place on the topic of load balancing in the past five or more years. This specific research topic had the burning coals of the dot-com barbeque under it, and the endless stream of investment money making it hotter. Although that has been all but extinguished, the product is pretty impressive!

The Association of Computing Machinery's Special Interest Group SIGMETRIC has published countless academic papers detailing concepts and approaches to modeling and evaluating load-balancing schemes. Having read many of these while doing research at the Center for Networking and Distributed Systems (CNDS) on the Backhand Project, I can say that the single biggest problem is that no one model applies equally well to all practical situations.

Far from the purely academic approach to the problem, countless autonomous groups were concurrently developing completely ad-hoc balancing solutions to be used in practice. Many were building tools to prove it was easy and that you didn't need to spend a fortune on hardware solutions; others were building them out of the desperate need for growth without venture funding.

As always, the most prominent solutions were those that were mindful of the progress on both fronts: maintaining the goal of building a valuable and usable product. Many excellent products are on the market today, software and hardware, open and proprietary, that make large web services tick.

IP-Friendly Services

Specifically with regard to the topic of web serving, it is impossible for two machines to share a single IP address on the same Ethernet segment because the address resolution protocol (ARP) poses a fundamental obstacle. As such, without a load-balancing device that provides virtual IP services, the rule is at least one distinct IP address per machine.

What does this mean? Well, a lot actually. DNS allows the exposure of multiple IP addresses for a single hostname. Multiple IP addresses are being used to provide the same service. It should be noted that nothing in the DNS specification guarantees an even distribution of traffic over the exposed IP addresses (or a distribution at all). However, in practice, a distribution is realized. Although the distribution is uniform over a large time quantum, the methodology is naive and has no underlying intelligence. Given its shortcomings, you will see its usefulness in specific environments in Chapter 6, "Static Content Serving for Speed and Glory."

For example, `dig www.yahoo.com` yields something like the following:

```
;; ANSWER SECTION:
www.yahoo.com.            1738    IN      CNAME    www.yahoo.akadns.net.
www.yahoo.akadns.net.     30      IN      A        216.109.118.70
www.yahoo.akadns.net.     30      IN      A        216.109.118.67
www.yahoo.akadns.net.     30      IN      A        216.109.118.64
www.yahoo.akadns.net.     30      IN      A        216.109.118.77
www.yahoo.akadns.net.     30      IN      A        216.109.118.69
www.yahoo.akadns.net.     30      IN      A        216.109.118.74
www.yahoo.akadns.net.     30      IN      A        216.109.118.73
www.yahoo.akadns.net.     30      IN      A        216.109.118.68
```

This means that you could visit any of the preceding IP addresses to access the Yahoo! World Wide Web service. However, consider secure hypertext transport protocol (HTTPS), commonly referred to as SSL (even though SSL applies to much more than just the Web).

The HTTP protocol allows for arbitrary headers to be added to any request. One common header is the `Host:` header used to specify which web real estate you want to query. This technique, called *name-based virtual hosting*, allows several web real estates to be serviced from the same IP address.

However, when using SSL, the client and server participate in a strong cryptographic handshake that allows the client to verify and trust that the server is who it claims to be. Unfortunately, this handshake is required to occur before HTTP requests are made, and as such no `Host:` header has been transmitted. This shortcoming of HTTP over SSL inhibits the use of name-based virtual hosting on secure sites. Although the question whether this is good or bad can be argued from both sides, the fact remains that servicing multiple secure websites from the same IP address is not feasible.

If you expose a single IP address for each web service, you need one IP address for each secure web real estate in service. But if multiple (N) IP addresses are used for each web service, you need N IP addresses for each secure web real estate. This can be wasteful if you manage thousands of secure websites.

There are two workarounds for this. The first is to run SSL on a different port than the default 443. This is a bad approach because many corporate firewalls only allow SSL connections over port 443, which can lead to widespread accessibility issues that are not easily rectified.

The second approach is to use a delegate namespace for all secure transactions. Suppose that we host www.example1.com through www.example1000.com, but do not want to allocate 1,000 (or N times 1,000) IP addresses for SSL services. This can be accomplished by using secure.example.com as the base site name for all secure transactions that happen over the hosted domains. This approach may or may not be applicable in your environment. Typically, if this is not a valid approach, it is due to the business issue of trust.

If you visit a site www.example1000.com and are transferred to secure.example.com for secure transactions, users will be aware that they were just tossed from one domain to another. Although it may not be so obvious with those domain names, consider a hosting company named acmehosting.com and a client named waldoswidgets.com. To preserve IP space, ACME hosting chooses to put all client SSL transactions through a single host named secure.acmehosting.com. However, the end customer who is expecting to purchase something from Waldo's Widgets is oblivious to the fact that Waldo chose ACME as a hosting company.

The end-user placed enough trust in waldoswidgets.com to conduct a secure transaction, but suddenly that user is placed on secure.acmehosting.com to conduct this transaction. Although the user can be put at ease by having seamless creative continuity between the two sites (both sites look the same), the URL in the browser has still changed, and that hand-off has diminished trust.

Although there is no real way to fix IP consumption issues with running a tremendous number of SSL sites, it can certainly be alleviated by running each secure site on at most one IP address. This approach brings up a scalability issue—which is why this discussion belongs in this chapter.

If you expose only a single IP address for a service, that IP must be capable of servicing all requests directed there. If it is a large site and the workload exceeds the capacity of a single web server, we have a problem that can only be solved by load balancing.

Web Switches

Web switches, or *black-box load balancers*, are by far the most popular technology deployed in the Internet for scaling highly trafficked websites. There are good and bad reasons for choosing web switches as the technology behind an end solution.

Throughout this book, we present the advantages of solutions followed by the disadvantages, usually leading to a better approach or a better technology that doesn't suffer the same shortcomings. With web switches, we'll take the opposite approach because web switches are sometimes the *only* viable solution given their features.

Web switches come in all shapes and sizes, from small 1U units to carrier-class units capable of aggregating the largest of environments. During the dot-com era, the marketplace had several key high availability and load balancing players, and competition was fierce. This led to stable, efficient products. The major players in the space are Nortel Networks, Foundry, Cisco, and Extreme Networks, just to name a few.

In layman's terms, web switches act like network address translation (NAT) capable routers—just backward. Your corporate firewall or your $50 wireless hub and cable modem can use NAT to allow multiples of your private machines (a few laptops and PCs) to share a single routable IP address to access the Internet. A web switch does the opposite by exposing the resources of several private machines through a single routable IP address to hosts on the Internet (that is, end-users) as shown in Figure 5.1.

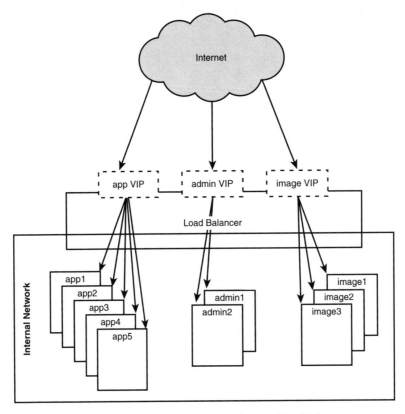

Figure 5.1   Example topology using front-end load balancer.

The one thing that truly sets web switches (at least the good ones) apart from other load-balancing solutions is their raw performance. Several switches on the market are capable of sustaining upwards of 15 million concurrent sessions and switching more than 50 gigabits/second of data. Those astounding performance metrics combined with simplistic balancing mechanics make for a solution that can drive the largest of Internet sites.

Arguing about the stability of these products seems to be a no-win endeavor. Everyone has his own unique experience. I have managed installations with chronic (weekly or daily) problems with high availability/load balancing device malfunctions, and I have deployed solutions that ran for three years without a single login.

However, one issue must be addressed: Do you really need a web switch? Chapter 4 discussed the irony of needing a high availability solution for your high availability/load balancing device. The irony may be amusing, but the accompanying price tag is not. These devices are useful when needed and cumbersome in many ways when they are not. The next few sections present several alternatives to web switches that may make more sense in architectures that don't need to sustain 15 million concurrent sessions or are capable of exposing their services over several IP addresses. Chapter 6 details a viable and proven solution that tackles a problem of considerable scale without employing the use of any web switches.

IP Virtual Servers

IP virtual servers (IPVS) are almost identical in purpose and use to web switches, the difference being only that they aren't specifically a piece of networking hardware. Instead, they are components that run on traditional (often commodity) servers and employ either a user space application, modified IP stack, or a combination of the two to provide a distribution point for IP traffic. By exposing a single virtual IP address for a service and distributing the traffic across a configured set of private machines, IPVS accomplishes the task of load balancing inbound traffic.

From a network topology perspective, a configuration using IPVS looks identical to a configuration based on web switches. Aside from the fact that web switches typically have several Ethernet ports to which servers can be connected and generally higher performance metrics, there is little difference between the placement and operation of IP virtual servers and web switches.

Application Layer Load Balancers

In stark comparison to web switches and IPVS systems, application layer load balancers operate entirely in user space. As such, they have a few feature advantages over their low-level counterparts. Along with these extra features come rather apparent limitations—specifically in the area of performance. These applications must play in the sandbox that is user space and as such are forced to deal with application programming interfaces (APIs) and limitations exposed therein.

A few examples of application-layer load balancers are

- Zeus Load Balancer
- Eddie
- Apache and mod_backhand

These products are fast and flexible, but the concurrency and performance they boast are pale when compared to the enterprise and carrier-class layer 4 and layer 7 switches available on the market. Layers 1 through 7 are defined by the OSI network model and are depicted in Figure 5.2.

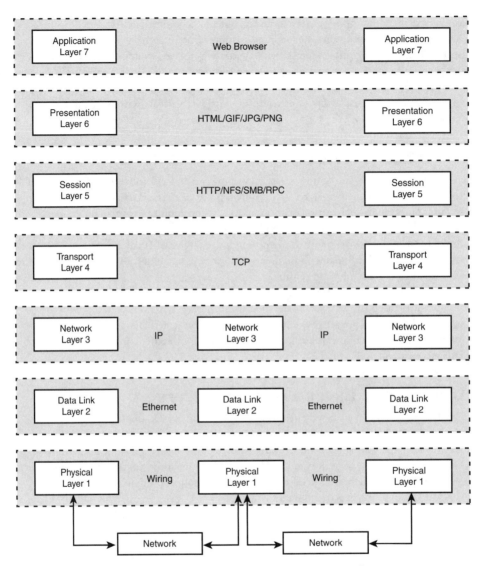

Figure 5.2   OSI network model applied to the Web.

The advantage of operating on layer 3 is that the solution does not need intimate knowledge of the application-specific protocols (in this case, SSL and HTTP). This advantage yields two benefits. First, layers 3 and under are fairly simple, and hardware accelerated solutions are much easier to come by. This results in performance that is orders of magnitude better than application-level solutions can provide. Second, because layer 3 is the foundation for almost everything that happens on the Internet, the solution is more versatile and can support a wide array of services such as SMTP, POP3, IMAP, DNS, FTP, and NTTP without understanding the intricacies of those high-level IP-based protocols.

Many layer 3 web switches claim to operate above layer 7. The truth is that some appear to work on layer 7 but actually act on layer 3. For the most part, this has advantages, but it also introduces some limitations. A web switch passes all traffic from connecting clients to real servers behind the switch. The same is true with IPVS systems. Although these devices can certainly inspect the traffic as it passes, they typically operate on the IP level with the capability to translate TCP/IP sessions to back-end servers. It is important to understand the difference between translation and proxying. When translating, the packets are simply manipulated (which can be done on an immense scale). Proxying requires processing all the data from the client and the real servers to which traffic is being sent, which includes reforming and originating all needed packets—that is substantially more expensive. Because these devices transit the web users' sessions, they can inspect the payload of packets to make decisions based on layer 7 information while affecting traffic on layer 3.

If a device can perform its duties without modifying packets above layer 5, why would you ever employ a technology like an application-level load balancer? Certain mechanisms cannot be employed without handling and fully processing information through the entire OSI network stack. These mechanisms are often safely ignored in large-scale architectures, but *often* is not *always*, so we stand to benefit discussing it here.

The following are some things that can be done by application-level load balancers that are difficult to do on web switches and IPVS devices:

- Requests can be allocated based on information in an encrypted SSL session.
- Requests of subsequent transactions in a pipelined HTTP session can be allocated to different real servers.
- Business rules can be used as the basis for customized allocation algorithms instead of predetermined vendor rules.

Certain high traffic environments have session concurrency requirements that make web switches and IPVS solutions more reasonable to deploy than an application-level solution. However, as should be apparent, requirements dictate the final solution more so than does convenience. If a web switch or IPVS simply can't fit the bill due to functional limitations, the solution is not bumped down the preference list; it is eliminated entirely.

A Real Use

A variety of uses of application-level load balancers can operate fully to layer 7. The most obvious are those that need to base allocation decisions on information in the request while employing SSL. SSL provides a mechanism for a client to validate the identity and authenticity of a server and optionally vice versa via a *public key infrastructure (PKI)*.

Additionally, using asymmetric cryptography, a symmetric key is negotiated and used to encrypt the session. Due to this safely negotiated keying, a man in the middle cannot compromise the information as it passes by.

Web switches and IPVS solutions typically do not terminate SSL connections. If they do, they are often application layer load balancing systems in disguise. Because they do not terminate the SSL session, they cannot see the payload and thus cannot use the information therein for decisions. Application-level load balancers, on the other hand, can.

Suppose that you have a news site serviced over SSL where three levels of users access the site. Premium customers are issued client SSL certificates and offered real-time news with stringent quality of service guarantees. Paying customers are given access to real-time data but less stringent quality of service guarantees. Nonpaying users access the site with no guarantees and no access to real-time data. The one kink in the plan is that all sites need to be serviced by the same URL schema. In other words, the complete URLs must be identical across all users because they tend to migrate from one service level to another on a regular basis, and it is essential that their bookmarks all continue to function and that naive users are not confused by different URLs or hostnames.

As such, you need something more than a load balancer. You need a resource allocation framework. Load balancers are, in effect, resource allocation frameworks; however, their allocation techniques are primarily focused on equalizing utilization across the machines for which they front. The beauty of application load balancers is that they implement all the plumbing necessary to proxy user-originating connections back to a set of real servers, and, because they are implemented as user-space applications, different decision-making algorithms are often easy to implement.

Both Eddie and mod_backhand can be used as general purpose resource allocation frameworks. This allows you to make simple modifications to the algorithms to accomplish the presented goal of your news site. The service requires the use of SSL, so the solution used must terminate the SSL connection to inspect the payload. As such, these frameworks are privy to the details of the connection, session, and payload. If an SSL certificate is presented by the client, this tier can validate the certificate, ensure that the user is still in good standing, and choose the appropriate real server based on more than just utilization. Figure 5.3 depicts a basic flow of this setup.

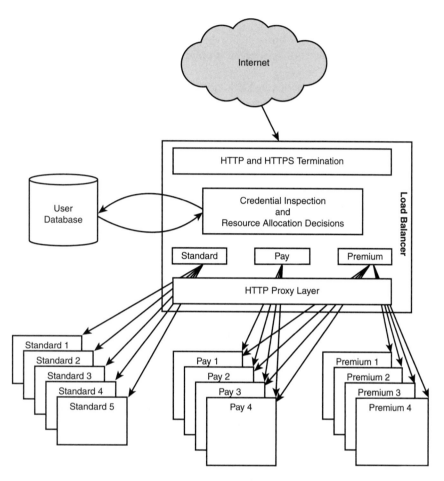

Figure 5.3   A full resource allocation system.

Abusing the Term

Load balancing is a consistently abused term. In the industry, it is used without thought to mean high availability and a linear scaling of services. Chapter 4 should have reinforced why load balancing and high availability, although partners in crime, are completely different concepts.

Linear scaling is simply a falsehood. By increasing a cluster from one server to two, we can only double the capacity if our algorithm for allocating requests across the machines was optimal. Optimal algorithms require future knowledge. The smallest inkling of reasoning tells us that because we lack knowledge of the future, we cannot be optimal, nor can we double our capacity by doubling our machinery, and thus the increase in performance due to horizontal scaling is sublinear. With one machine, we can realize 100% resource utilization. However, as more machines are added, the utilization is less impressive.

Although clustered systems that tackle long-term jobs (such as those tackled in super-computing environments) tend to have relatively good clusterwide utilization, web systems do not. High performance computing (HPC) systems boast up to 95% utilization with a steady stream of jobs. Due to the nature of web requests (their short life and rapid queueing), the error margins of algorithms are typically much higher. A good rule of thumb is to expect to achieve as low as 70% per-server utilization on clusters larger than three servers.

> **Capacity Planning Rule of Thumb**
>
> Expect to achieve an average of 70% utilization on each server in clusters with three or more nodes. Although better utilization is possible, be safe and bet on 70%.

Although the term *load balancing* is often used in situations where it means something else, there are some things to be gained by "abusing" the term. The first thing we talked about in this chapter was that balancing load isn't a good goal to have, so the name itself is off base. Twisting the definition slightly to suit the purpose of web requests, we arrive at the concept of equal resource utilization across the cluster.

Resources on the real servers should be allocated evenly to power a particular service...or should they? The bottom line is that load balancers should provide a framework or infrastructure for allocating real server resources to power a service. With a framework, the architect can decide how to approach resource allocation. This approach allows for architectural flexibility such as new and improved balancing algorithms or even intelligent artificial segmentation such as the one presented earlier in Figure 5.3.

The Web and Beyond

The Internet is much larger than the World Wide Web. Although more and more services are being built on top of HTTP due to its prevalence, a plethora of commonly used protocols are available for external and internal services. The distinct advantage of load balancing devices that do not operate above layer 4 is that they are multidisciplinary. Load balancing devices that operate on layer 3 or layer 4 (like most web switches and IPVS solutions) are capable of distributing service load across real servers for almost any IP-based protocol. A few of the most commonly load balanced IP-based protocols are

- Web Services (HTTP/HTTPS)
- Domain Name Service (DNS)
- Network News Transfer Protocol (NNTP)
- Local Directory Access Protocol (LDAP/LDAPS)

- Web Caching Systems (transparent HTTP)
- Internet Mail Access Protocol (IMAP/IMAPS)
- Post Office Protocol (POP/POPS)
- Simple Mail Transfer Protocol (SMTP)
- Local Mail Transfer Protocol (LMTP)
- File Transfer Protocol (FTP)

Regardless of the need, almost every large architecture has at least one load balancer deployed to distribute some IP traffic. For architectures that are centralized (single geographic installation), the choice to use an expensive, high-performance load balancer is usually sound. As illustrated in Chapter 4, load balancing does not provide high availability. Because there is still a single point of failure when deploying load balancers, two must be deployed, and a high availability solution must be instantiated between them. The "expensive" load balancer just doubled in price.

For centralized architectures, two devices often suffice, which makes the costs understood and usually reasonable. However, when an architecture decentralizes for political, business, or technical reasons, scalability is no longer efficient. The expensive price for dual load balancers now must be replicated across each cluster. Given four installations throughout the world, eight load balancers must be purchased for high availability, load balancing, and consistency. At that point, alternative approaches may be more appropriate.

Session Stickiness: A Fatal Misconception

The biggest misconception I'd like to lay to rest is that of mixing the concept of *balancing load* and *session stickiness*. Session stickiness is an approach to ensure that a specific visitor to the site is serviced by a machine in the cluster and that that visitor will continue to return to that machine throughout the life of his visit. If a request arrives at a load balancer and it assigns it to a machine based on information other than load metrics, it is not really balancing load.

One can argue that the attempt is to balance the load of a complete session rather than the load of an individual request. The Web exists on the terms of one short request after another. The act of bundling them into large composite transactions for the purpose of application design makes sense. However, doing this on the level of the load balancer leads to poor resource utilization and complicated resource allocation needs.

Many application programmers will tell you that all complicated web applications require application or web servers to store the state of the session locally (because sticking it in a centralized place is too expensive) and that this need mandates the use of session-sticky load balancing. Session information can be stored locally on the application or web server—this technique necessitates sticky sessions. Sticking a user to a specific web server because her session information is stored there and only there should have some pretty obvious implications on the fault-tolerance of the solution. If that server were to become unavailable, that user and every other user unfortunate enough to have been "stuck" to that server would certainly be aware of a single point of failure in your system architecture.

Sessions information can also be stored on some shared storage medium such as a database; this approach is common but can require tremendous horsepower. However, one other party is involved that web application designers always seem to forget about—the client.

Far too little attention is given to the art of cookies. At times, session information is so large that it could never conceivably fit in a user's cookie. However, I have yet to be presented with an architecture where a user's session data could not be split into rarely accessed or rarely updated components stored in a centralized backing store and frequently accessed or frequently updated components stored securely in a client's cookie. If this can be done, the load balancing techniques used in the architecture can be radically changed for the better.

So, Which One Is the Best?

Load balancing is a theoretically complicated problem. In and of itself, it is an academically difficult problem to solve completely. But, given the constrained nature of most web environments and a good engineer, many adequate solutions are available today.

Because load balancing is a tricky academic problem, most of the solutions available are ad-hoc systems for solving real-world, web-based, load-balancing problems. Some are naive, others are extremely insightful, but most importantly, all of them seem to have their place.

Throughout the rest of this book, we will look at various architectural challenges, and when load balancing is part of the solution, we will discuss why the technology presented is a good fit.

6

Static Content Serving
for Speed and Glory

APPLICATION DEVELOPERS PLACE so much focus on efficient web application design that it is easy to ignore an important and simple truth: Most content, by volume and by count, is static. From industries such as online pornography to common news sites, static content rules the screen, and the approaches to serving dynamic content are typically inefficient when used in the realm of static content serving.

What does it mean if static objects are served inefficiently? Pages on a website will appear to "hang" while loading or look incomplete during the process of acquiring all the embedded static objects. Some argue that good page coding can ensure that a page will load and display immediately, and the images will trickle in. Although this is important for users over slow dial-up connections, it is crazy to think this is a "solution" to the problem. Simply put, the images on a web page are there for a reason; if they haven't loaded yet, the user hasn't seen what you intended.

To understand what is efficient and what is not, it helps to establish some specific performance goals. So, let's assume that we are building a news serving site capable of servicing 3 million unique visitors per day. Let's also assume that, based on external research, during the peak hour, 15% of all traffic is served, so that 450,000 new visitors arrive during that hour. The average visitor visits five pages and then leaves the site.

Servicing 3 million visitors each with an initial page load and four subsequent page loads requires a capacity of 450,000/1h * 1h/3600s or 125 initial page loads per second. And the four subsequent page loads yield 500 subsequent page loads per second.

Why treat the initial page loads differently? The answer is browser cache. Browser caches hold images locally so that no time needs to be spent reloading the same image from the server to render it on a subsequent page that requires the same static content. We will look later at how to better estimate the peak requests per second.

What's So Tricky?

Static web serving doesn't seem so difficult at first. And, in truth, it isn't. However, as sites evolve and grow, they must scale, and the stresses of serving traffic in development and staging are different from those placed on an architecture by millions of visitors.

Let's walk through a typical approach to serving a website and then investigate that approach for inefficiencies. First, how much of the traffic is static? The answer to this is the basis for numerous timing, throughput, and other scalability calculations. Table 6.1 shows four sites: three real sites (one very small site and two that are huge) and a fourth site that is an example large site for discussion purposes whose page composition metrics are legitimized by the real data.

Table 6.1 **Page Object Analysis**

URI HTML (bytes)	Images (bytes)	External References	JS/CSS/etc. (bytes)	% static (bytes)
http://www.omniti.com/	1 (5098)	3 (46393)	2 (9163)	83.3% (93.6%)
(subsequent pages)	1 (8000)	0 (0)	0 (0)	0% (0%)
http://www.cnn.com/	1 (55941)	66 (96945)	5 (65211)	98.6% (74.3%)
(subsequent pages)	1 (32546)	8 (18234)	(0) 0	88.9% (24.6%)
http://amazon.com/	1 (65756)	46 (81574)	1 (2877)	97.9% (56.2%)
(subsequent pages)	1 (52590)	21 (131246)	0 (0)	95.2% (71.4%)
http://www.example.com/	1 (60000)	56 (87500)	2 (20000)	98.3% (64.2%)
(subsequent pages)	1 (35000)	9 (30000)	0 (0)	90% (46.2%)

As can be seen in Table 6.1, the number of requests for static content far outweighs the number of requests for possibly dynamic HTML pages. Additionally, the volume of static content served constitutes more than 50% of the total volume served.

Although browser cache reduces the number of queries for these static objects (particularly images) as can be seen in the "subsequent pages" rows, it does not eliminate them entirely. Sites that rarely change will benefit tremendously from browser-side caching, whereas other more dynamic sites will not. If you look at a popular online news source (such as CNN or BBC), you will notice that almost every news story that is added contains several new external objects whether an image, movie, or audio stream. As visitors come, they are unlikely to reread the same article, and thus unlikely to capitalize on the existence of the corresponding images in their browser's cache. While surfing on the CNN site, I calculated about an 88% cache hit rate for static objects within a page.

Additionally, ISPs, corporations, and even small companies employ transparent and nontransparent caching web proxies to help reduce network usage and improve user experience. This means that when Bob loads a page and all its images, Bob's ISP may cache those images on its network so that when another user from that ISP requests the page and attempts to fetch the embedded images, he will wind up pulling them (more quickly) from the ISP's local cache.

Where does this leave us? When a user first visits www.example.com, what happens on the network level? When I point my browser at www.example.com, it attempts to open seven TCP/IP connections to download the HTML base page and all the subsequent stylesheets, JavaScript includes, and images. Additionally, these seven connections are open for an average of 4 seconds.

Now, it should be obvious that only one of those TCP/IP connections was used to fetch the base document as it was fetched first and only once, and that the connection was reused to fetch some of the static objects. That leaves six induced connections due to page dependencies. Although subsequent page loads weren't so dramatic, the initial page loads alone provide enough evidence to paint a dismal picture.

Let's take the most popular web server on the Internet as the basis for our discussion. According to NetCraft web survey, Apache is the web server technology behind approximately 67% of all Internet sites with a footprint of approximately 33 million websites. It is considered by many industry experts to be an excellent tool for enterprise and carrier-class deployments, and it has my vote of confidence as well. For a variety of reasons, Apache 1.3 remains far more popular than Apache 2.0, so we will assume Apache 1.3.x to be core technology for our web installation at www.example.com.

Apache 1.3 uses a process model to handle requests and serve traffic. This means that when a TCP/IP connection is made, a process is dedicated to fielding all the requests that arrive on that connection—and yes, the process remains dedicated during all the lag time, pauses, and slow content delivery due to slow client connection speed.

Context Switching

How many processes can your system run? Most Unix-like machines ship with a maximum process limit between 512 and 20,000. That is a big range, but we can narrow it down if we consider the speed of a context switch. Context switching on most modern Unix-like systems is fast and completely unnoticeable on a workstation when 100 processes are running. However, this is because 100 processes *aren't* running; only a handful is actually running at any given time. In stark comparison, on a heavily trafficked web server, all the processes are on the CPU or are waiting for some "in-demand" resource such as the CPU or disk.

Due to the nature of web requests (being quick and short), you have processes accomplishing relatively small units of work at any given time. This leads to processes bouncing into and out of the run queue at a rapid rate. When one process is taken off the CPU and another process (from the run queue) is placed on the CPU to execute it, it is called a *context switch*. We won't get into the details, but the important thing to remember is that nothing in computing is free.

There is a common misconception that serving a web request requires the process to be switched onto the processor, where it does its job, and then gets switched off again, requiring a total of two context switches. This is not true. Any time a task must communicate over the network (to a client or to a database), or read from or write to disk, it has nothing to do while those interactions are being completed. At the bare minimum, a web server process must

- Accept the connection
- Read the request
- Write the response
- Log the transaction
- Close the connection

Each of these actions requires the process to be context switched in and then out, totaling 10 context switches. If multiple requests are serviced over the life of a single connection, the first and last events in the preceding list are amortized over the life of the connection, dropping the total to slightly more than six. However, the preceding events are the bare minimum. Typically, websites do something when they service requests, which places one or more events (such as file I/O or database operations) between reading the request and writing the response. In the end, 10 context switches is a hopeful lower bound that most web environments never achieve.

Assume that a context takes an average of 10μ (microseconds) to complete. That means that the server can perform 100,000 context switches per second, and at 10 per web request that comes out to 10,000 web requests per second, right? No.

The system could perform the context switches necessary to service 10,000 requests per second, but then it would not have resources remaining to do anything. In other words, it would be spending 100% of its time switching between processes and never actually running them.

Well, that's okay. The goal isn't to serve 10,000 requests per second. Instead, we have a modest goal of serving 1,000 requests per second. At that rate, we spend 10% of all time on the system switching between tasks. Although 10% isn't an enormous amount, an architect should always consider this when the CPU is being used for other important tasks such as generating dynamic content.

Many web server platforms in use have different design architectures than Apache 1.3.x. Some are based on a thread per request, some are event driven, and others take the extreme approach of servicing a portion of the requests from within the kernel of the operating system, and by doing so, help alleviate the particular nuisance of context switching costs.

As so many existing architectures utilize Apache 1.3.x and enjoy many of its benefits (namely stability, flexibility, and wide adoption), the issues of process limitation often need to be addressed without changing platforms.

Resource Utilization

The next step in understanding the scope of the problem requires looking at the resources required to service a request and comparing that to the resources actually allocated to service that request.

This, unlike many complicated technical problems, can easily be explained with a simple simile: Web serving is like carpentry. Carpentry requires the use of nails—many different types of nails (finishing, framing, outdoor, tacks, masonry, and so on). If you ask a carpenter why he doesn't use the same hammer to drive all the nails, he would probably answer: "That question shows why I'm a carpenter and you aren't."

Of course, I have seen a carpenter use the same hammer to drive all types of nails, which is what makes this simile so apropos. You can use the same web server configuration and setup to serve all your traffic—it will work. However, if you see a carpenter set on a long task of installing trim, he will pick up a trim hammer, and if he were about to spend all day anchoring lumber into concrete he would certainly use a hand sledge hammer or even a masonry nail gun.

In essence, it is the difference between a quick hack and a good efficient solution. A claw hammer can be used on just about any task, but it isn't always the most effective tool for the job.

In addition, if a big job requires a lot of carpentry, more than one carpenter will be hired. If you know beforehand that half the time will be spent driving framing nails, and the other half will be setting trim, you have valuable knowledge. If one person works on each task independently, you can make two valuable optimizations. The first is obvious from our context switching discussion above: Neither has to waste time switching between hammers. The second is the crux of the solution: A framing carpenter costs less than a trim carpenter.

Web serving is essentially the same even inside Apache itself. Apache can be compiled with mod_php or mod_perl to generate dynamic content based on custom applications. Think of Apache with an embedded scripting language as a sledge hammer and images as finishing nails. Although you can set finishing nails with a sledge hammer, your arm is going to become unnecessarily tired.

Listing 6.1 shows the memory footprint size of Apache running with mod_perl, Apache running with mod_php, and Apache "barebones" with mod_proxy and mod_rewrite all "in-flight" at a high traffic site.

Listing 6.1 **Apache Memory Resource Consumption**

PID	USER	PRI	NI	SIZE	RSS	SHARE	STAT	%CPU	%MEM	TIME	COMMAND
28871	nobody	15	0	37704	36M	8004	S	0.5	3.5	0:23	httpd-perl
26587	nobody	15	0	44920	34M	12968	S	0.7	3.4	2:25	httpd-perl
26572	nobody	16	0	46164	33M	10368	S	0.3	3.3	2:32	httpd-perl
26437	nobody	16	0	46040	33M	9088	S	0.3	3.3	2:40	httpd-perl
9068	nobody	15	0	5904	4752	2836	S	0.0	0.4	3:16	httpd-php
9830	nobody	15	0	5780	4680	2668	S	0.0	0.4	3:08	httpd-php
15228	nobody	15	0	4968	4112	2136	S	0.4	0.3	2:12	httpd-php
15962	nobody	15	0	4820	3984	2008	S	0.0	0.3	1:58	httpd-php
24086	nobody	9	0	3064	692	692	S	0.0	0.0	0:10	httpd-static
25437	nobody	9	0	2936	692	692	S	0.0	0.0	0:09	httpd-static
25452	nobody	9	0	3228	692	692	S	0.0	0.0	0:04	httpd-static
30840	nobody	9	0	2936	692	692	S	0.0	0.0	0:03	httpd-static

As can be seen, the static Apache server has a drastically smaller memory footprint. Because machines have limited resources, only so many Apache processes can run in memory concurrently. If we look at the `httpd-perl` instance, we see more than 20MB of memory being used by each process (RSS - SHARE). At 20MB per process, we can have fewer than 100 processes on a server with 2GB RAM before we exhaust the memory resources and begin to swap, which spells certain disaster. On the other hand, we have the `httpd-static` processes consuming almost no memory at all (less than 1MB across all processes combined). We could have several thousand `httpd-static` processes running without exhausting memory.

Small websites can get by with general-purpose Apache instances serving all types of traffic because traffic is low, and resources are plentiful. Large sites that require more than a single server to handle the load empirically have resource shortages. On our www.example.com site, each visitor can hold seven connections (and thus seven processes) hostage for 4 seconds or more. Assuming that it is running the `httpd-perl` variant shown previously to serve traffic and we have 2GB RAM, we know we can only sustain 100 concurrent processes: 100 processes / (7 processes * 4 second) = 3.58 visits/second. Not very high performance.

If we revisit our browsing of the www.example.com site and instruct our browser to retrieve only the URL (no dependencies), we see that only one connection is established and that it lasts for approximately 1 second. If we chose to serve only the dynamic content from the httpd-perl Apache processes, we would see 100 processes / (1 process * 1 second) = 100 visits / second. To achieve 100 visits per second serving all the traffic from this Apache instance, we would need 100/3.58 ≈ 30 machines, and that assumes optimal load balancing, which we know is an impossibility. So, with a 70% capacity model, we wind up with 43 machines.

Why were the processes tied up for so long when serving all the content? Well, pinging www.example.com yields 90ms of latency from my workstation. TCP requires a three-way handshake, but we will only account for the first two phases because data can ride on the heels of the third phase making its latency contribution negligible. So, as shown in Figure 6.1, establishing the connection takes 90ms. Sending the request takes 45ms, and getting the response takes at least 45ms. Our www.example.com visit requires the loading of 59 individual pieces of content spread over seven connections yielding about eight requests per connection. On average, we see that each connection spent at minimum one handshake and eight request/responses summing to 900ms.

This constitutes 900ms out of the 4 seconds, so where did the rest go? Well, as is typical, my cable Internet connection, although good on average, only yielded about 500Kb/s (bits, not bytes). Our total page size was 167500 bytes (or 1340000 bits). That means 2.7 seconds were spent trying to fetch all those bits. Now this isn't exact science as some of these seconds can and will overlap with the 900ms of latency shown in the previous paragraph, but you get the point—it took a while.

Now imagine dial-up users at 56Kb/s—the math is left as an exercise to the reader.

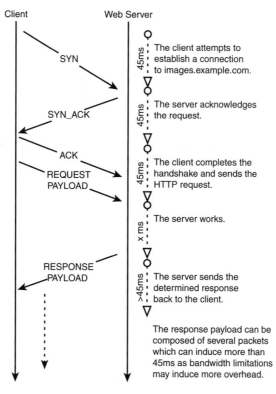

Figure 6.1   TCP state diagram for a typical web request.

The Goal

We've demonstrated that the Web is slow for most people. The goal is to speed it up, right? Yes, but that is more a secondary goal or side effect of accomplishing our real goal.

The real goal here is to *cost effectively* achieve a peak rate of 450,000 visitors per hour by making each visit take as few resources as possible, so that the same hardware (capital investment) can support many more visitors. This leads to scaling up (and down) the architecture more cost effectively.

Herein we will illustrate how to architect a web server solution that efficiently serves static content so that dynamic content web servers can continue to do their jobs. Only secondary is the goal of "accelerating" the end user's experience.

More specifically, we want to segregate our traffic to allow for static content services to be hosted and even operated independently. This means that scaling image services up and down can be done orthogonally to scaling the dynamic services. Note that we want to allow for this, not require it.

The first step of accomplishing this goal, before we build out the architecture, is to support it from within the web application. This requires a change (usually minimal) in the application, or none at all if some foresight was used in its construction. To segregate the static and dynamic content on the www.example.com domain, we will migrate all the static content to a new base domain name: images.example.com. Although any web developer should be able to tackle this task blindfolded, I present a simple approach that can be taken with a grain of salt.

You could go through all your content and change IMG SRC tags to use nonrelative URLs of the form http://images.example.com/path/to/image.jpg. However, doing so will only leave you in the same position if you want to change back, change domain names, or switch to a third-party service such as Akamai or EarthCache.

Instead, you should create a method or function that can be used to dynamically generate static URLs. A short example in PHP:

Request.inc

```
<?
    $default_http_static_base = 'http://images.example.com/';
    function imgsrc($img) {
        global $default_static_case;
        return $http_static_base.$img;
    }
?>
```

The php.ini file would be modified to `"auto_prepend_file"` Request.inc and in the PHP pages throughout the site, instead of placing images as `<img src="/images/toplogo.jpg">` place them as `<img src="<?php echo example_imgsrc('/images/toplogo.jpg') ?>">`. Using this methodology, to "scale down" and revert to the old method of a single instance for all traffic, simply change the `$default_http_static_base` back to `'http://www.example.com/'`.

Now that we have all our static content pointing to images.example.com, let's build a tuned cluster to support it.

Building the Cluster

The ultimate goal of this cluster is to serve static content more cost effectively than the main dynamic web servers can. Instead of being vague, let's have a specific goal.

We want to build a static image serving cluster to handle the static content load from the peak hour of traffic to our www.example.com site. We've described peak traffic as 125 initial page loads per second and 500 subsequent page loads per second. Optimizing the architecture that serves the 625 dynamic pages per second will be touched on in later chapters. Here we will just try to make the infrastructure for static content delivery cost effective.

Setting Goals

We need to do a bit of extrapolation to wind up with a usable number of peak static content requests per second. We can start with a clear upper bound by referring back to Table 6.1:

(125 initial visits / sec $\star$ 58 objects / initial visit) +
(500 subsequent visits / sec $\star$ 9 objects / subsequent visit) =
11750 objects/second

As discussed earlier, this is an upper bound because it does not account for two forms of caching:

- The caching of static content by remote ISPs—In the United States, for example, America Online (aol.com) subscribers constitute more than 20% of online users of several major websites. When ISPs such as AOL deploy web caches, they can cause a dramatic decrease in static content requests. In the best case, we could see 20% less static traffic.

- User browser caching—Many browsers aggressively cache static documents (even beyond the time desired by website owners). The previous numbers assume that the browser will cache images for the life of the session, but in truth that is a conservative speculation. Often images cached from prior days of web surfing may still reside in cache and can be utilized to make pages load faster. This also decreases the static request rate across the board.

The actual reduction factor due to these external factors is dependent on what forward caching solutions ISPs have implemented, and how many users are affected by those caches and the long-term client-side caches those users have.

We could spend a lot of time here building a test environment that empirically determines a reasonable cache-induced reduction factor, but that sort of experiment is out of the scope of this book and adds very little to the example at hand. So, although you should be aware that there *will* be a nonzero cache-induced reduction factor, we will simplify our situation and assume that it is zero. Note that this is conservative and errs on the side of increased capacity.

Putting Your Larger or Smaller Site in Perspective

We can calculate from Table 6.1 that our average expected payload is slightly less than 2500 bytes: 11,750 requests/second * 2500 bytes/request = 29,375,000 bytes/second or 235MB/s.

Tackling Content Distribution

We are going to build this rip-roaring static cluster serving traffic. First we'll approach the simplest of questions: How does the content get onto the machines in the first place?

A Priori Placement

A priori placement is just a fancy way of saying that the files need to be hosted on each node before they can be served from that node as depicted in Figure 6.2. This is one of the oldest problems with running clusters of machines, solved a million times over and, luckily for us, simplified greatly due to the fact that we are serving cacheable static content.

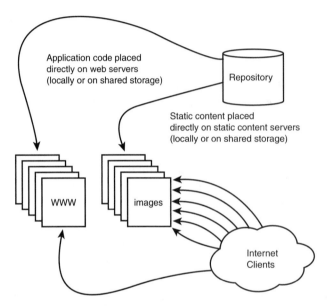

Figure 6.2   A priori placement of content.

Dynamic content typically performs some sort of business logic. As such, having one node execute the new version of code and another execute an older version spells disaster, specifically in multinode environments where each in the sequence of requests that compose a user's session may be serviced by different nodes. Although it is possible to "stick" a user to a specific node in the cluster, we already discussed in Chapter 5, "Load Balancing and the Utter Confusion Surrounding It," why this is a bad idea and should be avoided if possible.

Static content distribution, on the other hand, is a much simpler problem to address because we have already forfeited something quite important: control. To serve static content fast(er), we allow remote sites to cache objects. This means that we can't change an object and expect clients to immediately know that their cached copies are no longer valid. This isn't a problem logistically at all because new static objects are usually added and old ones removed because changing an object in-place is unreliable.

This means that no complicated semantics are necessary to maintain clusterwide consistency during the propagation of new content. Content is simply propagated and then available for use. Simply propagated... Hmmm...

The issue here is that the propagation of large sets of data can be challenging to accomplish in both a resource- and time-efficient manner. The "right" approach isn't always the most efficient approach, at least from a resource utilization perspective. It is important to align the techniques used to distribute content to your application servers and static servers in a manner that reduces confusion. If developers or systems administrators have to use different policies or take different pitfalls into consideration when pushing static content as opposed to dynamic content, mistakes are bound to happen.

This means that if you push code by performing exports directly from your revision control system, it may be easier to propagate static content via the same mechanism. Although an export may not be as efficient as a differential transfer of content from a "master server," only one mentality must be adopted—and remember: Humans confuse easily.

If no such infrastructure exists, we have several content distribution options.

NFS

Use a network file system. One copy of the content exists on a file server accessible by all web servers. The web servers mount this file system over IP and access the content directly. This is a popular solution in some environments, but poses a clear single point of failure because the clients cannot operate independently of the single file server. This approach also has certain deficiencies when used over a wide-area network.

AFS or CODA

AFS and CODA are "next-generation" network file systems. Both AFS and CODA allow for independent operation of the master file server by caching copies of accessed files locally. However, this technology is like implementing cache-on-demand on a different level in the application stack. Although these protocols are more friendly for wide areas, they still suffer from a variety of problems when operating in a disconnected manner.

Differential Synchronization

This technique involves moving only the data that has changed from the content distribution point to the nodes in need. You are probably familiar with the freely available (and widely used) tool called rsync that implements this. Rsync provides a mechanism for synchronizing the content from a source to a destination by first determining the differences and then transferring only what is needed. This is extremely network efficient and sounds ideal. However, the servers in question are serving traffic from their disks and are heavily taxed by the request loads placed on them. Rsync sacrifices local resources to save on network resources by first performing relatively inexpensive checksums across all files and then comparing them with the remote checksums so that unnecessary data transfers can be avoided.

The "relatively inexpensive" checksums don't seem so inexpensive when run on a highly utilized server. Plus, all our nodes need to sync from a master server, and, although rsync is only consuming marginal resources on each of the N nodes, it is consuming N times as many resources on the master server.

Hence, the world needs a network-efficient, resource-efficient 1 to N content distribution system with rsync's ease of use. Consider this a call to arms.

Exports from Revision Control

Directly exporting from revision control, assuming that your content is stored in some revision control system (as it certainly should be), has tremendous advantages. All the uses for revision control of code directly apply to static content: understanding change sets, backing out changes, and analyzing differences between tags or dates.

Most systems administrators are familiar with some version of revision control, and all developers should be fluent. This means that revision control is not only philosophically compatible with the internal control of static content but also is familiar, intuitive, and usable as well.

With so much praise, why isn't this approach used by everyone? The answer is efficiency. CVS is the most popular revision control system around due to its licensing and availability. CVS suffers from terrible tag times, and exports on large trees can be quite painful. Even with commercial tools and newer open free tools such as Subversion, the efficiency of a large checkout is, well, inefficient.

Most well-controlled setups implement exports from revision control on their master server and use a tool such as rsync to distribute that content out to the nodes responsible for serving that traffic, or opt for a pure cache-on-demand system.

Cache-on-Demand

Cache-on-demand uses a different strategy to propagate information to a second (or third, or fourth) tier. A variety of commercial solutions are available that you simply "plug in" in front of your website, and it runs faster. These solutions typically deploy a web proxy in reverse cache mode.

Web caches were originally deployed around the Internet in an attempt to minimize bandwidth usage and latency by caching commonly accessed content closer to a set of users. However, the technologies were designed with high throughput and high concurrency in mind, and most of the technologies tend to outperform general-purpose web servers. As such, a web cache can be deployed in front of a busy website to accomplish two things:

- Decrease the traffic directed at the general web servers by serving some of the previously seen content from its own cache.

- Reduce the amount of time the general purpose web server spends negotiating and tearing down TCP connections and sending data to clients by requiring the general purpose web server to talk over low-latency, high-throughput connections.

The web cache is responsible for expensive client TCP session handling and spoon-feeding data back to clients connected via low-throughput networks.

Web caches handle client requests directly by serving the content from a local cache. If the content does not exist in the local cache, the server requests the content from the "authoritative" source once and places the resulting content in the local cache so that subsequent requests for that data do not require referencing the "authoritative" source. This architecture is depicted in Figure 6.3.

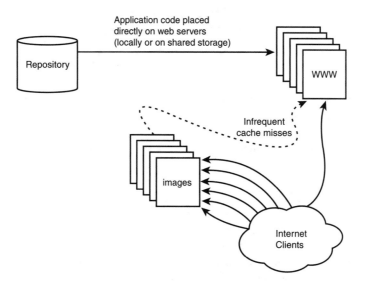

Figure 6.3   Typical cache-on-demand architecture.

Web caches that operate in this reverse proxying fashion are often called *web accelerators*. Apache with `mod_proxy` and Squid are two popular, widely adopted caching solutions commonly deployed in this configuration. Figure 6.3 shows a configuration in which the authoritative source is the main website. We can remove this marginal load from the dynamic servers by placing the content a priori on a single static content server that is hidden from the public as seen in Figure 6.4.

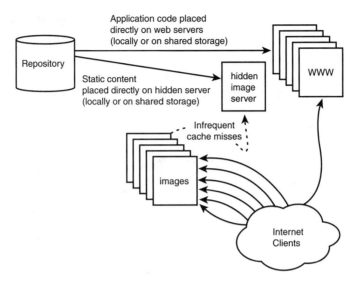

Figure 6.4 A more controlled cache-on-demand architecture.

Choosing a Web Serving Platform

Let's continue our route of using free software, as Apache is already at the core of our architecture. Apache 1.3.x with a relatively vanilla install clocks in at about 800 requests per second on our server. Our goal is to service 11,750 requests per second, and we don't want to exceed 70% capacity, which leaves us with a need for (11,750/70%)/800 = 20 servers. Each server here is capable of pushing about 16MB/s. Although commodity servers such as this have a list price of around $2,000 each, totaling at a reasonable $40,000, 20 servers for static images seems, well, less than satisfying.

Because we are serving static traffic, several other web server technologies could be used with little or no effort, instead of Apache. A quick download and compile of thttpd yields better results at approximately 3500 requests per second on the same server pushing about 70MB/s. Repeating the previous server calculations with our new metrics, we now need five servers—(11,750/70%)/3,500 rounded up.

A valuable feature exists in Apache and is notably absent in thttpd. This is reverse-proxy (web cache) support. This feature is useful because it allows you to build a cluster with a different strategy and adds elegance and simplicity to the overall solution. thttpd requires a priori placement of content, whereas Apache can use both a priori placement of content and cache-on-demand via the mod_proxy module. As we have seen, it takes 20 servers running Apache to meet the capacity requirements of our project, so let's find a higher performance caching architecture.

Apache is slower than `thttpd` in this particular environment for several reasons:

- It is more flexible, extensible, and standard.
- It is more complicated and multipurposed.
- It uses an architectural model that allocates more resources to each individual connection.

So, logically, we want to find a web server capable of proxying and caching data that is single-purposed, simple, and extremely efficient on a per-connection basis. Some research leads us to Squid (www.squid-cache.org). Architecturally, it is similar to `thttpd`, but single-purposed to be a web cache.

Cache-on-demand systems are inherently less efficient than direct-serve content servers because extra efforts must be made to acquire items that are requested but not yet in the cache and to ensure that data served from cache is still valid. However, a quick test of Squid is a good indication as to whether such a performance degradation is acceptable.

By installing Squid in http acceleration mode, we can benchmark on the same hardware around 2,800 requests per second. This is 20% slower. However, we see that this only increases our single location requirements to (11,750/70%)/2,800 and thus six servers.

Several commercial products boast higher performance than Squid or Apache. The adoption of any such device is really up to the preference of the operations group. Growing a solution based on open-sourced technologies tends to have clear technical and financial advantages for geographically distributed sites because costs multiply rapidly when commercial technologies are used in these situations. This is basically the same argument that was made in Chapter 4, "High Availability. HA! No Downtime?!" Adding a high performance appliance to a setup is often an easy way to accomplish a goal, just remember you need two for high availability. Although this may make good sense at a single highly trafficked location, if the site were to want a presence at four geographically unique locations, you have just committed to six more of these appliances (two at each site). Whether that is right is a decision you need to make for yourself.

Six servers are better than 20 for more reasons than capital hardware costs. A smaller cluster is easier and cheaper to manage, and, as discussed in previous chapters, it simplifies troubleshooting problems. Because this cluster serves only the simplest of content, we are not impressed with the extra added features of Apache and its modules, and do not find them to be a compelling reason to choose it over a smaller, simpler, and faster solution for our project at hand.

Examining Our Availability Requirements

The architecture supporting the static content for www.example.com must maintain the same (or stricter) availability requirements as the dynamic systems because it is a necessary part of the overall service. Our peak traffic is expected to be 11,750 requests per second, so we should be able to satisfy that metric with four servers, leaving us two for truly unexpected traffic surges and hardware failures.

This means that we must build a two-fault tolerant system that has remedial balancing of traffic. Multiple DNS RR A records should be sufficient for distributing incoming requests naively across the six machines, leaving an IP availability issue that can easily be solved by Wackamole.

Choosing an OS

For this cluster, we will use FreeBSD 4.9. Why? Simply because. This is not because FreeBSD is better than Linux is better than Solaris is better the Joe's OS, and so on. Honestly, any of these Unix and Unix-like systems should work like a charm. So, why do we choose FreeBSD as an example?

- It is a popular platform on which to run Squid, so community support for Squid on this platform will likely be of a higher caliber. Additionally, Squid supports the kqueue event system on FreeBSD allowing it to boast higher concurrency at lower CPU utilization than some other platforms.

- Wackamole supports FreeBSD more thoroughly than Solaris or Linux. More tested installations means less likelihood of failure.

- For the sake of an example in literature, the whole "which Linux distribution" religious war can be avoided.

We install six commodity servers with a FreeBSD 4.9 default install and assign each its public management IP address, 192.0.2.11 through 192.0.2.16, and name them image-0-1 through image-0-6, respectively.

Appropriate firewall rules should be set to protect these machines. Although this is outside the scope of this book, we can discuss the traffic we expect to originate from and terminate at each box.

- Inbound port 80 TCP and the associated established TCP session (for web serving)

- Inbound port 22 TCP and the associated established TCP session (ssh for administration)

- Outbound port 53 UDP and the corresponding responses (for DNS lookups)

- Inbound/Outbound Port 3777 UDP/TCP and 3778 UDP (to peer machines for Spread needed by Wackamole)

It is important to note that the six IP addresses above the management IPs and all client-originating web traffic will arrive to the IP published through DNS for this service.

Wackamole

Wackamole is a product from the Center for Networking and Distributed Systems at the Johns Hopkins University and is an integral part of the Backhand Project (www.backhand.org).

Wackamole's goal is to leverage the powerful semantics of group communication (Spread specifically) to drive a deterministic responsibility algorithm to manage IP address assignment over a cluster of machines. The technology differs from other IP failover solutions in that it can flexibly support both traditional active-passive configuration, as well as power multi-machine clusters where all nodes are active.

In Chapter 4, we briefly discussed the technical aspects of Wackamole; now we can discuss why it is the "right" solution for this problem.

Reasoning

There are several reasons for choosing Wackamole aside from my clearly biased preference toward the solution. The alternative solutions require placing a machine or device in front of this cluster of machines. Although this works well from a technical standpoint, its cost-efficiency is somewhat lacking. As discussed in Chapter 4, to meet any sort of high-availability requirements, the high-availability and load-balancing (HA/LB) device needs to be one of a failover pair.

You also might argue that you already have a hardware load balancer in place for the dynamic content of the site, and you can simply use those unsaturated resources as shown in Figure 6.5. This is a good argument and a good approach. You have already swallowed the costs of owning and managing the solution, so it does not incur additional costs while the management of a Wackamole-based solution does. However, another reason has not been mentioned yet—growth.

The last section of this chapter discusses how to split the solution geographically to handle higher load and faster load times for users. Clearly, if this architecture is to be replicated twice over, the costs of two HA/LB content switches twice over will dramatically increase the price and complexity of the solution.

Although it is arguable that Wackamole is not the right solution for a single site if an HA/LB content-switching solution is already deployed at that site, it will become clear that as the architecture scales horizontally, it is a cost-effective and appropriate technology.

Installation

Wackamole, first and foremost, requires Spread. Appendix A, "Spread," details the configuration and provides other tips and tricks to running Spread in production. For this installation, we will configure Spread to run listening to port 3777.

Wackamole is part of the Backhand project and can be obtained at www.backhand.org. Compiling Wackamole is simple with a typical `./configure; make; make install`. For cleanliness (and personal preference), we'll keep all our core service software in /opt. We issue the following commands for our install:

```
./configure -prefix=/opt/wackamole
make
make install
```

Installed as it is, we want a configuration that achieves the topology portrayed in Figure 6.6. This means that the six machines should manage the six IP addresses published through DNS. Now the simplicity of peer-based failover shines.

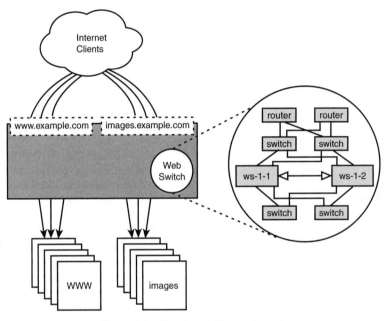

Figure 6.5 Simple HA/LB configuration.

Which machine should get which IP address? As a part of the philosophy of peer-based HA, that question is better left up to the implementation itself. Wackamole should simply be told to manage the group of IP addresses by creating a wackamole.conf file as follows:

```
Spread = 3777
Group = wack1
SpreadRetryInterval = 5s
Control = /var/run/wack.it

Prefer None
VirtualInterfaces {
```

```
    { fxp0:192.0.2.21/32 }
    { fxp0:192.0.2.22/32 }
    { fxp0:192.0.2.23/32 }
    { fxp0:192.0.2.24/32 }
    { fxp0:192.0.2.25/32 }
    { fxp0:192.0.2.26/32 }
}

Arp-Cache = 90s
mature = 5s

Notify {
    # Let's notify our router
    fxp0:192.0.2.1/32
    # And everyone we've been speaking with
    arp-cache
}
```

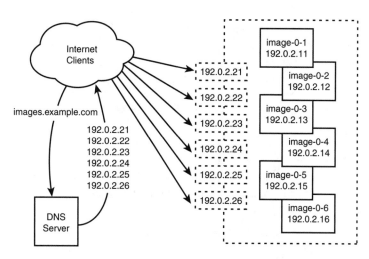

Figure 6.6   Peer-based high-availability configuration.

Let's walk through this configuration file step-by-step before we see it in action:

- Spread—Connects to the Spread daemon running on port 3777.

- Group—All Wackamole instances running this configuration file will converse over a Spread group named wack1.

- SpreadRetryInterval—If Spread were to crash or otherwise become unavailable, Wackamole should attempt to reconnect every 5 seconds.

- `Control`—Wackamole should listen on the file /var/run/wack.it for commands from the administrative program wackatrl.

- `Prefer`—Instructs Wackamole that no artificial preferences exist toward any one IP. In other words, all the Wackamoles should collectively decide which servers will be responsible for which IP addresses.

- `VirtualInterfaces`—Lists the IP addresses that the group of servers will be responsible for. These are the IP addresses published through DNS for images.example.com that will "always be up" assuming that at least one machine running Wackamole is alive and well.

- `Arp-Cache`—Instructs each instance to sample the local machine's ARP cache and share it with the other cluster members. The ARP cache contains the IP address to Ethernet MAC address mapping that is used by the operating system's network stack to communicate. It contains every IP address that a machine has been communicating with "recently." If machine A fails, and B is aware of the contents of A's ARP cache, B can inform all the necessary machines that have been communicating with A that the MAC addresses for the services they need have changed.

- `Mature`—To reduce "flapping," 5 seconds are allowed to pass before a new member is eligible to assume responsibility for any of the virtual interfaces listed.

- `Notify`—When Wackamole assumes responsibility for an IP address, it informs its default route at 192.0.2.1 and every IP address in the cluster's collective ARP cache. This is an effort to bring quick awareness of the change to any machines that have been using the services of that IP address.

Testing the High Availability

Now that Wackamole is installed, let's crank it up and see whether it works. First we will bring up Spread on all the machines (it should be in the default start scripts already) and test it as described in Appendix A. Next, we start Wackamole on `image-0-1`:

```
root@image-0-1# /usr/local/sbin/wackamole
root@image-0-1# /usr/local/sbin/wackatrl -l
Owner: 192.0.2.11
     *    fxp0:192.0.2.21/32
     *    fxp0:192.0.2.22/32
     *    fxp0:192.0.2.23/32
     *    fxp0:192.0.2.24/32
     *    fxp0:192.0.2.25/32
     *    fxp0:192.0.2.26/32

root@image-0-1# ifconfig fxp0
fxp0: flags=8843<UP,BROADCAST,RUNNING,SIMPLEX,MULTICAST> mtu 1500
        inet 192.0.2.11 netmask 0xffffff00 broadcast 192.0.2.255
```

```
        inet6 fe80::202:b3ff:fe3a:2e97%fxp0 prefixlen 64 scopeid 0x1
        inet 192.0.2.21 netmask 0xffffffff broadcast 192.0.2.21
        inet 192.0.2.22 netmask 0xffffffff broadcast 192.0.2.22
        inet 192.0.2.23 netmask 0xffffffff broadcast 192.0.2.23
        inet 192.0.2.24 netmask 0xffffffff broadcast 192.0.2.24
        inet 192.0.2.25 netmask 0xffffffff broadcast 192.0.2.25
        inet 192.0.2.26 netmask 0xffffffff broadcast 192.0.2.26
        ether 00:02:b3:3a:2e:97
        media: Ethernet autoselect (100baseTX <full-duplex>)
        status: active
```

So far, so good. Let's make sure that it works. From another location, we should ping all six of the virtual IP addresses to ensure that each is reachable. After successfully passing ICMP packets to these IP addresses, the router or firewall through which `image-0-1` passes packets will have learned that all six IP addresses can be found at the Ethernet address 00:02:b3:3a:2e:97.

Now we bring up `image-0-2`:

```
root@image-0-2# /usr/local/sbin/wackamole
root@image-0-2# /usr/local/sbin/wackatrl -l
Owner: 192.0.2.11
    *    fxp0:192.0.2.21/32
    *    fxp0:192.0.2.22/32
    *    fxp0:192.0.2.23/32
Owner: 192.0.2.12
    *    fxp0:192.0.2.24/32
    *    fxp0:192.0.2.25/32
    *    fxp0:192.0.2.26/32

root@image-0-2# ifconfig fxp0
fxp0: flags=8843<UP,BROADCAST,RUNNING,SIMPLEX,MULTICAST> mtu 1500
        inet 192.0.2.12 netmask 0xffffff00 broadcast 192.0.2.255
        inet6 fe80::202:b3ff:fe3a:2f97%fxp0 prefixlen 64 scopeid 0x1
        inet 192.0.2.24 netmask 0xffffffff broadcast 192.0.2.24
        inet 192.0.2.25 netmask 0xffffffff broadcast 192.0.2.25
        inet 192.0.2.26 netmask 0xffffffff broadcast 192.0.2.26
        ether 00:02:b3:3a:2f:97
        media: Ethernet autoselect (100baseTX <full-duplex>)
        status: active
```

Everything looks correct, but we should make sure that `image-0-1` sees the same thing. Because the output of `wackatrl -l` will certainly be the same, `ifconfig` is the true tool to make sure everything is the same. Subsequent to bringing image-0-2's Wackamole instance up, we see the appropriate message in `/var/log/message`, and `ifconfig` shows that the three complementary IP addresses are assigned to `image-0-1`.

```
root@image-0-1# tail /var/log/message | grep wackamole
image-0-1 wackamole[201]: DOWN: fxp0:192.0.2.24/255.255.255.255
image-0-1 wackamole[201]: DOWN: fxp0:192.0.2.25/255.255.255.255
image-0-1 wackamole[201]: DOWN: fxp0:192.0.2.26/255.255.255.255

root@image-0-1# ifconfig fxp0
fxp0: flags=8843<UP,BROADCAST,RUNNING,SIMPLEX,MULTICAST> mtu 1500
        inet 192.0.2.11 netmask 0xffffff00 broadcast 192.0.2.255
        inet6 fe80::202:b3ff:fe3a:2e97%fxp0 prefixlen 64 scopeid 0x1
        inet 192.0.2.21 netmask 0xffffffff broadcast 192.0.2.21
        inet 192.0.2.22 netmask 0xffffffff broadcast 192.0.2.22
        inet 192.0.2.23 netmask 0xffffffff broadcast 192.0.2.23
        ether 00:02:b3:3a:2e:97
        media: Ethernet autoselect (100baseTX <full-duplex>)
        status: active
```

Although the local configuration on each server looks sound, there is more to this than meets the eye. The traffic from other networks is being delivered to and from this one server through a router, and that router has an ARP cache. If the ARP cache was not updated, the router will continue to send packets to 192.0.2.24, 192.0.2.25, and 192.0.2.26 to image-0-1. Although we can be clever and send ICMP packets to each IP address and use a packet analyzer such as tcpdump or ethereal to determine whether the ICMP packets are indeed being delivered to the correct machine, there is a simpler and more appropriate method of testing this—turn off image-0-1.

Wackamole employs a technique called *ARP spoofing* to update the ARP cache of fellow machines on the local Ethernet segment. Machines use their ARP cache to label IP packet frames for delivery to their destination on the local subnet. When two machines on the same Ethernet segment want to communicate over IP, they each must ascertain the Ethernet hardware address (MAC address) of the other. This is accomplished by sending an ARP request asking what MAC address is hosting the IP address in question. This request is followed by a response that informs the curious party with the IP address and MAC address. The crux of the problem is that this result is cached to make IP communications efficient.

After we yank the power cord from the wall, we should see image-0-2 assume responsibility for all the IP addresses in the Wackamole configuration. Now a ping test will determine whether Wackamole's attempts to freshen the router's ARP cache via unsolicited ARP responses was successful.

If pings are unsuccessful and suddenly start to work after manually flushing the ARP cache on our router, we are unfortunate and have a router that does not allow ARP spoofing. The only device I am aware of that acts in this fashion is a Cisco PIX firewall, but I am sure there are others lingering out there to bite us when we least expect it.

If a server is communicating over IP with the local router, that router will inevitably have the server's MAC address associated with that server's IP address in its ARP cache.

However, if that server were to crash and another machine was to assume the responsibilities of one of the IP addresses previously serviced by the crashed machine, the server will have the incorrect MAC address cached. Additionally, it will not know that it needs to re-ARP for that IP. So, Wackamole will send ARP response packets (also known as *unsolicited* or *gratuitous ARPing*) to various machines on the local Ethernet segment if an IP address is juggled from one server to another.

Assuming that all has gone well, our cluster is ready for some serious uptime. After bringing up all six Wackamole instances, we will see the following output from `wackatrl -l`.

```
root@image-0-2# /usr/local/sbin/wackatrl -l
Owner: 192.0.2.11
    *     fxp0:192.0.2.21/32
Owner: 192.0.2.12
    *     fxp0:192.0.2.22/32
Owner: 192.0.2.13
    *     fxp0:192.0.2.23/32
Owner: 192.0.2.14
    *     fxp0:192.0.2.24/32
Owner: 192.0.2.15
    *     fxp0:192.0.2.25/32
Owner: 192.0.2.16
    *     fxp0:192.0.2.26/32
```

Now, even if five of these machines fail, all six virtual IP addresses will be publicly accessible and serving whatever services necessary. Granted, our previous calculations let us know that one machine would never be capable of coping with the peak traffic load, but we still should be able to have two of them offline (unexpectedly or otherwise) and be able to handle peak load.

The next step is to advertise these six IP addresses via DNS so that people visiting images.example.com will arrive at our servers.

The DNS RR records for this service should look as follows:

```
$ORIGIN example.com.
images    900    IN    A    192.0.1.21
          900    IN    A    192.0.1.22
          900    IN    A    192.0.1.23
          900    IN    A    192.0.1.24
          900    IN    A    192.0.1.25
          900    IN    A    192.0.1.26
```

This sample bind excerpt advertises the six listed IP addresses for the name images.example.com, and clients should "rotate" through these IP addresses. Clients, in this context, are not actually end users but rather the caching name server closest to the client. Each name server is responsible for cycling the order of the records it presents from response to response. So each new query for images.example.com results in a list of IP addresses in a new order. Typically, web browsers tend to use the name service resolution provided by the host machine that they run on, and most hosts choose the first DNS RR record when several are presented. That means different clients accessing the same name server will contact different IPs, and there will be a general distribution across all the advertised IPs.

The balancing will not be even, but you should see roughly the same number of requests per second across each of the IP addresses. For example, in our production reference implementation, we see an average 30% deviation from machine to machine on a second-to-second basis, and less than 3% deviation from minute to minute. So, although the balancing is not perfect, it is entirely sufficient.

Serving Content

Now that we have six servers clustered together, we need to set up a high-performance web serving platform to meet our needs—a peak demand of 11,750 requests per second.

Installing Squid is fairly straightforward with a familiar ./configure; make; make install. However, configuring it can be complicated.

The main squid.conf file should be modified to make the Squid instance act as an HTTP accelerator only for images.example.com.

```
http_port 80 accel vhost vport=80 defaultsite=images.example.com

acl all src 0.0.0.0/0.0.0.0
acl manager proto cache_object
acl localhost src 127.0.0.1/255.255.255.255
acl to_localhost dst 127.0.0.0/8
acl Safe_ports port 80
acl CONNECT method CONNECT
http_access allow manager localhost
http_access deny manager
http_access deny !Safe_ports
http_access deny to_localhost
http_access deny CONNECT
http_access allow all

acl acceld dstdomain images.example.com
always_direct allow acceld
```

This allows requests to this cache from anywhere but only pulls content to satisfy those requests of images.example.com. images.example.com should be added to the local /etc/hosts file to be the published IP of www.example.com. This configuration achieves the content placement approach shown previously in Figure 6.3.

World Domination

Our news site is now cranking along, serving static content to visitors. The solution we have built works well. Visitors from all around the world visit www.example.com and fetch images from our small and efficient cluster. As with any good system, however, there is always room for improvement.

Of course, nothing initiates improvements like a change in requirements. The site has been performing adequately from a technical point of view, but example.com has been overperforming on the business side—we all should be so lucky. We have been tasked by management to increase the capacity of the whole system by a factor of four to meet expected demand.

Scaling the systems downward that we built before could not be easier. Unplugging, moving from the cabinets, and liquidating some of the static servers would have done the trick—no administration required. However, scaling up requires some work. The goal is to have a technology base that is sound and efficient enough to be grown without core change. We will see that we have accomplished this.

The one aspect of image serving that is deficient, aside from our sudden lack of capacity, is our ability to capitalize on user proximity. Essentially, everyone in the world is visiting our site in San Jose, California, in the United States. Although this is probably great for people on the West Coast of the United States, it leaves a lot to be desired for visitors from the United Kingdom, the rest of Europe, Asia, Africa, and even the East Coast of the United States.

Figure 6.7 shows this configuration from a global perspective. Earlier, we analyzed the resource costs of latency and found that the resources idly tied up by the latency in a TCP connection to a web server is second only to that incurred by low-bandwidth connections. Although a single intercontinental or cross-continental TCP request for a single object may not be painfully slow, six connections for 58 objects certainly is. By providing a static cluster closer to the end user, we intrinsically reduce latency and have a good chance of increasing throughput by reducing the number of possibly congested networks through which packets flow.

Ideally, we want to place static content servers in a position to serve the bulk of our visitors with low latency. Upon further investigation into the business issues that sparked this needed capacity, we find that the reason is a doubling of traffic in the United States and good penetration into the European and Asian markets.

With this in mind, a placement in Japan, Germany, New York, and San Jose would be reasonably close to the vast majority of our intended audience. However, special care should be taken. The system must be designed correctly, or what we hope to accomplish will backfire. We want users to visit the content distribution point closest to them. However, the architecture, in its raw form, affords the opportunity to have users visit a distribution point that is very far away, as shown in Figure 6.8.

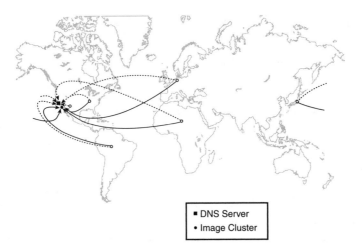

Figure 6.7 Centralized image serving cluster.

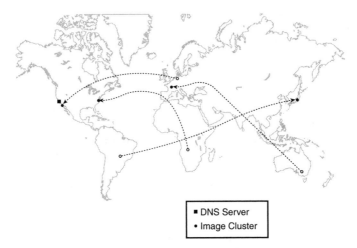

Figure 6.8 Geographically separate image serving clusters with undesirable access patterns.

Clearly this type of introduced inefficiency is something to avoid. So, how do we make sure that users in Europe visit our content distribution point in Europe and likewise for other countries and locations? We'll take a very short stab at answering this question and then talk about why it is the wrong question to ask.

To have users in Europe visit our installation in Germany, we can determine where in the world the user is and then direct them to a differently named image cluster. For example, Germany could be images.de.example.com, and Japan could be images.jp.example.com. To determine "where" the user is, there are two basic options. The first is to ask the user where she is and trust her response. This is sometimes used to solve legal issues when content must differ from viewer to viewer, but we do not have that issue. The second is to guess the location from the client's IP address. Unfortunately, both these methods have a high probability of being inaccurate.

We have gone astray from our goal with a subtly incorrect assumption. Our goal was to reduce latency and possibly increase throughput by moving the origin of content closer to the user. So far, so good. Then we conjectured about how we should determine whether a user is geographically closer to one location or another. Somehow, that "geographical" qualifier slipped in there, likely because people prefer to think spatially. The truth of the matter is that you don't care where in the world (literally) the user is, just where on the Internet the user is. The proximity we should be attempting to capitalize on is the user's proximity on the network.

The problem has been more clearly defined and is now feasible to solve using some network-based techniques.

DNS Round-Trip Times

The DNS Round-Trip Times method relies on each local name server tracking the round-trip time of packets as it performs recursive name service resolution. Over time, the local recursive name server will favor authoritative servers with the lowest latency. This "optimization strategy" results in resolution being performed against the authoritative DNS server "closest" to the client's name server with respect to the network—or so the theory goes.

Rephrased and simplified a bit, the client attempts to resolve images.example.com from each authoritative name server, eventually settling on the name server with the quickest responses.

So, all we need to do is put a publicized, authoritative name server for images. example.com alongside each image cluster at our four locations. Each name server will serve the IP addresses of the onsite image servers. As shown in Figure 6.9, the name server in Germany serves the IP addresses for the cache servers in Germany, the name server in Japan serves the IP addresses for the cache servers in Japan, and so on.

This method is easy to implement and requires no special infrastructure, but it suffers from some rather serious shortcomings. The most obvious is that the algorithm calls for the "eventual" convergence on the closest name server, and until each client's local name server converges, you have misdirection. Additionally, sudden changes in network topology, such as a collapsed route or the peering relationship between two autonomous systems (ASs) changing, will cause the answer we spent so much time reaching to be suboptimal. The Internet is a rapidly changing place—a sea of endpoints. Point A will most likely always be able to communicate with point B, but the routers and networks those packets traverse can change at any moment.

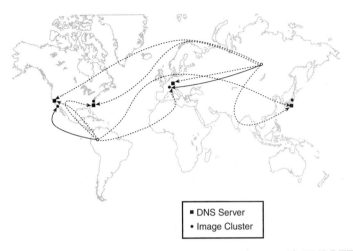

Figure 6.9   Geographically separate image serving clusters with DNS RTT-based convergence.

Anycast—Shared IP

There is another method to find the closest server on the network that copes well with the nature of the Internet by leveraging the fundamentals of efficient network routing (that is, delivering packets to an IP address over the shortest path).

By giving two different servers on the Internet the same IP address and requesting the networks to which we are attached to announce the routes to those IP addresses (as is normally done), we employ the technique now called *Anycast*.

The tricky part about using Anycast is that, at any moment in time, routes can change. This means that the next packet sent to that IP address might very well find its way to a different host. What does this mean in terms of IP? Given that all DNS traffic and web serving happens over IP, this is an important question.

If host image-2-1.example.com in Germany and image-3-1.example.com in Japan share the same IP address, the following scenario is possible. A client attempts to establish a TCP connection to images.example.com. The client first resolves the name to an IP address to which the client sends a SYN packet (sent as the first step in establishing a TCP connection) that finds its way to image-2-1.example.com (in Germany). The ACK packet is sent back to the client, and the client then sends back the first data packet containing the http request. All is well until now. Then a route flaps somewhere on the Internet, and the closest path from that client to the destination IP address now delivers packets to image-3-1.example.com (in Japan).

image-2-1 returns a data packet to the client, and it gets there because the shortest path from image-2-1 to the client does not lead the packet astray (there is only one machine on the Internet with that client's IP address). However, when the client responds to that packet, it goes to Japan (the new shortest path back to the server IP). This is where things go sour. When the packet arrives at image-3-1, it is part of a preexisting TCP session with image-2-1 of which image-3-1 knows nothing. The only reasonable response to this is to send a TCP RST packet, which aborts the TCP session, and that's no good at all.

So, what good is Anycast? Well, we've demonstrated the shortcomings with respect to TCP. But these shortcomings hinge on the connectedness of that transport protocol. UDP, on the other hand, is a connectionless protocol. Services such as DNS typically only require a single request and response UDP packet to accomplish a task. So, where does this leave us?

We know that each node in each image cluster needs a unique IP address to avoid the problem described previously. If we place DNS servers next to each image cluster and all DNS servers share the same IP address (via Anycast) and each DNS server offers the IP addresses of the image cluster nodes nearest to it, we achieve our proximity objectives. Figure 6.10 shows our globally distributed system based on Anycast.

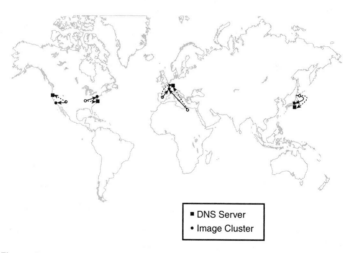

Figure 6.10   Geographically separate image serving clusters with ideal access patterns.

Anycast ensures that a client's DNS requests will be answered by the DNS server closest to him on the network. Because the DNS server handed back the IP addresses associated with the image server to which it is adjacent, we know that (as the DNS request traversed the Internet) this image cluster was the closest to the client. That's pretty powerful mojo.

A Final Review

We now know how to construct a static content distribution network capable of servicing a peak load of 47,000 queries per second (assuming full utilization on each cluster). More importantly, we have accomplished the following goals:

- Build a static content acceleration server to make our news site faster.
- Reduce the latency and potentially increase the throughput for most users' requests to the site.
- Build something from scratch that is easy to maintain, inexpensive to build, and inexpensive to operate in the long run.

Our final architecture has four identical cluster installs that are globally and strategically placed.

- Each cluster is completely functional and standalone. Six inexpensive commodity machines running Wackamole for IP failover provide high availability and high performance.
- The architecture runs Squid and acts as a cache-on-demand system that needs no out-of-band content synchronization.
- DNS servers using Anycast ensure that clients are delivered to the most network-appropriate cluster.

Was It Worth It?

Earlier a statement was made: "It will become clear that as the architecture scales horizontally, it is a cost-effective and appropriate technology." Let's look at this a bit more to better understand the drastic savings resulting from this architecture choice over a classic "white-paper" approach.

Figure 6.5 shows what the architecture would look like if the image cluster was fronted by the same web switch that drives the load-balancing for the dynamic content cluster. The "web switch" in that diagram is really two routers, four wiring-closet switches, and two web switches. When we presented the architecture depicted in Figure 6.7 in context, it was reasonable because that infrastructure was already there to support the dynamic application, so there was no investment to be made. However, by placing the image clusters at three other locations in the world, we would now need that same "web switch" in front of each.

In all fairness, we can't just ignore all that hardware. We will need portions of it in the new architecture—namely two routers and two switches at each location for high availability. But immediately we see that we can avoid purchasing six wiring-closet switches and six web switches. Let's put some dollars on that.

Web switches capable of actually load-balancing more than 200Mbs of traffic carry a pretty price tag—often more than $50,000 each. Wiring-closet switches often run around $5,000 each. That adds up to $625,000. Well worth it if you ask me.

7

Static Meets Dynamic
Adding Caches to Reduce Costs

CHAPTER 6, "STATIC CONTENT SERVING FOR SPEED AND GLORY," walked you through building a high-capacity static content serving system using a web caching system as the core technology. That software was responsible for fetching static content from "master" servers and peddling the cached content efficiently and inexpensively.

Why is the problem so different when the content is no longer static? Why can't we use the exact same solution presented in Chapter 6 for dynamic content?

Think of a website as if it were a phone book. A cache is a piece of paper that sits next to your phone book on which you record all the numbers you look up. Sounds like a good idea, right? So much so that you will probably tape that piece of notebook paper to the front of your phone book because you are likely to be interested only in a small subset of the information contained in the book and just as likely to be interested in the same information time and time again. Sounds perfect, right? But the analogy is flawed. Static content on a website is like a phone book, but imagine how difficult it would be to use your "paper cache" if the numbers inside the phone book constantly changed or if numbers differed based on who was looking them up. This is why caching dynamic content poses a more difficult problem than caching static content.

One misconception about caches is due to the misalignment of the computing-centric definition and the English definition of the word *cache*. In English, a *cache* is a place to store things often out of sight or in secret, and that definition assumes that it will be there when you return for it. A *computer cache* is only meant to speed acquisition of data; if it is missing when you look for it, you incur what is called a *cache miss*. This miss costs you nothing but time.

Caches are everywhere, from the "registers" on your CPU to L1/L2 CPU cache to disk drives to name servers to web systems—and the list goes on. Caches are fundamental engineering tools both inside and outside technology. If they are everywhere, how do you tell if a cache is a web cache? Let's define our web architecture as components directly creating browser-digestible content. This definition eliminates many architectural components that use caches: load balancers, databases, networking equipment, disk drives, and so on. This leaves us with web servers and application servers (glorified web servers).

Web servers are squished right in the middle of our spectacular architectural sandwich. Web caches are caching components of any type that operate directly on web servers or between web servers and their adjacent layers as depicted in Figure 7.1.

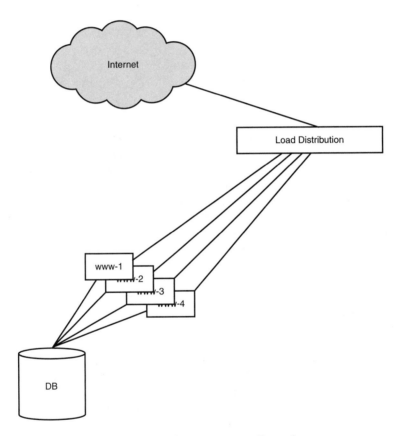

Figure 7.1   Typical architecture surrounding web servers.

Performance Tuning Has Its Limits

Why are we talking about caching and not application performance tuning? This is an important question and deserves attention. Our goal is to demonstrate techniques that can be used as building blocks for scalable systems—and caching is such a technique. Application tuning can only increase performance, and you'll note that the title of this book is *not* High Performance Internet Architectures. That is not to say that the concepts herein do not perform well, but rather that they focus on scalability and leave high-performance programming, tuning, and tweaking to other books.

Why are scalability and performance different? This is explored in detail in the introduction, but it deserves a few more words. No matter how fast you make your application, you will be limited if it does not scale horizontally.

To put it another way, if your application performance can be increased by 10%, 5%, or perhaps 1% by doubling your hardware, you are in big trouble. Moore's law says that your computer will be twice as fast in 18 months, so if you want to double your capacity, call me in a year and a half. On the other hand, if your application and architecture are designed to be able to leverage 60% or more performance by doubling your architecture, you can scale your system up today. Those percentages are arbitrary, and each architecture will have its own horizontal scaling efficiency. 100% means a perfectly (horizontally) scalable architecture, and 0% means an architecture that scales vertically, so performance tuning is your only option—so aim high.

Types of Caches

There are five basic types of caching approaches when dealing with content distribution. Each has pros and cons, and more importantly each has its place. Often it is awkward, or simply impossible, to implement a specific caching approach due to the nature of the underlying data.

Layered/Transparent Cache

The transparent (or layered) cache should be well understood by now. This is the technology deployed to solve our image-serving problem in Chapter 6. The caching proxy is placed in front of the architecture and all requests arrive at the proxy. The proxy attempts to service the request by using its private cache. If the response to that request has not yet been cached (or the cache has expired or otherwise been destroyed), the cache is (re)populated by issuing a request for the content to the authoritative source and storing the response.

This technique is ideal for static content because it is often easy to build commodity proxy caches capable of holding the entire static content store (capacity-wise). This means that as time goes on, the cache will closely resemble the authoritative source, and nearly 100% of all requests issued to the cache can be satisfied on the spot from its local copy.

This technology is called *transparent* because many implementations allow you to place a cache in front of web servers without any configuration changes. In Chapter 6, we chose not to use the technology in this fashion because we wanted to play tricks with our domain name (images.example.com). In a local web environment, the cache can intercept data and proxy it back to web servers by acting as a bridge or as a configured part of the architecture in the form of an IP gateway. Either way, web clients have no knowledge of its placement in the architecture, and it has no noticeable side effects from their perspective.

These proxy caches have an additional added value discussed briefly in Chapter 6. This value is *acceleration* and it is appropriate to delve into it more deeply now. Web clients (users with browsers) will most certainly be connecting to the website over a long-haul link that has a distinctly poorer performance than the main egress point of the website to the Internet. This means that the website *could* push the request content back to the client very rapidly if it wasn't for the slow connection over which it must feed the data. This is often referred to as *spoon-feeding* clients.

Application servers differ from static content servers in that they have more work to do. A static server interprets a request and hands back the appropriate content to the client. A dynamic server interprets a request and is responsible for *constructing* the content and then handing it back to the client. The act of constructing the content often requires more expensive resources than simply serving it (more RAM and faster processors). This means that application servers sport a higher price tag than their static counterparts.

At the end of the day, you do not want to look back and find that you spent a considerable amount of resources on your application servers spoon-feeding clients. An application server should be generating content and delivering it as fast as possible so that it can proceed to the next dynamic content generation job in its queue. This is where proxy caches shine.

A *proxy cache* is an "accelerator" if it sits between the client and the application server. In this configuration, the connection between the proxy cache and application server is a local area one that boasts high throughput and low latency (shown in Figure 7.2). This means that the response from the application server can be completed quickly and stored on the proxy cache allowing the application server to proceed to the next request. The proxy cache then spoon-feeds the content to the slow client and acts as a cost-effective buffer preventing slow clients from affecting the application servers.

If most pages served from an application server are unique, it is clear that caching the data on a transparent cache will be of little value because the cache hit-rate will be nearly 0%. However, the accelerating aspect of the technology alone is often worth the investment.

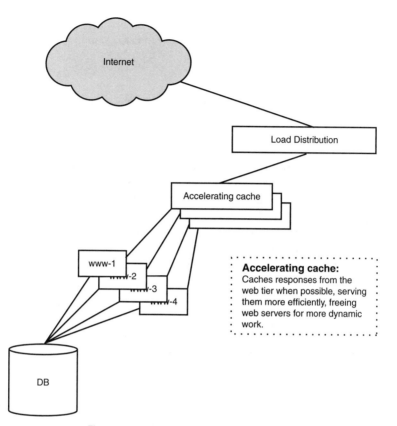

Figure 7.2 An accelerating web proxy cache.

Integrated (Look-Aside) Cache

An *integrated cache* steps far away from the transparent caching in both implementation and mentality. Transparent caching is simply a black-box architectural component that can be placed in front of an architecture for added benefit. Integrated caching is, as you might assume, integrated into the architecture—more specifically into the application. Integrated caching is most similar to the programming technique of computational reuse where we store the results of expensive computations on the side so that they don't need to be repeated.

Computational Reuse

Computational reuse is a programming technique that attempts to capitalize on situations where the cost of storing the results of a computation and later finding them again is less expensive than performing the computation again. The classic computer science example of computational reuse is the computation of Fibonacci numbers.

The nth Fibonacci number is defined as $F(n) = F(n-1) + F(n-2)$ where $F(0) = 0$ and $F(1) = 1$. A small perl function to calculate the nth Fibonacci number would be as follows:

```perl
sub fib {
    my $o = shift;
    die "Only natural number indexes." if($o < 0 || $o != int($o));
    return $o if ($o < 2);
    return fib($o-2) + fib($o-1);
}
```

Running `fib(30)` on my laptop takes approximately 6.1 seconds. Why is this simple calculation so slow? When I calculate `fib(28)` and then proceed to calculate `fib(29)`, I end up calculating `fib(28)` again. I calculate `fib(28)` twice, `fib(27)` three times, `fib(26)` five times, `fib(25)` eight times...and `fib(2)` 514229 times! (Do you see the sequence there? Math is fascinating.)

Let's make a simple attempt at storing the result of each calculation so that every subsequent time we are asked for `fib(n)` we look up the answer instead of calculating it:

```perl
my %fib_cache;
sub fib_cr {
    my $o = shift;
    die "Only natural number indexes." if($o < 0 || $o != int($o));
    return $o if($o < 2);
    # Here we return a cached result if one exists.
    return $fib_cache{$o} if(exists($fib_cache{$o}));
    # Here we cache the result and return it.
    return $fib_cache{$o} = fib_cr($o-2) + $fib_cr($o-1);
}
```

Running `fib_cr(30)` on my laptop takes less than 0.01 seconds—roughly a 61000% speed up. This painfully obvious example demonstrates the value of computational reuse. This particular example's simplicity and obvious benefit are the reasons for its place as the "poster child" of computational reuse.

Real Application

Although the Fibonacci example may seem contrived, it illustrates a simple concept: It is often cheaper to store a previous calculation and retrieve it later than it is to perform the calculation again from scratch. This is true in all arenas of computer science, engineering, and life.

Integrated caches are most similar to computational reuse because the application itself attempts to remember (cache) any acquisition of data (or transformation of data) considered by the developer to be frequently used and sufficiently expensive.

Computational reuse itself can be applied directly to core application code, but when the problem is extrapolated to an architecture with multiple interdependent components, the technique evolves from computational reuse to integrated caching; and with that evolution comes complexity.

It is important to digress for a moment and understand that the gain from computation reuse is a performance gain and does not imply scalability. Computation reuse is an edict of high-performance computer programming, and although high-performance does not ensure scalability, low performance is a death warrant.

The gain from integrated caching is a step toward horizontal scalability (although not always a good step to take, as you will see). Integrated caching allows one component in an architecture to use another component less. A good example is the use of a database as the backing store for content on a website. You could query the database every time a specific page was requested, or you could cache the results and future requests would not require a database query.

The concept of an application code cache is to allow the application to store the result of an expensive operation and determine an answer to that query more quickly by referencing local data than by requerying the authoritative source (see Figure 7.3).

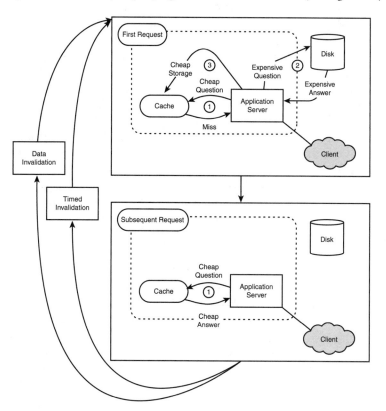

Figure 7.3   An integrated look-aside cache.

Although computational reuse is a good approach in computer programming, it makes the assumption that the result of a particular question will not change. The 19th

Fibonacci number isn't going to change when we aren't looking. However, if we were to cache a user's preferences or another result of an expensive database query, the answer *is* likely to change when we aren't looking.

This leaves us with the challenge of architecting a cache invalidation infrastructure or "fudging it" by setting cache timeouts—basically accepting that an answer is good for some magical amount of time, and if it changes in that time, we will be stuck with the old incorrect answer.

A beautiful example of integrated caching is that which is inside recursive domain name system (DNS) servers. When I perform a lookup on www.example.com, I issue a simple question to my local recursive DNS server and expect a simple response. My DNS server must query root servers to determine who is responsible for the example.com domain and then query the responsible party—and this is the simplest case. If my DNS server did this every time I needed www.example.com, the Internet would be a wholly unsatisfying (slow) place. Instead, my DNS server caches the answer for some amount of time so that subsequent identical requests can be answered on the spot.

Why can't we use the same technique in our web applications? The technique clearly applies, but DNS has the advantage (called good engineering) that every piece of data is distributed with a time-to-live (TTL). Unlike web applications, every DNS system has insight into how long it is allowed to cache the result before it must throw away that answer as stale and then requery.

In web applications, the queries performed typically do not have an explicit TTL and the only implicit TTL for data is the life of the request itself. This means that the data changes, and we don't know how fast it will change. These circumstances make caching beyond the life of a single web request difficult to maintain and debug, and often lead to compromises that can be avoided by using data caches or write-thru caches.

Although integrated caches in their most simple form are an awkward fit for large-scale web architectures, we can use aspects of this technology combined with write-thru caches and distributed caches to realize true horizontal scalability.

Data Cache

The data cache is a simple concept. It is effectively computational reuse on a lower level than the integrated cache. With a data cache, we expect our core services (those on which the application relies) to employ computational reuse and extensive caching.

As we defined web caching, this doesn't exactly fit. The idea here is to have a database or other core service that efficiently uses a cache so that the web application can transparently benefit. The only reason that data caches are relevant is that it is possible to place a database replica on each web server and then we can more legitimately call data caching a form of web caching.

The intrinsic problem with integrated caching is that the cache is distributed and uncoordinated. If one node running the application performs an SQL query against a database and stores the answer, it has no sound way of determining whether the underlying data that formed the response has changed. As such, it has no good way of knowing whether it will receive the same answer if it issues the same question. However, one system *does* know whether the data has changed—the database.

We will just accept the fact that the vast majority of Internet architectures use a relational database management system (RDBMS) to store their data. All queries for that data are posed to the RDBMS, and it is responsible for answering them.

MySQL, for example, employs a data cache calling it a *query cache*. Essentially, it caches the complete answers to questions that are asked of it. Along with those answers it stores a reference to the data on which their accuracy depends. If that data changes, the answer is efficiently invalidated.

This is a simpler solution than an integrated cache on the web application level because a single product is in complete control of both the caching infrastructure and the authoritative data.

What does this buy you? The vast majority of data that powers Internet sites has a high read-to-write ratio, meaning that questions are asked of the database far more often than data is placed in the database. Although databases are fast and robust, they still must spend time answering queries, and that time is precious.

Write–Thru and Write–Back Caches

Write-back caches are classic computer engineering. You will find this technology in every computer processor, code optimizer, and disk drive. Any time that it is expensive to save a piece of data that is also commonly accessed, you will find a write-back cache. A write-back cache means that all modifications of data are performed on the cache. When the cache is full and entries are removed, they are then written to the backing store if needed. This simple design is depicted in Figure 7.4.

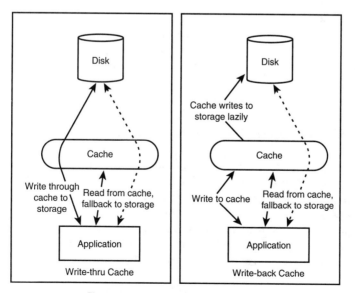

Figure 7.4   Write-thru and write-back caches.

If you stop reading here and get a cup of coffee, you should be able to come up with a few catastrophic problems with the write-back architecture.

A cache on most systems is a faster storage medium than the authoritative source for which it caches. In a web proxy cache, it is the cheap disk drive on the cheap box serving static content—no data is modified on those drives, so a failure cannot incur data loss. In a disk drive, volatile memory (DRAM) is faster than the physical disk drives. If data is written to the volatile cache on a drive and that cache operates in write-back mode, what happens when the power fails? Data does not make it back to disk, and you have inconsistency, corruption, and lost data.

Some IDE drives enable write-back cache that cannot be turned off! External RAID arrays often use write-back caches and have expensive battery units capable of keeping all the drives up and running long enough to completely journal its cache back to permanent storage.

You may be wondering how in the world you would incorporate a write-back cache paradigm in a distributed/cluster web application architecture? Well, there is certainly no good concrete example I can find. The concept does not adapt well to web systems; but, let's jump to write-back's brother named write-thru.

Write-thru caches operate in an interesting fashion. They exploit the fact that reads and writes in many systems are temporally relative. What does this mean? Reads often occur on data most recently written. A concrete example is the addition of a news article to a database. New news is read more often than old news. The news most recently added to the system will be the news most frequently requested from the system.

A write-thru cache writes the data to the cache *and* to the backing store knowing that a read request (or many read requests) are likely to follow for that data.

Distributed Cache

Distributed caching is a loosely defined term. Any time more than a single machine is being used to cache information you can argue that the solution is distributed. Herein, we refine our view of distributed caches to those that are collaborative. What does this really mean?

In a distributed cache, when a particular node computes and stores the results in its cache, other nodes will benefit. In effect, it is no longer "its" cache, but rather "the" cache. All the nodes participating in the cluster share a common cache where information is shared.

This sounds a lot like putting the cache in a centralized database. However, there is one distinct difference. Distributed caches are distributed, which means that the data is not stored in any single place. Typically, all data is stored at every node. Chapter 8, "Distributed Databases Are Easy, Just Read the Fine Print," touches on more complicated data replication techniques that will have information placed on some plural subset of machines within a cluster. In both situations, the data is available *on* the nodes that use the cache, and any single system failure will not pose a threat to availability.

Distributed systems are pretty tricky in general. What seem like simple problems at first, turn out to be complicated to solve in a general case. Let's look at a simple distributed cache that operates like a dictionary of keys and values both of which are simple strings. Caching techniques apply directly to countless technologies, but we will look at stock quotes and SSL session caching as two acutely different examples.

Simple Distributed Information Caches

For simplicity's sake, we will assume that we have real-time stock quotes feeding in from ACME Tickers. One of the services on our news site is real-time stock quotes on every page if the user opts for that in her personal preferences. We want all the information on these stock quotes on every web server so as not to stress or rely on any single point for the information. If we were to use a centralized database and it were to go down, all stock quotes would be unavailable. However, if we were to keep a cached copy on every box, and the main distribution point were to become unavailable, information would be stale but available until the distribution point was once again operational. This is a spectacular example of why people think distributed caches are easy.

In this example, changes are effected at a single point in the architecture and propagated from there. It is *not* the generalized case of distributed caching. It is a specific, distributed cache that operates on a one-to-many replication paradigm shown in Figure 7.5.

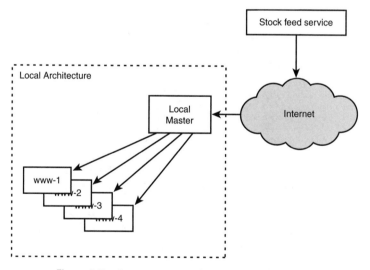

Figure 7.5   One-to-many replication for stock quotes.

This sort of information dissemination can be accomplished via asynchronous database replication (discussed in Chapter 8), as well as a simple, reliable multicast approach using a technology such as Spread.

Not-So-Simple Distributed Information Caches

Now look at an SSL session cache. When an SSL connection is established, a session key and a corresponding session context are established. When a browser has a session ID and initiates another request, if it is found in the server's session cache, an expensive asymmetric key negotiation can be avoided.

In a clustered environment where we want to capitalize on all of our resources as efficiently as possible, we want to be able to allocate a request to the machine that has the most sufficient resources to satisfy it. In a typical SSL environment, subsequent requests are often sent back to the same server to avoid expensive cryptographic computations—even if that server is overloaded.

Alternatively, the SSL session information can be placed in a distributed cache (shown in Figure 7.6) so that subsequent requests can be serviced by any machine in the cluster without unnecessary overhead induced by an "absent" SSL session.

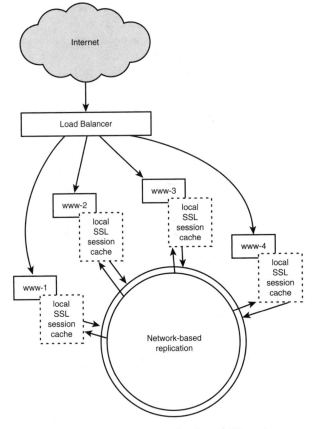

Figure 7.6   Commutative replication of SSL sessions.

This problem is distinctly different from the stock quote problem. In this system, we must publish from all participating nodes and as such, the issues of partitions and merges of the network arise.

Ben Laurie's Splash! SSL session caching system based on Spread tackles some of these issues, and Spread Concept's Replicated Hash Table (RHT) product, although it doesn't integrate directly with SSL session caching systems, tackles all the commutative replication requirements for such a distributed caching architecture.

Deploying Caches

There are two aspects of deploying caches. First, you must choose the right technology or combination of technologies to fit the problem at hand. Then you must place it in the architecture.

The true beauty of a cache is that it isn't needed for operation, just performance and scalability. As seen in Chapter 6, with the static cache, images *could* be served of the main site, but a cache was used for performance and scalability. If such immense scalability is no longer required, the architecture can easily be reverted to one without a caching system.

Most caching systems (except for transparent layered caches) do not have substantial operational costs, so their removal would not provide a substantial cost savings. In these cases, after an effective and efficient caching mechanism is deployed, it is senseless to remove it from the architecture unless it will be replaced by a better solution.

After that long-winded explanation of different caching technologies, we can concentrate on the only one that really applies to scalable web architectures: distributed caching. However, the concepts from write-thru caching can be cleverly applied to distributed caching for further gain.

As mentioned previously, increasing performance isn't our primary goal. Caching solutions speed up things by their very nature, but the goal remains scalability. To build a scalable solution we hope to leverage these caches to reduce contention on a shared resource. Architecting a large site with absolutely no shared resources (for example, a centralized database or network attached storage) is challenging and not always feasible.

Serving a News Site

Let's go back to our wildly popular news site www.example.com. In Chapter 6 we tackled our static content distribution problem, which constitutes the bulk of our bandwidth and requests. However, the dynamic content constitutes the bulk of the work.

So far we have talked about our news site in the abstract sense. Let's talk about it now in more detail so that you know a bit more about what it is and what it does.

Figure 7.7 displays a sample article. This page shows two elements of dynamic content:

- The main article content—Including author, publication time, title, content, and reader feedback.
- The left navigation bar—Each user can choose what he wants in that bar and the order in which it should be displayed.

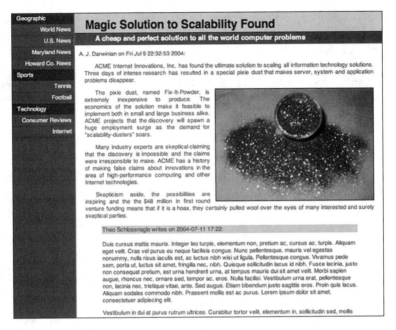

Figure 7.7   Screenshot from our news website.

All information for the site must be stored in some permanent store. This store is the fundamental basis for all caches because it contains all the original data.

First let's look at this architecture with no caching whatsoever. There is more complete code for the examples used throughout this chapter on the Sams website. We will just touch on the elements of code pertinent to the architectural changes required to place our caches.

> **Note**
>
> Remember that this book isn't about how to write code; nor is it about how to build a news site. This book discusses architectural concepts, and the coding examples in this book are simplified. The pages are the bare minimum required to illustrate the concepts and benefits of the overall approach being discussed.
>
> The concepts herein can be applied to web architectures regardless of the programming language used. It is important to consider them as methodologies and not pure implementations. This will help you when you attempt to apply them to an entirely different problem using a different programming language.

For no reason other than the author's intimate familiarity with perl, our example news site is written in perl using Apache::ASP, and an object-oriented approach was used when developing the application code. Apache::ASP is identical to ASP and PHP with respect to the fashion in which it is embedded in web pages.

Three important classes (or *packages* in perl) drive our news pages that display articles:

- An SIA::Article object represents a news article and has the appropriate methods to access the article's title, author, publication date, content, and so on.

- An SIA::User object represents a visitor to the website and has the methods to retrieve all of that visitor's personal information including website preferences such as the desired structure of the left navigation bar.

- An SIA::Cookie object represents the cookie and can fetch and store information in the cookie such as the user's ID.

Simple Implementation

With these objects, we can make the web page shown in Figure 7.7 come to life by creating the following Apache::ASP page called /hefty/art1.html:

```
 1: <%
 2:  use SIA::Cookie;
 3:  use SIA::Article;
 4:  use SIA::User;
 5:  use SIA::Utils;
 6:  my $articleid = $Request->QueryString('articleid');
 7:  my $article = new SIA::Article($articleid);
 8:  my $cookie = new SIA::Cookie($Request, $Response);
 9:  my $user = new SIA::User($cookie->userid);
10: %>
11: <!DOCTYPE HTML PUBLIC "-//W3C//DTD HTML 4.01//EN"
12:  "http://www.w3.org/TR/html4/st
13: rict.dtd">
14: <html>
15: <head>
16: <title>example.com: <%= $article->title %></title>
17:    <meta http-equiv="Content-Type" content="text/html">
18:    <link rel="stylesheet" href="/css/main.css" media="screen" />
19: </head>
20: <body>
21:   <div id="leftnav">
22:     <ul>
23:     <% foreach my $toplevel (@{$user->leftNav}) { %>
24:       <li class="type"><%= $toplevel->{group} %></li>
25:       <% foreach my $item (@{$toplevel->{type}}) { %>
26:         <li><a href="/sia/news/page/<%= $item->{news_type} %>">
27:              <%= $item->{type_name} %></a></li>
28:       <% } %>
29:     <% } %>
30:     </ul>
31:   </div>
```

```
32:    <div id="content">
33:      <h1><%= $article->title %></h1>
34:      <h2><%= $article->subtitle %></h2>
35:      <div id="author"><p><%= $article->author_name %>
36:                on <%= $article->pubdate %>:</p>
37:      <div id="subcontent">
38:        <%= $article->content %>
39:      </div>
40:      <div id="commentary">
41:        <%= SIA::Utils::render_comments($article->commentary) %>
42:      </div>
43:    </div>
44:  </body>
45:  </html>
```

Before we analyze what this page is doing, let's fix this site so that article 12345 isn't accessed via /hefty/art1.html?articleid=12345. This looks silly and prevents search indexing systems from correctly crawling our site. The following mod_rewrite directives will solve that:

```
RewriteEngine On
RewriteRule ^/news/article/(.*).html \
            /data/www.example.com/hefty/art1.html?articleid=$1 [L]
```

Now article 12345 is accessed via http://www.example.com/news/articles/12345.html, which is much more person- and crawler-friendly. Now that we have that pet peeve ironed out, we can look at the ramifications of placing a page like this in a large production environment.

The left navigation portion of this page is a simple two-level iteration performed on lines 22 and 24. The method $user->leftNav performs a single database query to retrieve a user's preferred left navigation configuration.

The main content of the page is completed by calling the accessor functions of the $article object. When the $article object is instantiated on line 6, the article is fetched from the database. From that point forward, all methods called on the $article object access information that has already been pulled from the database with the noted exception of the $article->commentary call on line 38. $article->commentary must perform fairly substantial database queries to retrieve comments posted in response to the article and comments posted in response to those comments, and so on.

To recap, three major database interactions occur to render this page for the user. So what? Well, we now have this code running on a web server...or two...or twenty. The issue arises that one common resource is being used, and because it is required every time article pages are loaded, we have a contention issue. Contention is the devil.

Don't take my word for it. Let's stress this system a bit and get some metrics.

Looking at Performance

We don't need to go into the gross details of acquiring perfect (or even good) performance metrics. We are not looking for a performance gain directly; we are looking to alleviate pressure on shared resources.

Let's run a simple ab (Apache Benchmark) with a concurrency of 100 against our page and see what happens. The line we will take note of is the average turn-around time on requests:

```
Time per request:   743 - (mean, across all concurrent requests)
```

This tells us that it took an average of 743ms to service each request when serving 100 concurrently. That's not so bad, right? Extrapolating this, we find that we should be able to service about 135 requests/second. The problem is that these performance metrics are multifaceted, and without breaking them down a bit, we miss what is really important.

The resources spent to satisfy the request are not from the web server alone. Because this page accesses a database, some of the resources spent on the web server are just time waiting for the database to perform some work. This is where performance and scalability diverge.

The resources used on the web server are easy to come by and easy to scale. If whatever performance we are able to squeeze out of the system (after performance tuning) is insufficient, we can simply add more servers because the work that they perform is parallelizable and thus intrinsically horizontally scalable. Figure 7.8 illustrates scalability problems with nonshared resources.

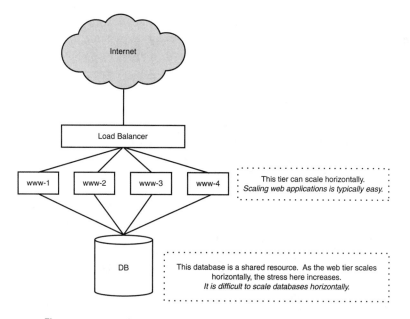

Figure 7.8   A web tier using a shared, nonscalable database resource.

On the other hand, the database is a shared resource, and, because requests stress that resource, we can't simply add another core database server to the mix. Chapter 8 discusses why it is difficult to horizontally scale database resources.

The performance metrics we are interested in are those that pertain to components of the architecture that do not scale. If we mark up our database abstraction layer a bit to add time accounting for all query preparation, execution, and fetching, we run the same test and find that, on average, we spend 87ms performing database operations. This isn't necessarily 87ms of stress on the database, but then again, that depends on perspective. One can argue that the database isn't actually working for those 87ms and that much of the time it is waiting for packets to fly across the network. However, there is a strong case to be made that during those 87ms, the client still holds a connection to the database and thus consumes resources. Both statements are true, especially for databases such as Oracle where an individual client connection requires a substantial amount of memory on the database server (called a *shadow process*). MySQL, on the other hand, has much less overhead, but it is still quantifiable.

Where are we going with this? It certainly isn't to try to tune the database to spend less resources to serve these requests. Although that is an absolute necessity in any large environment, that is a performance issue that sits squarely on the shoulders of a DBA and should be taken for granted when analyzing architectural issues. Rather, our goal is to eliminate most (if not all) of the shared resource usage.

Each request we passed through the server during our contrived test required 743ms of attention. Of that time, 87ms was *not* horizontally scalable, and the other 656ms was. That amount—87ms—may not seem like much, and, in fact, it is both small and completely contrived. Our tests were in a controlled environment with no external database stress or web server stress. Conveniently, we were simply attempting to show that some portion of the interaction was dependent on shared, nonscalable resources. We succeeded; now how do we fix it?

Introducing Integrated Caching

There are a variety of implementations of integrated caching. File cache, memory cache, and distributed caches with and without replication are all legitimate approaches to caching. Which one is the best? Because they all serve the same purpose (to alleviate pressure on shared resources), it simply comes down to which one is the best fit in your architecture.

Because our example site uses perl, we will piggyback our implementation of the fairly standard `Cache` implementation that has extensions for file caching, memory caching, and a few other external caching implementations including `memcached`.

With integrated caching, you need to make a choice up front on the semantics you plan to use for cached data. A popular paradigm used when caching resultsets from complicated queries is applying a time-to-live to the data as it is placed in the cache. There are several problems with this approach:

- The result set often carries no information about the period of time over which it will remain valid.

- The arbitrary timeouts provided by application developers are not always accurate.

- The underlying data may be changed at any time, causing the cached result set to become invalid.

Let's look at the alternative and see what complications arise. If we cache information without a timeout, we must have a cache invalidation infrastructure. That infrastructure must be capable of triggering removals from the cache when an underlying dataset that contributed to the cached result changes and causes our cached view to be invalid. Building cache invalidation systems can be a bit tricky. Figure 7.9 shows both caching semantics.

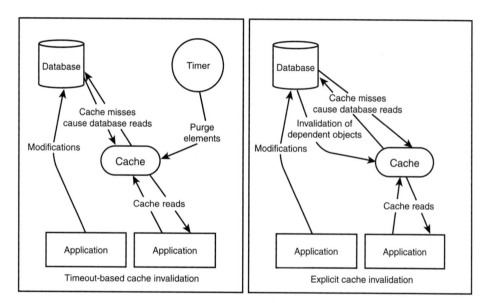

Figure 7.9   Timeout-based caches (left) and explicitly invalidated caches (right).

Basically, the two approaches are "easy and incorrect" or "complicated and correct." But "incorrect" in this case simply means that there is a margin of error. For applications that are tolerant of an error-margin in their caching infrastructures, timeout-based caches are a spectacularly simplistic solution.

If we choose a timeout for our cached elements, it means that we must throw out our cached values after that amount of time, even if the underlying data has not changed. This causes the next request for that data to be performed against the database, and the result will be stored in the cache until the timeout elapses once again.

It should be obvious after a moment's thought that if the overall application updates data infrequently with respect to the number of times the data is requested, cached data will be valid for many requests. On a news site, it is likely that the read-to-write ratio for news articles is 1,000,000 to 1 or higher (new user comments count as writes). This means that the cached data could be valid for minutes, hours, or days.

However, with a timeout-based cache, we cannot capitalize on this. Why? We must set our cache element timeout sufficiently low to allow for newly published articles to be "realized" into the cache. Essentially, the vast majority of cache purges will be wasted just to account for the occasional purge that results in a newer replacement.

Ideally, we want to cache things forever, and when they change, we will purge them. Because we control how articles and comments are published through the website, it is not difficult to integrate a cache invalidation notification into the process of publishing content.

We had three methods that induced all the database costs on the article pages: $user->leftNav, $article->new, and $article->comments. Let's revise and rename these routines by placing an _ in front of each and implementing caching wrappers around them:

```
sub leftNav {
  my $self = shift;
  my $userid = shift;
  my $answer = $global_cache->get("user_leftnav_$userid");
  return $answer if($answer);
  $answer = $self->_leftNav($userid);
  $global_cache->set("user_leftnav_$userid", $answer);
  return $answer;
}
```

Wrapping SIA::Article methods in a similar fashion is left as an exercise for the reader.

In the startup code for our web server, we can instantiate the $global_cache variable as so:

```
use Cache::Memcached;
$global_cache = new Cache::Memcached {
  'servers' => [ "10.0.2.1:11211", "10.0.2.2:11211",
                 "10.0.2.3:11211", "10.0.2.4:11211" ],
  'debug' => 0,
};
```

Now we start a memcached server on each web server in the cluster and voila! Now, as articles and their comments are requested, we inspect the cache. If what we want is there, we use it; otherwise, we perform the work as we did before, but place the results in the cache to speed subsequent accesses. This is depicted in Figure 7.10.

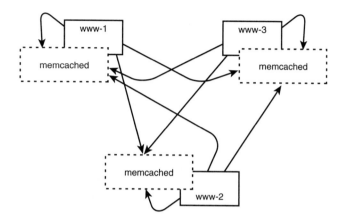

Figure 7.10   A memcached cluster in use.

What do we really gain by this? Because our data is usually valid for long periods of time (thousands or even millions of page views), we no longer have to query the database on every request. The load on the database is further reduced because memcached is a distributed caching daemon. If configured as a cluster of memcached processes (one on each machine), items placed into the cache on one machine will be visible to other machines searching for that key. Because it is a cache, if a machine were to crash, the partition of data that machine was caching would disappear, and the cache clients would deterministically failover to another machine. Because it is a cache, it was as if the data was prematurely purged—no harm, no foul.

We have effectively converted all the article queries to cache hits (as we expect our cache hit rate for that data to be nearly 100%). Although the cache hit rate for the user information is not as high, the data is unique per user, and the average user only visits a handful of pages on the site. If the average user visits five pages, we expect the first page to be a cache miss within the $user->leftNav method. However, the subsequent four page views will be cache hits, yielding an 80% cache hit rate. This is just over a 93% overall cache hit rate. In other words, we have reduced the number of queries hitting our database by a factor of 15—not bad.

How Does memcached Scale?

One of the advantages of memcached is that it is a distributed system. If 10 machines participate in a memcached cluster, the cached data will be distributed across those 10 machines. On a small and local-area scale this is good. Network connectivity between machines is fast, and memcached performs well with many clients if you have an operating system with an advanced event handling system (epoll, kqueue, /dev/poll, and so on).

However, if you find that memcached is working a bit too hard, and your database isn't working hard enough, there is a solution. We can artificially segment out memcached clusters so that the number of nodes over which each cache is distributed can be controlled (see Figure 7.11).

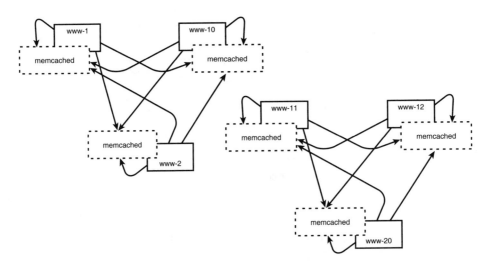

Figure 7.11   An artificial segmented memcached system.

This administrative segmentation is useful when you have two or more clusters separated by an expensive network link, or you have too many concurrent clients.

Healthy Skepticism

We could stop here. Although this is an excellent caching solution and may be a good stopping point for some caching needs, we have some fairly specialized data that is ripe for a better caching architecture. The first step is to understand what is lacking in our solution up to this point. Two things are clearly missing: We shouldn't have to go to another machine to fetch our article data, and the cache hit rate on our user preferences data is abysmally low.

Unfortunately, memcached isn't replicated, so these accesses still require a network access. If N machines participate in the memcached cluster, there is only 1/N chance that the cached item will reside on the local machine, so as the cluster size grows, the higher the probability that a cache lookup will visit a remote machine. Memcached counts on local network access to another machine running memcached is cheaper than requerying the database directly. Although this is almost always true, "cheaper" doesn't mean "cheapest," and certainly not free.

Why is lack of replication unfortunate? The article data will have nearly a 100% cache hit rate, and it is accessed often. This means that every machine will want the data, and nearly every time it gets the data, it will be identical. It should be a small mental leap that we can benefit from having that data cached locally on every web server.

> **For Those Who Think Replication Is Expensive**
>
> Many argue that replicating data like this is expensive. However, both active and passive replications are possible in this sort of architecture.
>
> The beauty of a cache is that it is not the definitive source of data, so it can be purged at will and simply be "missing" when convenient. This means that replication need not be atomic in many cases.
>
> Simply propagating the cache by publishing the cache operations (add/get/delete) to all participating parties will work most of the time. Propagation of operations as they happen is called *active replication*.
>
> Alternatively, in a nonreplicated distributed system such as memcached, we find that one machine will have to pull a cache element from another machine. At this point, it is essentially no additional work to store that data locally. This is passive replication (like cache-on-demand for caches). Passive caching works well with timeout-based caches. If the cached elements must be explicitly invalidated (as in our example), active replication of delete and update events must still occur to maintain consistency across copies.
>
> Because we are not dealing with ACID transactions and we can exercise an "if in doubt, purge" policy, implementing replication is not so daunting.
>
> As an alternative to memcached, Spread Concept's RHT (Replicated Hash Table) technology accomplishes active replication with impressive performance metrics.
>
> These simplistic replication methods won't work if operations on the cache must be atomic. However, if you are using a caching facility for those types of operations, you are likely using the wrong tool for the job—in Chapter 8 we will discuss replicated databases.

What else isn't optimal with the integrated caching architecture? The user information we are caching has an abysmally low cache hit rate—80% is awful. Why is it so bad? The problem is that the data itself is fetched (and differs) on a per-user basis. In a typical situation, a user will arrive at the site, and the first page that the user visits will necessitate a database query to determine the layout of the user's left navigation. As a side effect, the data is placed in the cache. The concept is that when the user visits subsequent pages, that user's data will be in the cache.

However, we can't keep data in the cache forever; the cache is only so large. As more new data (new users' navigation data, article data, and every other thing we need to cache across our web architecture) is placed in the cache, we will run out of room and older elements will be purged.

Unless our cache is very large (enough to accommodate all the leftnav data for every regular user), we will end up purging users' data and thereby instigating a cache miss and database query upon subsequent visits by those users.

Tackling User Data

User data, such as long-term preferences and short-term sessions state, has several unique properties that allow it to be cached differently from other types of data. The two most important properties are use and size:

- The use of the data usually only has the purpose of shaping, transforming, or selecting other data. In our left navigation system, the user's preferences dictate which of the navigation options should be displayed and in what order to display them. This does not change often and is specific to that user.

- The size of the data is usually less than a few kilobytes, often between 100 and 500 bytes. Although it can take some creative measure to compact the representation of the data into as little space as possible, you will soon see how that can be wonderfully beneficial.

Now, because this is still the chapter on application caching, we still want to cache this. The problem with caching this data with memcached is that each piece of user data will be used for short bursts that can be days apart. Because our distributed system is limited in size, it uses valuable resources to store that data unused in the cache for long periods of time. However, if we were to increase the size of our distributed system dramatically, perhaps the resources will be abundant and this information can be cached indefinitely...and we just happen to have a multimillion node distributed caching system available to us—the machine of every user.

The only tricky part about using a customer's machine as a caching node is that it is vital that only information pertinent to that customer be stored there (for security reasons). Cookies give us this.

The cookie is perhaps the most commonly overlooked jewel of the web environment. So much attention is poured into making a web architecture's load balancing, web servers, application servers, and databases servers fast, reliable, and scalable that the one layer of the architecture that is the most powerful and very scalable is simply overlooked.

By using a user's cookie to store user-pertinent information, we have a caching mechanism that is user-centric and wildly scalable. The information we store in this cache can also be semipermanent. Although we can't rely on the durability of the information we store there, we can, in most cases, rely on a long life. Again, this is a cache; if it is lost, we just fetch the information from the authoritative source and replace it into the cache.

To accomplish this in our current article page, we will add a method to our SIA::Cookie class that is capable of "acting" just like the leftNav method of the SIA::User class, except that it caches the data in the cookie for the user to store locally. We'll need to pass the $user as an argument to leftNav in this case so that method can run the original action in the event of an empty cookie (also known as a cache miss). We'll add the following two methods to our SIA::Cookie package:

```perl
sub setLeftNav {
  my ($self, $ln) = @_;
  my $tight = '';
  foreach my $toplevel (@$ln) {
    $tight .= "\n" if(length($tight));
    $tight .= $toplevel->{group}."$;";
    $tight .= join("$;", map { $_->{news_type}.",".$_->{type_name} }
                          @{$toplevel->{type}}));
```

```
  }
  ($tight = encode_base64($tight)) =~ s/[\r\n]//g;
  $self->{Response}->Cookies('leftnav', $tight);
  return $ln;
}

sub leftNav {
  my ($self, $user) = @_;
  my $tight = $self->{Request}->Cookies('leftnav');
  return $self->setLeftNav($user->leftNav) unless($tight);
  $tight = decode_base64($tight);
  my @nav;
  foreach my $line (split /\n/, $tight) {
    my ($group, @vals) = split /$;/, $line;
    my @types;
    foreach my $item (@vals) {
      my ($nt, $tn) = split /,/, $item, 2;
      push @types, { news_type => $nt, type_name => $tn };
    }
    push @nav, { group => $group, type => \@types };
  }
  return \@nav;
}
```

We now copy /hefty/art1.html to /hefty/art2.html and change it to use these new SIA::Cookie methods by replacing the original line 22:

```
22:     <% foreach my $toplevel (@{$user->leftNav}) { %>
```

with one that incorporates the $cookie->leftNav method invocation:

```
22:     <% foreach my $toplevel (@{$cookie->leftNav($user)}) { %>
```

You don't really need to understand the code changes as long as you understand what they did and what we gain from them and their size (a mere 31 new lines, and 1 line of change).

SIA::Cookie::setLeftNav executes our original $user->leftNav, serializes the results, base64 encodes them (so that it doesn't contain any characters that aren't allowed in cookies), and sends it to the user for permanent storage.

SIA::Cookie::leftNav checks the user's cookie, and if it is not there, calls the setLeftNav method. If it is there, it base64 decodes it and deserializes it into a useable structure.

In our original design, our application required a database query on every page load to retrieve the data needed to render the left navigation bar. With our first stab at speeding this up using integrated caching, we saw good results with an approximate 80% cache hit rate. Note, however, that the database queries and cache lookups stressed a limited number of machines that were internal to the architecture. This contention is the arch enemy of horizontal scalability.

What we have done with cookies is simple (32 lines of code) but effective. In our new page, when a user visits the site for the first time (or makes a change to her preferences), we must access the database because it is a cache miss. However, the new caching design places the cached value on the visitor's machine. It will remain there forever (effectively) without using our precious resources. In practice, aside from initial cache misses, we now see a cache hit rate that is darn near close to 100%.

Addressing Security and Integrity

Because this is a cache, we are not so concerned with durability. However, the nature of some applications requires that the data fed to them to be safe and intact. Any time authentication, authorization, and/or identity information is stored within a cookie, the landscape changes slightly. Although our news site isn't so concerned with the security and integrity of user preferences, a variety of other applications impose two demands on information given to and accepted from users.

The first demand is that a user cannot arbitrarily modify the data, and the second is that the user should not be able to determine the contents of the data. Many developers and engineers avoid using a user's cookie as a storage mechanism due to one or both of these requirements. However, they do so wrongly because both issues can be satisfied completely with cryptography.

In the previous example, immediately before base64 encoding and after base64 decryption, we can use a symmetric encryption algorithm (for example, AES) and a private secret to encrypt the data, thereby ensuring privacy. Then we can apply a secure message digest (for example, SHA-1) to the result to ensure integrity.

This leaves us with a rare, but real argument about cookie theft (the third requirement). The data that we have allowed the user to store may be safe from both prying eyes and manipulation, but it is certainly valid. This means that by stealing the cookie, it is often possible to make the web application believe that the thief is the victim—identity theft.

This debacle is not a show-stopper. If you want to protect against theft of cookies, a time stamp can be added (before encrypting). On receiving and validating a cookie, the time stamp is updated, and the updated cookie is pushed back to the user. Cookies that do not have a time stamp with X of the current time will be considered invalid, and information must be repopulated from the authoritative source, perhaps requiring the user to reauthenticate.

Two-Tier Execution

Now that we have user preferences just about as optimal as they can get, let's move on to optimizing our article data caching. We briefly discussed why our memcached implementation wasn't perfect, but let's rehash it quickly.

Assuming that we use memcached in a cluster, the data that we cache will be spread across all the nodes in that cluster. When we "load balance" an incoming request to a web server, we do so based on load. It should be obvious that no web server should be uniquely capable of serving a page, because if that web server were to crash that page would be unavailable. Instead, all web servers are capable of serving all web pages.

So, we are left with a problem. When a request comes in and is serviced by a web server, and when it checks the memcached cache for that request, it will be on another machine n-1 times out of n (where n is the number of nodes in our cluster). As n grows, the chance of not having the cached element on the local machine is high. Although going to a remote memcached server is usually much faster than querying the database, it still has a cost. Why don't we place this data on the web server itself?

We can accomplish this by an advanced technique called *two-tier execution*. Typically in a web scripting language (for example, PHP, ASP, Apache::ASP, and so on), the code in a page is compiled and executed when the page is viewed.

Compilation of scripts is a distributed task, and no shared resources are required. Removing the compilation step (or amortizing it out) is a technique commonly used to increase performance. PHP has a variety of compiler caches including APC, Turk MMCache, PHP Accelerator, and Zend Performance Suite. Apache::ASP uses mod_perl as its underlying engine, which has the capability to reuse compiled code. Effectively, recompiling a scripted web page is more of a performance issue than one of scalability, and it has been solved well for most popular languages.

Execution of code is the real resource consumer. Some code runs locally on the web server. XSLT transforms and other such content manipulations are great examples of horizontally scalable components because they use resources only local to that web server and thus scale with the cluster. However, execution that must pull data from a database or other shared resources takes time, requires context switches, and is generally good to avoid.

So, if we have our data in a database and want to avoid accessing it there, we stick it in a distributed cache. If we have our data distributed cache and want to avoid accessing it there, where can be put it? In our web pages.

If we look back at our /hefty/art2.html example, we see two types of code executions: one that generates the bulk of the page and the other that generates the left navigation system. So, why are they so different? The bulk of the page will be the same on every page load, no matter who views it. The left navigation system is different for almost every page load. This is the precise reason that a transparent caching solution will not provide a good cache hit rate—it is only capable of caching entire pages.

To eliminate database or cache requests for the main content of the page, we could have the author code the page content directly into the HTML. Is this an awful idea? Yes. Authors do not need to know about the page where the data will reside; they should concentrate only on content. Also, the content (or some portion of the content) will most likely be used in other pages. It is simply not feasible to run a news site like the old static HTML sites of the early 90s.

However, we can have the system do this. If we augment our scripting language to allow for two phases of execution, we can have the system actually run the script once to execute all the slowly changing content (such as article information and user comments) and then execute the result of the first execution to handle dynamic content generation that differs from viewer to viewer.

To accomplish this, we will do three things:

1. Write a `/hefty/art3.html` page that supports our two-tier execution.

2. Write a small two-tier page renderer that stores the first phase execution.

3. Use `mod_rewrite` to short-circuit the first phase of execution if it has been performed already.

```
 1: <%
 2:    use SIA::Article;
 3:    use SIA::Utils;
 4:    my $articleid = $Request->QueryString('articleid');
 5:    my $article = new SIA::Article($articleid);
 6: %>
 7: <[%
 8:    use SIA::User;
 9:    use SIA::Cookie;
10:    my $cookie = new SIA::Cookie($Request, $Response);
11:    my $user = new SIA::User($cookie->userid);
12: %]>
13: <!DOCTYPE HTML PUBLIC "-//W3C//DTD HTML 4.01//EN"
14:    "http://www.w3.org/TR/html4/strict.dtd">
15: <html>
16: <head>
17: <title>example.com: <%= $article->title %></title>
18:    <meta http-equiv="Content-Type" content="text/html">
19:    <link rel="stylesheet" href="/sia/css/main.css" media="screen" />
20: </head>
21: <body>
22:    <div id="leftnav">
23:    <ul>
24:    <[% foreach my $toplevel (@{$cookie->leftNav($user)}) { %]>
25:      <li class="type"><[%= $toplevel->{group} %]></li>
26:      <[% foreach my $item (@{$toplevel->{type}}) { %]>
27:        <li><a href="/sia/news/page/<[%= $item->{news_type} %]>">
28:           <[%= $item->{type_name} %]></a></li>
29:      <[% } %]>
30:    <[% } %]>
31:    </ul>
32:    </div>
33:    <div id="content">
34:      <h1><%= $article->title %></h1>
35:      <h2><%= $article->subtitle %></h2>
36:      <div id="author"><p><%= $article->author_name %>
37:           on <%= $article->pubdate %>:</p>
38:      <div id="subcontent">
39:        <%= $article->content %>
40:      </div>
```

```
41:    <div id="commentary">
42:      <%= SIA::Utils::render_comments($article->commentary) %>
43:    </div>
44:   </div>
45: </body>
46: </html>
```

As you can see, no new code was introduced. We introduced a new script encapsulation denoted by `<[%` and `%]>`, which `Apache::ASP` does not recognize. So, upon executing this page (directly), `Apache::ASP` will execute all the code within the usual script delimiters (`<%` and `%>`), and all code encapsulated by our new delimiters will be passed directly through to the output.

We will not ever directly execute this page, however. Our renderer is responsible for executing this page and for transforming all `<[%` and `%]>` to `<%` and `%>` in the output, so that it is ready for another pass by `Apache::ASP`. This intermediate output will be saved to disk. As such, we will be able to execute the intermediate output directly as an `Apache::ASP` page:

```
<%
use strict;
use Apache;
die "Direct page requests not allowed.\n" if(Apache->request->is_initial_req);

my $articleid = $Request->QueryString('articleid');
# Make sure the article is a number
die "Articleid must be numeric" if($articleid =~ /\D/);

# Apply Apache::ASP to our heavy template
my $doc = $Response->TrapInclude("../hefty/art3.html");

# Reduce 2nd level cache tags to 1st level cache tage
$$doc =~ s/<\[?(\[*)%/<$1%/gs;
$$doc =~ s/%\]?(\]*)>/%$1>/gs;

# Store our processed heavy tempalate to be processed by Apach::ASP again.
my $cachefile = "../light/article/$articleid.html";
if(open(C2, ">$cachefile.$$")) {
  print C2 $$doc; close C2;
  rename("$cachefile.$$", $cachefile) || unlink("$cachefile.$$");
}
# Short circuit and process the ASP we just wrote out.
$Response->Include($doc);
%>
```

Now for the last step, which is to short-circuit the system to use `/light/article/12345.html` if it exists. Otherwise, we need to run our renderer at `/internal/render.html?articleid=12345`. This can be accomplished with `mod_rewrite` as follows:

```
RewriteEngine On

RewriteCond %{REQUEST_URI} news/article/(.*)
RewriteCond /data/www.example.com/light/$1 -f
RewriteRule $news/(.*) /data/www.example.com/light/$1 [L]

RewriteRule ^news/article/(.*).html$
            /data/www.example.com/internal/render.html?articleid=$1 [L]
```

Cache Invalidation

This system, although cleverly implemented, is still simply a cache. However, it caches data as aggressively as possible in a compiled form. Like any cache that isn't timeout-based, it requires an invalidation system.

Invalidating data in this system is as simple as removing files from the file system. If the data or comments for article 12345 have changed, we simply remove `/data/www.exmaple.com/light/article/1.html`. That may sound easy, but remember that we can (and likely will) have these compiled pages on every machine in the cluster. This means that when an article is updated, we must invalidate the cache files on all the machines in the cluster.

If we distribute *cache delete* requests to all the machines in the cluster, we can accomplish this. However, if a machine is down or otherwise unavailable, it may miss the request and have a stale cache file when it becomes available again. This looks like a classic problem in database synchronization; however, on closer inspection, it is less complicated than it seems because this data isn't crucial. When a machine becomes unavailable or crashes, we simple blow its cache before it rejoins the cluster.

Caching Is Powerful

Two things should be clear by now. First, caching systems vary widely in their implementation, approach, and applicability. Second, on analysis you can determine which caching approach is right for a specific component to achieve dramatic improvements with respect to both performance and scalability.

In our original article page we witnessed three substantial database operations on every page. After implementing a variety of dynamic caching solutions we were able to achieve an acceptably high cache-hit rate (nearly 100%) and all but eliminate database queries from our pages. After users log in for the first time, their left navigation preferences are stored in their cookie, and it is unlikely that they will ever lose their cookie and require a database query to reset it. Articles data, which once required two queries to retrieve, are now compiled into a valid web page to be served directly by Apache, alleviating both database access and the dependency on an external caching mechanism.

Although the examples in this chapter are implemented in perl using the `Apache::ASP` embedding system, all the caching techniques presented can be implemented using almost any interpreted scripting language. The goal was to present concepts. Aside from the two-tier execution approach, all the concepts presented can be implemented in any language and in any architecture—even outside the Web.

The key to successful caching is understanding the true nature of your data: how frequently it is changed and where it is used.

8

Distributed Databases Are Easy, Just Read the Fine Print

DISTRIBUTED DATABASES ARE PROBABLY THE most consistently misunderstood technology component in the world. I hear the strangest things on a regular basis. Business folks say, "I need my data in more than one place; replicate it," or "We pay for two databases; I want to use both of them." Techies constantly explain that either there are no solutions to the problem or the problem is very hard, or they say "That's easy, just use MySQL."

This chapter discusses distributed databases and helps you understand why these one-sentence, context-absent technical explanations make nontechnical decision-makers confused and irate—and rightfully so.

What Is a Distributed Database?

To better understand this question and its answer, it is necessary first to clearly define the problem space. There are several business and technical problems that distributed database technologies attempt to solve.

Data Resiliency

Data resiliency is perhaps the most common reason for deploying such a technology. The goal is not to change the way the architecture works or performs but to ensure that if primary architecture is lost (due to a natural disaster or a terrorist attack), a complete, consistent, and current copy of the data is located elsewhere in the world. The technique can also be applied on a local level to maintain a copy of production data on a second server local to the production architecture to protect against hardware failures. This often entails shipping modifications to the production dataset in near real-time off to a second location.

Operational Failover

Operational failover is above and beyond data resiliency. The goal is to have both data resiliency and the capability to assume normal operations in case of a catastrophe. This technique is often referred to as *warm-standby* or *hot-standby*.

The difference between warm- and hot-standby is not related so much to the type of replication but rather to the effort involved in having the production architecture start using the second database in the event of a failure. Hot-standby means that it is automatic, and engineers are informed that a failure has occurred, as well as a failover. Warm-standby, on the other hand, means that when a failure occurs, an engineer must perform actions to place the standby into the production architecture.

Operational failover is the most common implementation of distributed database technology. The only difference between this technique and plain data resiliency is the need for a usable, production-grade architecture supporting the replica.

Increased Query Performance

Databases are the core technologies at the heart of most IT infrastructures, be it back office or the largest dot com. As a site scales up, the demands placed on the database are increased, and the database must keep up. Most architectures (but notably not all) have a high read-to-write ratio. This means that most of the time the database is being used to find stored information, not store new information.

There is a delineation between high read/write ratio architectures and others because when databases are distributed, compromises must be made. Database usage like this can allow for compromises that are infeasible in more write-intensive scenarios.

The approach here is to set up one or more databases and maintain on them an up-to-date copy of the production dataset (just as in an operation failover situation). However, we can guarantee that these databases will never become a master and that no data modification will occur on any system. This allows clients to perform read-only queries against these "slave" systems, thereby increasing performance. We will discuss the ramifications and limits placed on clients in the "Master-Slave Replication" section later in this chapter.

Complete Reliability

The operational failover (as a hot-standby) sounds like it will provide seamless failover and perfect reliability. This, however, is not necessarily true because the technique used ships changes to the production dataset in near real-time. As anyone in the banking industry will tell you, there is a big difference between nearly accurate and accurate.

For nonstop reliability, transactions that occur on one server must *not* be allowed to complete (commit) until the second server has agreed to commit them; otherwise, transactions that occur on one machine immediately prior to a complete failure *may* never make it to the second machine. It's a rare edge condition, right? Tell me that again when one of the mysteriously missing transactions is a million-dollar wire transfer.

This master-master (parallel server) technology is common at financial institutions and in other systems that require nonstop operation. The compromise here is speed. What was once a decision for a single database to make (whether to commit or not) now must be a collaborative effort between that database and its peer. This adds latency and therefore has a negative impact on performance.

Geographically Distributed Operation

This is the true distributed database. Here we have the same needs as master-master, but the environment is not controlled. In a geographically distributed operation the large, long-distance networking circuits (or even the Internet) connect various databases all desperately attempting to maintain atomicity, consistency, isolation, and durability (ACID).

Even in the best-case scenario, latencies are several orders of magnitude higher than traditional parallel server configurations. In the worst-case scenario, one of the database peers can disappear for seconds, minutes, or even hours due to catastrophic network events.

From a business perspective, it does not seem unreasonable to ask that a working master-master distributed database be geographically separated for more protection from real-world threats. However, "simply" splitting a master-master solution geographically or "simply" adding a third master to the configuration is anything but simple.

Why Is Replication So Hard?

Why is replication such a challenging problem? The short answer is ACID. Although this isn't intended to be a databases primer, you do need a bit of background on how databases work and what promises they make to their users. Here is what ACID buys us:

- Atomicity—All the data modifications that occur within a transaction must happen completely or not at all. No partial transaction can be recorded even in the event of a hardware or software failure.

- Consistency—All changes to an instance of data must be reflected in all instances of that data. If $300 is subtracted from my savings account, my total aggregated account value should be $300 less.

- Isolation—The elements of a transaction should be isolated to the user performing that transaction until it is completed (committed).

- Durability—When a hardware or software failure occurs, the information in the database must be accurate up to the last committed transaction before the failure.

Databases have been providing these semantics for decades. However, enforcing these semantics on a single machine is different from enforcing them between two or more machines on a network. Although it isn't a difficult technical challenge to implement, the techniques used internally to a single system do not apply well to distributed databases from a performance perspective.

Single database instances use single system specific facilities such as shared memory, interthread and interprocess synchronization, and a shared and consistent file system buffer cache to increase speed and reduce complexity. These facilities are fast and reliable on a single host but difficult to generalize and abstract across a networked cluster of machines, especially wide-area networked.

Instead of attempting to build these facilities to be distributed (as do single-system-image clustering solutions), distributed databases use specific protocols to help ensure ACID between more than one instance. These protocols are not complicated, but because they speak over the network they suffer from performance and availability fluctuations that are atypical within a single host.

People have come to expect and rely on the performance of traditionally RDBMS solutions and thus have a difficult time swallowing the fact that they must make a compromise either on the performance front or the functionality front.

Multimaster Replication

Multimaster replication is the "holy grail" of distributed databases. In this model, all data is located at more than one node, and all nodes are completely capable of processing transactions. Most systems do not require what multimaster replication offers. However, traditionally most nontechnical people (and even many technical people) assume this model when speaking of database replication. As time goes on and replicated databases become common in both small and large architectures, this interpretation will change. It is my hope that people will lean toward more descriptive names for their replication setups. For now, when we say replication, we'll refer to the whole kit and caboodle—multimaster replication.

Why is this problem so hard? Let's step back and look what ACID requires:

- Atomicity seems to be a simple thing to ensure. It simply means we do all or nothing, right? Yes; however, when at the end of a transaction, we must commit. Now, it is not as simple as closing out the transaction. With a single instance, we commit, and if anything goes horribly wrong we return an error that the transaction could not be committed. In a distributed system, we must commit on more than one node, and all must succeed or all must fail, or an inconsistency is introduced.

- Consistency requires that all instances of perspectives on a datum are updated when a transaction is complete. In and of itself this isn't a problem. However, we have introduced a complication in the "scheduling" of database operations. When operating in a single instance, the database engine will arbitrarily order concurrent transactions so that one commit takes place before another. Concurrent transactions take on a whole new meaning when transactions operating on the same data can initiate and run their course at different nodes. It means that there must be a consistent global ordering of transaction commits—not so easy.

- Isolation is not really affected by the fact that transactions are happening at the same time in different places.

- Durability requires that in the event of a crash, the copy must correctly reflect all information through the last committed transaction and not any information that was part of an uncommitted transaction. When multiple copies of the same data exist on separate machines, this task proves more difficult because agreeing on clusterwide commits is now necessary.

Although there are several technical approaches to the problem of multimaster database replication and several real-world implementations, they often require sacrifices—such as decreased performance, network topology limitations, and/or application restrictions—that are impossible to make.

Suppose that you have a database that performs 2,000 transactions per second. The obvious goal is to have that replicated in three locations around the world and be able to increase the transactional throughput to 6,000 transactions per second. This is a pipe dream—a pure impossibility for general database uses. Increasing a cluster's size by a factor of three resulting in a threefold increase in performance would be an optimal solution. We know that optimal solutions don't exist for general problems. However, what the true performance "speedup" is may be alarming. Although read-only query performance can often be increased almost linearly, the total transactional throughput decreases if the transactions affect the same data.

There is a special case where an almost linear performance gain can be achieved. That case is when replication takes the pure form of data aggregation. If the operations on the datasets at each location are disjointed, and this is an assumption in the architecture of the replication technology itself, atomicity and consistency can be enforced without collaboration. Because this is an edge case, we'll ignore it for now.

Two-Phase Commit (2PC)

Two-phase commit (and to a lesser degree three-phase commit) has been used for decades to safely and reliably coordinate transactions between two separate database engines. The basic idea is that the node attempting the transaction will notify its peers that it is about to commit, and they will react by preparing the transaction and notifying the originating node that they are ready to commit. The second phase is noticing any aborts in the process and then possibly following through on the commit (hopefully everywhere).

The two-phase commit is not perfect, but it is considered sufficient for applications such as stock trading and banking—which are considered to be the most stringent industries when it comes to data consistency, aside from perhaps aerospace operations.

The glaring problem with 2PC is that it requires the lock-step progress on each node for a transaction to finish. With a single node down, progress can be halted. If a node is marked offline to allow progress, resynchronization must occur. This approach simply isn't ideal for wide-area replication against hostile networks (the Internet is considered a hostile network in this case).

Despite its shortcomings, the only common "correct" multimaster replication technique used today is the 2PC, and, due to its overhead costs, it is not widely used for geographic replication.

EVS Engine

Extended virtual synchrony (EVS) is a concept from the world of group communications. The EVS Engine itself is a product of the group communication world and has been commercialized by Spread Concepts, LLC. The theoretical approach to this replication technique is well documented and proven correct in the PhD thesis of Yair Amir (one of the Spread Concepts guys).

If you just sit back and consider for a moment who would have the best ideas on how to get multiple computers to communicate, organize, and collaborate on an effort to accomplish some goal (say ACID), it would be the group communications people. On the other hand, the only people you trust your data to are the database people. The requirement that these two groups must collaborate poses a roadblock for the evolution of more advanced data replication approaches.

Techniques from the group communication world can help overcome the challenges posed by disconnected networks and network partitions. In typical multimaster replication configurations all nodes must concur that an operation will happen and then execute on it using 2PC. This might work well in two-node scenarios; however, when more nodes are involved and they are not local with respect to each other, serious complications are introduced that can seriously affect progress in these systems.

To take a conceptually simple architecture for multimaster replication, we can look at a company in the United States that has offices in six states. Each office wants a local copy of the enterprise's database. To modify the content in that database, that database must know that it will not produce a conflict with any of its peers. This sounds simple until one of the long-haul networking circuits used to transit information goes down. This will cause some partition in the working set of databases, and it is likely that there will be two or more views of the participating databases.

Assume that we have two West Coast, two East Coast, and two Midwest databases. After a networking disaster, a VPN failure, or some other unexpected but probable event, a partition in the working set of databases will occur. Those on the West Coast and in the Midwest can all see each other and believe that the eastern nodes have crashed, while the two eastern nodes can see each other and believe that the four nodes to their west have gone down. This is called a *network partition*. When network partitions occur, you have two options: manual magic and quorums.

Manual Magic

The first step is to stop all operations; after any data modification on any database node you will not be able to effectively perform a commit because you cannot form a unanimous vote to do so. In this model, an operator must intervene and instruct the participating machines that they only need a consensus across a newly defined set of the nodes.

For example, the eastern operators do nothing, and the western operators reconfigure their replication scheme to exclude the two nodes that are unavailable to them. This is often the case in local area replication schemes because the expectation is that network partitions will not occur and that if a node becomes unavailable it is because something disastrous happened to that node. Aside from the manual intervention required to allow progress in the event of a network partition, techniques and procedures must be developed to handle resynchronizing those machines excluded from the replication configuration during the time of the partition—this is hard—it's magic…black magic.

Quorums

The second option is to establish a quorum. Our friends in the group communication field have had to deal with this problem from the beginning of the exploration of their field. It isn't a concept at all related to databases but rather one related to group decision making. A *quorum* is defined as an improper subset of the total possible group that can make a decision. A correct quorum algorithm ensures that regardless of the number of machines, as long as every machine follows that algorithm there will exist at most one quorum at any time. The most simple quorum algorithm to imagine is one when a majority of the total configuration is represented in the working set. With the six machine configuration just described, this would be any time a group of four or more machines can communicate. That grouping is the quorum. More complicated quorum algorithms exist that are more robust than the simple majority algorithm, but they are outside the scope of this book.

By establishing and executing a quorum algorithm, the overall replication configuration can guarantee progress in the event of arbitrary network configuration changes that could induce partitions and subsequent merges. Some believe the downside of this is that an administrator could make better business decisions on which partition should be allowed to make progress because they have access to outside influence and information. However, it should be recognized that quorum algorithms can be efficient in preserving business continuity if the proper considerations are incorporated into the adoption or development of the quorum algorithm used in the system.

If we introduce the fact that our New York database (one of the two eastern databases) is at the corporate headquarters and that, if at all possible, it should be able to make progress, we can change our quorum algorithm to reflect that. For example, if the group of connected nodes contains the New York database, it is a quorum. Probably safer than that is a quorum defined by either five of the six machines or any two machines if one is in New York.

On top of this quorum system, EVS Engine allows reliable, ordered messaging among members without the cost of 2PC. A message is sent to the current group; an EVS system guarantees that when it is delivered, you will know the exact membership of the group at the time of delivery and that everyone else who received the message also saw the same membership at the time of delivery. Using this, it proves that you can replicate ACID databases.

Although EVS Engine is available in some fashion or another from Spread Concepts, LLC., it has a long way to go before it is accepted as a standard approach to multimaster replication. It has considerable opposition from the database community for unsubstantiated reasons, but when that intergroup dynamic resolves, you can expect replication over extended virtual synchrony to be the de facto replication paradigm.

In the end, multimaster replication isn't ready for prime time in most environments for the sole reason that people tend to want multimaster replication for increased availability and performance, and it isn't possible to have both.

As an interesting aside, the PostgreSQL Slony-II project is implementing an algorithm similar in nature to EVS Engine. Its algorithm replaces some of the more challenging problems tackled by EVS Engine with more simple (and practical) solutions. The Slony-II project is positioned to lead the industry with respect to achieving scalable and efficient geographically separated multimaster database configurations.

Master–Master Replication

A special case of the multimaster replicated database approach is when we limit the system to exactly two nodes with a low latency interconnect (like local Ethernet). This is master-master replication, and the common distributed consistency protocols such as 2PC and 3PC don't pose an unreasonable overhead.

Even over a wide area network, there is no advantage to using newer, less tried, and more complicated replication techniques that are emerging in the multinode multimaster replication environments. So, in two-node systems, 2PC is "how replication is done."

Many commercial databases support database replication via the two-phase commit method. Although this is really useful and fundamental in highly available systems design, it certainly doesn't add any scalability to a solution. Given this, we won't dig much deeper.

Master–Slave Replication

Master-slave replication is indeed replication, yet it satisfies an entirely different need than that of multimaster schemes. It does not provide the same availability and fault tolerance guarantees as do multimaster techniques. If there is one thing I hope you walk away from this book with, it would be "the right tool for the job" mentality. Despite the fact that master-slave replication is different from multimaster replication, it is vital that this difference not be interpreted as a weakness. It is a different tool with different applications, and there are many places where it is simply an excellent tool for the job at hand.

Changing the Scope of the Problem

Master-slave replication is a solution for a different problem. In this configuration, data modification may occur only at the master because there is no attempt to coordinate atomic transactions or view consistency between the slaves and their master. If you can't modify data at the slaves, what good are they? Clearly you can perform both simple and complicated read-only operations against the slaves.

By replicating authoritative data from a master to many slave nodes, you can increase the performance of read-intensive database applications almost linearly and sometimes super-linearly. How does this help with write-intensive applications? That is a complicated answer and depends heavily on the underlying replication technology used to push database modification from the master to its slaves. Understanding this will debunk some myths about the performance gains of master–slave replication systems.

Operation and Changeset Replication

When a database processes a request for data modification (commonly referred to as *DML*, which stands for *data modification language*), it does a bit of work behind the scenes.

The first step is to understand the question and what datasets are required to answer the question. This is the parsing and planning phase of processing DML. Because SQL is a complicated language that can consist of arbitrarily complicated queries that feed into the modification being performed, after the database arrives at a satisfactory plan to answer the question, it attempts to process it and apply the required changes. The changes are applied, or the operation is rolled back and the transaction is complete.

There are two common methods to replicate a master database to a set of slaves based on the preceding transaction flow. The first is to replicate the operation—that is, distribute the statement that resulted in the change to all the slave nodes and allow them to plan and then execute the operation to (hopefully) arrive at the same result. The second technique consists of tracking the actual data changes (called a *changeset*) and distributing the data that has changed to each slave. We will call the first *DML replication*, and the second *DML log replication* because the first replicates the actual data modification language, whereas the second replicates the log of what happened due to the data modification language.

One of these methods may seem much better than the other, and that is typically the case. However, half the population thinks DML replication is better, whereas the other half thinks DML log replication is better. Who is right?

Each of these techniques has trade-offs. After you have a clear understanding of your own problems, you can better match your issues to the trade-offs to arrive at the best solution.

To understand better where these techniques both excel and fall short, let's define four types of DML:

- Cheap DML with small data change—This would be a query such as UPDATE USERS SET LAST_LOGON=SYSDATE WHERE USERID=:userid, where the column userid has a unique index. It is computationally cheap and guaranteed to affect at most a single row.

- Expensive DML with small data change—This would be a query such as INSERT INTO REGISTRATION_SUMMARY SELECT TRUNC(SYSDATE), a.CNT, b.CNT FROM (SELECT COUNT(*) AS CNT FROM USERS WHERE TRUNC(REG_DATE)=TRUNC

(SYSDATE-1)) a, (SELECT COUNT(*) AS CNT FROM HITS WHERE TRUNC(HIT_DATE)=TRUNC(SYSDATE-1)) b. Although we could have an index on REG_DATE and HIT_DATE, it still requires an index scan and could process millions of rows of data, all to insert just a single row. This is computationally expensive, and yet will never affect more than a single row.

- Expensive DML with large data change—This would be a query such as UPDATE USERS SET ACCESS='ineligible' WHERE USERID IN (SELECT USERID FORM HITS WHERE HIT_CODE='opt-out' MINUS SELECT USERID FROM PAYMENT_HISTO-RY WHERE STATUS='approved'), which may induce a massive data change and is relatively expensive to perform because we are revoking access to users who opted out but have never successfully purchased anything, and the HITS table could have a billion rows and PAYMENT_HISTORY tables could have several hundred thousand rows.

- Cheap DML with large data change—Perhaps the easiest to demonstrate are queries that are simple to calculate, but dramatic data-level changes ensue. Queries such as DELETE FROM HITS WHERE HIT_DATE < SYSDATE-30, which would delete all rows in a table older than 30 days, could induce multimillion row data changes with little or no computation effort by the database.

So, ask yourself which of the preceding examples characterizes the queries run against the database that you want to replicate. Expensive DML with large changesets and cheap DML with small changesets have similar costs under both replication models—they don't compel a choice one way or the other. It is difficult to ascertain whether you will spend more time planning and executing on the slave node than you would shipping over the changes and applying them directly.

On the other hand, the difference between the other two usage patterns is astounding. Cheap DML operations that result in massive data updates mean that you ship over the query and have the slave node delete or update a slew of rows (using DML replication), or you can ship over every single row that has changed as a result of the query and reapply each individually to each slave (using DML log replication). That sounds awful. However, you really should not be performing massive data changes on an online transaction processing (OLTP) data system. So, if you classify many of your queries in this category, perhaps you should revisit your queries and data model and determine a way to avoid them in the first place.

Expensive DML operations that result in small data updates mean that you spend hours on the master performing a query that ultimately changes a few rows of data and then ships that query to each slave so that they can perform several hours of computational mimicking to update the same few rows of data (using DML replay). However, using the DML log replay technique, the master spends several hours calculating the resultset (which is unavoidable) and then ships a few snippets of data change to the clients. If you classify many of your queries in this category, DML log replay is a huge win. However, just as with cheap DML with massive changes, this type of operation should be rare in a production OLTP environment.

So, where does that leave us? Both solutions are good. In my personal experience, changeset is more reliable and adapts more easily to cross-platform database replication (such as Oracle to PostgreSQL or Oracle to MySQL), which can be useful to get the best of all worlds.

Looking at Oracle

Oracle's primary method of master-slave replication is via changeset replication. As data is changed, the changes are shipped to slave instances and applied. This is commonly called *applying archive redo logs*. This means that if you have a write-intensive database usage pattern on the master node, the slave node will be able to keep up so long as there is sufficient network bandwidth to transmit the changes and sufficient I/O bandwidth on the slave to apply the changes. This makes Oracle's replication lackluster in the cases where cheap DML is applied, resulting in massive data updates. However, it is perfect for expensive DML that results in small data updates, meaning that if you run a lot of reporting and statistical aggregation on the master, the slaves can be much weaker machines and still have no issues "keeping up" with the master's replication needs.

Looking at MySQL

MySQL, on the other hand, has the concept of a *binlog* that stores every query that induced a data modification. This binlog is transferred to slave MySQL databases, and the operations are re-performed. This makes a million-row delete very quick to replicate to slaves, but it also means that if the updates were expensive to plan and execute, you will pay that cost on every single slave.

Some costs cannot be avoided, but some can. Simple updates with complicated `where` clauses that induce a nontrivial amount of load to execute are difficult to engineer around. However, the example for expensive DML with small data change that was used previously was an `INSERT INTO SELECT` ... statement that would insert a single row. This type of load can be avoided on the slave nodes by splitting the queries into two. Because the binlog contains only queries that induce data modification, if the expensive `SELECT` is run in the application and then the result is inserted back into the database via a subsequent `INSERT` statement, the cost will be negligible on the slave nodes.

Choosing

Given that most online transaction processing systems have many queries that are inexpensive and induce small data change, choosing between operation and changeset replication is really a "six to one, half-dozen to another" argument. As such, sticking to your existing database vendor is most likely a good approach unless your typical usage patterns unequivocally fall into one of the other two DML patterns.

In general on local area networks, network bandwidth and I/O bandwidth are cheaper than CPU cycles and memory. This makes changeset replication ideal for local clusters. For wide area replication where network bandwidth can easily be more expensive than CPU cycles and memory, operation replication makes more sense.

News Site Revisited

After the preceding discussion of replication technologies, you might be thoroughly confused about what a good replication strategy is. This confusion isn't a bad thing—it is the decision in disguise. The goal here is scalability, and as such we need to ensure that we can scale horizontally. This means that if we need more power we want to be able to simply add more nodes for a linear performance benefit. Although a linear speed-up is a theoretical best, it's still our goal, and we should design the system to target that goal.

Master-master replication is two nodes. As such, adding nodes is not possible. Multimaster replication using two-phase commit is too expensive to scale horizontally. If you attempt a 100-node configuration, the cost of each node performing 2PC with 99 other systems will cause everything to come crashing down. Master-slave replication is the only approach left standing.

Choosing Technologies and Methods

For the increased interest of this discussion, assume that our news site is running against Oracle. Why Oracle? The demands on the OLTP system that drives the site are intense (remember, we are trying to solve that here), and a tremendous amount of maintenance and auditing goes on in stored procedures. Additionally, there is a need for extensive data mining against an operational data store that pulls information from the OLTP system and exposes it to analysts. That operational data store runs Oracle because the analysts requested to use some of the data mining and reporting tools that Oracle provides. The real answer, of course, is that the architect, VP of Engineering, and CTO sat down with a group of vendors and liked what they heard from Oracle. All that matters is that the system is running Oracle, it is way too busy, and we want to scale to many more users.

The site's dynamic content is serviced centrally via a small cluster of web application servers directly referencing the master OLTP Oracle database that services the end-user and an even smaller set of web application servers that serve administrative users (columnists, editors, and so on). The operational data store hangs off the OLTP database and services some administrative users to perform business tasks and in-depth analysis. Figure 8.1 illustrates this architecture.

We could simply deploy slave Oracle instances (two) onsite with each web cluster location and perform master-slave replication. Technically this would work, but financially—not a chance. Let's assume that we have content web servers in each of our four worldwide locations as shown in Figure 6.10 in Chapter 6, "Static Content Serving for Speed and Glory." Assuming 10 dual processor machines in each location, that would be Oracle licenses for 4 clusters x 2 nodes/cluster x 2 processors/node = 16 processors! The price for that would make more than a casual dent in the year's operating budget. If you aren't familiar with Oracle's licensing policies, it is typically on a per-feature, per-processor basis. This policy is friendly for those who want to vertically scale their solutions, but as discussed, the goal is horizontal scalability.

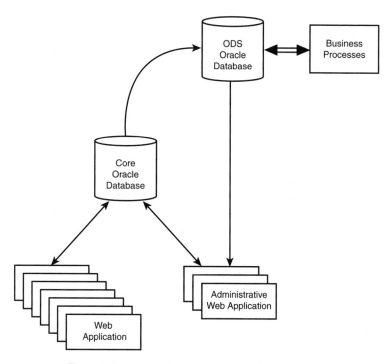

Figure 8.1   A centralized, vertically scalable architecture.

It is important to remember that Oracle does not "enable" our architecture. It is a relational database solution that can be queried via SQL, and, most importantly, there are many others just like it. We could switch our infrastructure to use something less costly knowing now that we want to scale out to many more nodes; however, one rule of thumb is don't change what works if you can help it.

We really want to make as few changes as possible to our existing core architecture but enable the web application deployed at each data center to have a locally accessible database with an accurate copy of data managed at the core. We want to be able to scale up and down without incurring a large operating expense or a large capital expense. It so happens that our developers' expertise is against Oracle, and we want to leverage as much of that as possible. Between PostgreSQL and MySQL, PostgreSQL is more similar in feature set and usage to Oracle than is MySQL.

An Oracle core infrastructure with 16 PostgreSQL replicas (shown in Figure 8.2) is an architecture that does not pose a substantial financial risk or an enormous technical risk with respect to leveraging existing application developer expertise.

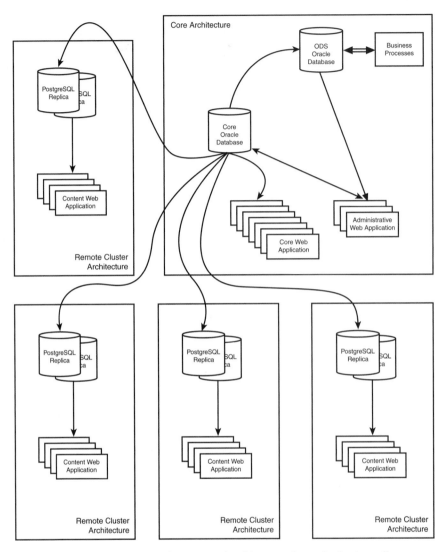

Figure 8.2 A master-slave oriented architecture that scales horizontally.

What we hope to leverage here is the replication of heavily queried data to our various clusters. The data, as with most heavily used website data, changes infrequently with respect to the frequency it is referenced in read-only operations. In other words, the read-to-write ratio is high. In our case, we need to replicate the news articles, administrative users (authors, editors, approvers), and customers (the end-user). Of course, this book isn't only on this topic, so the example here will aim to be complete and accurate with respect to the limited problem we are going to tackle. An actual implementation would likely encompass much more data. Here we will talk about three tables, but I've used this technique before to handle a multiterabyte schema with more than 1,200 tables.

Implementing Cross-Vendor Database Replication

Implementing cross-vendor database replication in a generic manner can revolutionize the way problems are tackled in an architecture. If done correctly, it can allow you to truly choose the right tool for the job when it comes to databases. If we have some tasks that can be solved using features only found in MySQL or Postgres or Oracle or SQL Server, we simply replicate the necessary information to and from them and our problem is solved.

As discussed, there are a variety of database replication techniques, and what each offers is different. Our goals are met by master-slave database replication, which fortunately is easy to implement in an application external to the source and destination databases.

Specifically, we have three tables in Oracle that we want to replicate to 16 PostgreSQL nodes: AdminUsers is rather small with only about 5,000 rows; SiteUsers is large, and we see about 0.1% change on that table (by row count) on a daily basis (that is, of the 100 million rows, about 100,000 rows change during the course of a normal day). NewsArticles contains the articles that are published, and this can be between 50 and 2,000 new articles per day, and many more updates as articles are written, edited, and approved. The code listing for source database CREATE TABLE DDL follows:

```
CREATE TABLE AdminUsers (
  UserID INTEGER PRIMARY KEY,
  UserName VARCHAR2(32) NOT NULL UNIQUE,
  Password VARCHAR2(80) NOT NULL,
  EmailAddress VARCHAR2(255) NOT NULL
);
CREATE TABLE SiteUsers (
  SiteUserID INTEGER PRIMARY KEY,
  CreatedDate DATE NOT NULL,
  UserName VARCHAR2(32) NOT NULL UNIQUE,
  Password VARCHAR2(80) NOT NULL,
  EmailAddress VARCHAR2(255) NOT NULL,
  Country VARCHAR2(3) NOT NULL,
  PostalCode VARCHAR2(10) NOT NULL
);
CREATE TABLE NewsArticles (
  ArticleID INTEGER PRIMARY KEY,
  Author INTEGER NOT NULL REFERENCES AdminUsers(UserID),
  Editor INTEGER REFERENCES AdminUsers(UserID),
  Approver INTEGER REFERENCES AdminUsers(UserID),
  CreatedDate DATE NOT NULL,
  LastModifiedDate DATE NOT NULL,
  PublishedDate DATE,
  Title VARCHAR2(200),
  AbstractText VARCHAR2(1024),
```

```
    BodyText CLOB,
    isAvailable INTEGER DEFAULT 0 NOT NULL
);
```

The SiteUsers table in particular has far fewer rows than we would expect our real site to have. But all tables are kept a bit thin on columns only to help the brevity of the example.

The basic concept here is to replicate the changes that happen against these tables to another database. So, the obvious first step is to attempt to keep track of the changes. Changes in databases all come in one of three forms: addition, removal, and change (that is, INSERT, DELETE, and UPDATE).

DML Replay Replication

Keeping track of INSERT, DELETE, and UPDATE is actually easy because SQL provides a trigger on each of these. Before we jump the gun and write ourselves a trigger to track the changes, we'll need some place to stick the data itself. This is where the techniques can vary from one approach to another.

In our model, we care only about representing the most recent view available, and it isn't vitally important for us to play each transaction on the source forward and commit them individually on the destination. Although it isn't any more difficult to do this sort of thing, we simply want to know all the missed transactions and replay them to achieve a "current" resultset. As such, we don't care how the record changed, just that it is likely different. It is wholly sufficient to track just the primary key of the records that have been modified in some way.

The first step is to create the tables that will store the primary keys that get modified. We will tackle the NewsArticles and SiteUsers tables this way and leave the AdminUsers for the next section. We need to know what row changed (by primary key), and it would make our lives easier if we knew what transaction the changes happened in (so that we can more easily track what we have done already) and for database maintenance (such as cleaning out the DML log because when it gets old we should track the time at which the modification took place). The code listing for DDL to create DML logs follows:

```
CREATE TABLE SiteUsersDML (
    TXNID VARCHAR2(20) NOT NULL,
    SiteUserID INTEGER NOT NULL,
    InsertionDate DATE NOT NULL
);
CREATE INDEX SiteUsersDML_TXNID_IDX ON SiteUsersDML(TXNID);
CREATE INDEX SiteUsersDML_InsertionDate_IDX ON SiteUsersDML(InsertionDate);

CREATE TABLE NewsArticlesDML (
    TXNID VARCHAR2(20) NOT NULL,
    ArticleID INTEGER NOT NULL,
    InsertionDate DATE NOT NULL
);
```

```
CREATE INDEX NewsArticlesDML_TXNID_IDX ON NewsArticlesDML(TXNID);
CREATE INDEX NewsArticlesDML_InsertionDate_IDX ON NewsArticlesDML(InsertionDate);
```

Now that we have some place to track our changes, let's do it. Each time we insert or update data, we want to place the new primary key (SiteUserID for SiteUsers and ArticleID for NewsArticles) into the DML table along with the current time and the transaction ID. Any time we delete data, we want to take the same action except on the old primary key (in SQL talk, there is no "new" row for a delete because it is gone). The code listing for DML tracking triggers follows:

```
CREATE OR REPLACE TRIGGER SiteUsersDMLTracker
  AFTER INSERT OR UPDATE OR DELETE
  ON SiteUsers
  REFERENCING NEW as NEW OLD as OLD
  FOR EACH ROW
BEGIN
  IF (deleting)
  THEN
    INSERT INTO SiteUsersDML
                (TXNID, SiteUserID, InsertionDate)
        VALUES (DBMS_TRANSACTION.local_transaction_id,
                :OLD.SiteUserID, SYSDATE);
  ELSE
    INSERT INTO SiteUsersDML
                (TXNID, SiteUserID, InsertionDate)
        VALUES (DBMS_TRANSACTION.local_transaction_id,
                :NEW.SiteUserID, SYSDATE);
  END IF;
END;


CREATE OR REPLACE TRIGGER NewsArticlesDMLTracker
  AFTER INSERT OR UPDATE OR DELETE
  ON NewsArticles
  REFERENCING NEW as NEW OLD as OLD
  FOR EACH ROW
BEGIN
  IF (deleting)
  THEN
    INSERT INTO NewsArticlesDML
                (TXNID, ArticleID, InsertionDate)
        VALUES (DBMS_TRANSACTION.local_transaction_id,
                :OLD.ArticleID, SYSDATE);
  ELSE
    INSERT INTO NewsArticlesDML
                (TXNID, ArticleID, InsertionDate)
        VALUES (DBMS_TRANSACTION.local_transaction_id,
```

```
                :NEW.ArticleID, SYSDATE);
   END IF;
END;
```

After these triggers are in place, every modification to a row in both the SiteUsers and
NewsArticles tables will be tracked in this table as well. The InsertionDate in these tables
is only for removing rows from these DML tables after they have been applied to all the
slave nodes; however, it cannot be used for tracking replication progress.

The next step is for a slave to connect to the master server and request all the transactions that have occurred since the last time it ran. You might think that it would be correct to have the slave store the last (latest) InsertionDate time stamp it witnessed as a
high water mark and request all DML that has occurred since that point in time. This is
terribly wrong.

The concept of "since" applies intuitively to time. However, in databases, what has
happened "since" the last time you looked has nothing to do with when it *happened* but
rather when it was *committed*. Oracle, unfortunately, does not expose the ability to place a
trigger before commit, so there is no way to tell when all the rows inserted into our
DML log left the isolation of their transaction and were actually committed for others to
see. Our replication process is one of those "others," so this is a big issue. If we relied on
time, we could have a race condition (shown in Figure 8.3), which would lead to a
wholly inconsistent copy on the slaves.

Instead of playing back by time, we should play back by transaction ID. This, unfortunately, requires us to maintain a list of transactions that each node has processed so that it
can determine which transactions are "new" on each subsequent run. The code listing
for the DDL to create tables for replication progress follows:

```
CREATE TABLE SiteUsersDMLProcessed (
  NodeName VARCHAR2(80) NOT NULL,
  TXNID VARCHAR2(20) NOT NULL,
  PRIMARY KEY(NodeName, TXNID)
);
CREATE INDEX SiteUsersDMLP_NN_IDX ON SiteUsersDMLProcessed(NodeName);
CREATE TABLE NewsArticlesDMLProcessed (
  NodeName VARCHAR2(80) NOT NULL,
  TXNID VARCHAR2(20) NOT NULL,
  PRIMARY KEY(NodeName, TXNID)
);
CREATE INDEX NewsArticlesDMLP_NN_IDX ON NewsArticlesDMLProcessed(NodeName);
```

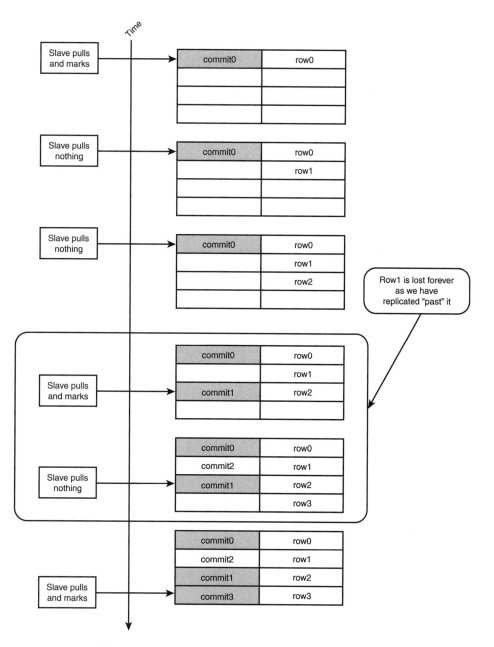

Figure 8.3   The race condition in replaying DML by time.

Now that we have all our building blocks in place on the master, we can tackle the actual replication from the slave's perspective.

Clearly we can't put any data into our PostgreSQL replica until we have the necessary tables in place. We need tables to hold the SiteUsers and NewsArticles as well as stored procedures (or functions in PostgreSQL) to apply changes as they come in. The code listing for DDL to create target tables in PostgreSQL follows:

```
CREATE TABLE SiteUsers (
  SiteUserID INTEGER PRIMARY KEY,
  CreatedDate TIMESTAMP NOT NULL,
  UserName VARCHAR(32) NOT NULL UNIQUE,
  Password VARCHAR(80) NOT NULL,
  EmailAddress VARCHAR(255) NOT NULL,
  Country VARCHAR(3) NOT NULL,
  PostalCode VARCHAR(10) NOT NULL
);
CREATE TABLE NewsArticles (
  ArticleID INTEGER PRIMARY KEY,
  Author INTEGER NOT NULL,
  Editor INTEGER,
  Approver INTEGER,
  CreatedDate TIMESTAMP NOT NULL,
  LastModifiedDate TIMESTAMP NOT NULL,
  PublishedDate TIMESTAMP,
  Title VARCHAR(200),
  AbstractText VARCHAR(1024),
  BodyText TEXT,
  isAvailable INTEGER NOT NULL DEFAULT 0
);
```

Now that we have our tables in place, we need to write the stored procedures (or functions) in PostgreSQL for each table to apply the changes that we pull from our master Oracle instance. These stored procedures are fairly generic, and you could write an automated procedure for generating them from DDL information. The code listing for SiteUsers_Apply and NewsArticles_Apply follows:

```
01: CREATE FUNCTION
02: SiteUsers_Apply(integer, integer, timestamp, varchar,
03:                 varchar, varchar, varchar, varchar)
04: RETURNS void
05: AS $$
06: DECLARE
07:    v_refid ALIAS FOR $1;
08:    v_SiteUserID ALIAS FOR $2;
09:    v_CreatedDate ALIAS FOR $3;
10:    v_UserName ALIAS FOR $4;
11:    v_Password ALIAS FOR $5;
12:    v_EmailAddress ALIAS FOR $6;
```

```
13:    v_Country ALIAS FOR $7;
14:    v_PostalCode ALIAS FOR $8;
15: BEGIN
16:   IF v_SiteUserID IS NULL THEN
17:     DELETE FROM SiteUsers WHERE SiteUserID = v_refid;
18:     RETURN;
19:   END IF;
20:   UPDATE SiteUsers
21:     SET SiteUserID = v_SiteUserID, CreatedDate = v_CreatedDate,
22:         UserName = v_UserName, Password = v_Password,
23:         EmailAddress = v_EmailAddress, Country = v_Country,
24:         PostalCode = v_PostalCode
25:   WHERE SiteUserID = v_refid;
26:   IF NOT FOUND THEN
27:     INSERT INTO SiteUsers
28:             (SiteUserID, CreatedDate, UserName, Password,
29:              EmailAddress, Country, PostalCode)
30:     VALUES (v_SiteUserID, v_CreatedDate, v_UserName, v_Password,
31:             v_EmailAddress, v_Country, v_PostalCode);
32:   END IF;
33: END;
34: $$ LANGUAGE 'plpgsql';
35:
36: CREATE FUNCTION
37: NewsArticles_Apply(integer, integer, integer, integer, integer,
38:                    timestamp, timestamp, timestamp, varchar,
39:                    varchar, text, integer)
40: RETURNS void
41: AS $$
42: DECLARE
43:    v_refid ALIAS FOR $1;
44:    v_ArticleID ALIAS FOR $2;
45:    v_Author ALIAS FOR $3;
46:    v_Editor ALIAS FOR $4;
47:    v_Approver ALIAS FOR $5;
48:    v_CreatedDate ALIAS FOR $6;
49:    v_LastModifiedDate ALIAS FOR $7;
50:    v_PublishedDate ALIAS FOR $8;
51:    v_Title ALIAS FOR $9;
52:    v_AbstractText ALIAS FOR $10;
53:    v_BodyText ALIAS FOR $11;
54:    v_isAvailable ALIAS FOR $12;
55: BEGIN
56:   IF v_ArticleID IS NULL THEN
57:     DELETE FROM NewsArticles WHERE ArticleID = v_refid;
58:     RETURN;
```

```
59:    END IF;
60:    UPDATE NewsArticles
61:       SET ArticleID = v_ArticleID, Author = v_Author,
62:           Editor = v_Editor, Approver = v_Approver,
63:           CreatedDate = v_CreatedDate,
64:           LastModifiedDate = v_LastModifiedDate,
65:           PublishedDate = v_PublishedDate,
66:           Title = v_Title, AbstractText = v_AbstractText,
67:           BodyText = v_BodyText, isAvailable = v_isAvailable
68:     WHERE ArticleID = v_refid;
69:    IF NOT FOUND THEN
70:      INSERT INTO NewsArticles
71:            (ArticleID, Author, Editor, Approver, CreatedDate,
72:             LastModifiedDate, PublishedDate, Title,
73:             AbstractText, BodyText, isAvailable)
74:      VALUES (v_ArticleID, v_Author, v_Editor, v_Approver,
75:             v_CreatedDate, v_LastModifiedDate, v_PublishedDate,
76:             v_Title, v_AbstractText, v_BodyText, v_isAvailable);
77:    END IF;
78: END;
79: $$ LANGUAGE 'plpgsql';
```

The basic concept behind these two routines is the same. The program that will pull changes from Oracle and apply them to PostgreSQL will know the original primary key of the row that was changed and the new full row (primary key and other columns) as it is in Oracle. The original primary keys are the *reference* primary keys, and the new full row represents how that referenced row should now appear. We have three cases to deal with:

- If the new full row has a NULL value in the nonreference primary key, it means that the row was not in the master. This means that we should delete the row from the slave (based on the reference primary key). Lines: 16–19 and 56–59.

- If the new full row has a valid (not NULL) primary key and the reference primary key exists in the slave table already, we must update that row to reflect the new information provided. Lines: 20–25 and 60–68.

- If the new full row has a valid (not NULL) primary key and the reference primary key does not exist in the slave table, we must insert this new row. Lines: 26–32 and 69–77.

We now have the necessary back-end infrastructure in place in Oracle and PostgreSQL and must write the actual workhorse. We'll use Perl for this example because the DBI (Database independent interface for Perl) is simple, sweet, and entirely consistent across all the DBDs (database drivers), including the one for Oracle and the one for PostgreSQL.

Although the concept of tracking your changes using triggers is straightforward, there are several moving parts. The slave side is much simpler in both concept and implementation. Basically, a slave does the following:

1. Connects to the master

2. Requests all modifications it has not yet processed

3. Applies those modifications

4. Informs the master it has applied them

5. Commits at the slave and the master

6. Repeats

A majority of the legwork here is authoring the queries that will serve to interact with the master and slave. We will make an effort to generalize the query generation so that adding new tables is easy. You should note that writing this as a single procedural Perl script is likely not the best way to go about putting a piece of critical infrastructure into your system. Making this into a clean, well-separated Perl replication framework is left as an exercise for the reader (and a rather simple one at that). Here it is as one procedural script so that we can walk through it section by section to match it against our six-item checklist without chasing down different classes and methods. The code listing for dml_replay.pl follows:

```
001: #!/usr/bin/perl
002:
003: use strict;
004: use DBI;
005: use POSIX qw/uname/;
006: use Getopt::Long;
007: use vars qw/%db %sql_ops %ops %tableinfo
008:              $nodename $interval $print_usage $verbose/;
009:
010: ($nodename = [POSIX::uname]->[1]) =~ s/\..*//; # short hostname
011: $interval = 5;                                 # 5 sec default
012:
013: sub vlog { printf STDERR @_ if($verbose); }
014:
015: GetOptions( 'n|nodename=s' => \$nodename,
016:             'i|interval=i' => \$interval,
017:             'v|verbose'    => \$verbose,
018:             'h|help'       => \$print_usage );
019:
020: if($print_usage) {
021:   print "$0 [-n node] [-i seconds] [-v] [-h]\n";
022:   exit;
023: }
024:
025: $db{master} = DBI->connect("dbi:Oracle:MASTER", "user", "pw",
```

```perl
026:                           { AutoCommit => 0, RaiseError => 1 } ) ||
027:    die "Could not connect to master";
028: $db{slave}  = DBI->connect("dbi:Pg:database=slave", "user", "pw",
029:                           { AutoCommit => 0, RaiseError => 1 } ) ||
030:    die "Could not connect to slave";
031:
032: # define our tables (names, keys, and other columns)
033: %tableinfo = (
034:    'SiteUsers' =>
035:      { 'keys'    => [ 'SiteUserID' ],
036:        'columns' => [ 'CreatedDate', 'UserName', 'Password',
037:                       'EmailAddress', 'Country', 'PostalCode'],
038:      },
039:    'NewsArticles' =>
040:      { 'keys'    => [ 'ArticleID' ],
041:        'columns' => [ 'Author', 'Editor', 'Approver', 'CreatedDate',
042:                       'LastModifiedDate', 'PublishedDate', 'Title',
043:                       'AbstractText', 'BodyText', 'isAvailable' ],
044:      },
045: );
046:
047: %sql_ops = (
048:    master => {
049:      fetchlogs => sub {
050:        my ($table, $pks, $cols) = @_;
051:        return qq{
052:        SELECT l.txnid, }.join(',', map { "l.$_" } (@$pks)).", ".
053:              join(',', map { "t.$_" } (@$pks, @$cols)).qq{
054:          FROM $table t, ${table}DML l, ${table}DMLProcessed p
055:        WHERE l.txnid = p.txnid(+) /* left join l to p and from */
056:          AND p.nodename(+) = ?    /* our node's view to remove */
057:          AND p.txnid is NULL      /* all seen txnids in p      */
058:          /* then left join against t on the primary key to    */
059:          /* pull the changed row even if it has been deleted. */
060:          AND }.join(' AND ', map { "l.$_ = t.$_(+)" } @$pks).qq{
061:        ORDER BY l.txnid};
062:      },
063:      record => sub {
064:        my ($table, $pks, $cols) = @_;
065:        return qq{
066:        INSERT INTO ${table}DMLProcessed (txnid, nodename)
067:                             VALUES (?, ?)
068:        };
069:      },
070:    },
071:    slave => {
```

```
072:     apply => sub {
073:        my ($table, $pks, $cols) = @_;
074:        # reference primary keys, new primary keys, new columns
075:        return qq{ SELECT ${table}_Apply(}.
076:          join(',', map { "?" } (@$pks, @$pks, @$cols)).
077:            ')';
078:     }
079:   }
080: );
081:
082: # transform %sql_ops into %ops where the operations are now
083: # DBI statement handles instead of SQL text.
084: while (my($table,$props) = each %tableinfo) {
085:   for my $connection ('master', 'slave') {
086:     while(my($op,$tsql) = each %{$sql_ops{$connection}}) {
087:       # use our template to build sql for this table
088:       # ($tsql is coderef that generates our SQL statements)
089:       my $sql = $tsql->($table,$props->{keys},$props->{columns});
090:       $ops{$connection}->{$table}->{$op} =
091:         $db{$connection}->prepare($sql) ||
092:           die "Could not prepare $sql on $connection";
093:     }
094:   }
095: }
096:
097: sub dml_replay($) {
098:   my $table = shift;
099:   my $rows = 0;
100:   my %seen_txns;
101:   eval {
102:     my $master = $ops{master}->{$table};
103:     my $slave = $ops{slave}->{$table};
104:     vlog("Fetch the $table logs from the master\n");
105:     $master->{fetchlogs}->execute($nodename);
106:     while(my @row = $master->{fetchlogs}->fetchrow()) {
107:       # txnid is the first column, pass the remaining to apply
108:       my $txnid = shift @row;
109:       vlog("[$txnid] Apply the changed row to the slave\n");
110:       $slave->{apply}->execute(@row);
111:       $seen_txns{$txnid}++;
112:       $rows++;
113:     }
114:     foreach my $txnid (keys %seen_txns) {
115:       vlog("[$txnid] Record the application to the master\n");
116:       $master->{record}->execute($txnid, $nodename);
117:     }
118:     $master->{fetchlogs}->finish();
```

```
119:    if($rows) {
120:        my $txns = scalar(keys %seen_txns); # get a count
121:        vlog("[$table] commit $txns txns / $rows rows\n");
122:        for ('slave', 'master') { $db{$_}->commit(); }
123:    }
124:  };
125:  if($@) {
126:    vlog("rollback DML replication on $table: $@\n");
127:    for ('slave', 'master') { eval { $db{$_}->rollback(); }; }
128:  }
129: }
130:
131: my $stop;
132: $SIG{'INT'} = sub { $stop = 1; };
133: while(!$stop) {
134:   foreach my $table (keys %tableinfo) {
135:     dml_replay($table);
136:   }
137:   sleep($interval);
138: }
139:
140: vlog("Disconnecting...\n");
141: for my $connection ('slave', 'master') {
142:   $db{$connection}->disconnect();
143: }
```

Let's walk over the checklist again and cross-reference it with our script:

1. Connect to the master. This is handled in lines 25–30.

2. Request all modifications it has not yet processed. The method for generating the SQL is defined in lines 49–62. That method is used and the result prepared on the database handle in lines 82–95. The request and the loop over the response set are in lines 105–106.

3. Apply those modifications. The SQL for applying the changes to the slave table is defined in lines 63–69 and prepared as a statement handle in lines 82–95. The resultset of the previous step is then applied to the slave table, and the transaction IDs that are applied are tracked in lines 107–112.

4. Inform the master that it has applied them. The SQL for recording applied transactions with the master is defined in lines 72–78 and prepared as a statement handle in lines 82–95. Lines 114–117 execute this statement handle to inform the master of the transactions we applied in the previous step.

5. Commit at the slave and the master. The changes are committed in lines 119–123. If there was an error during any of the previous steps, the eval block would be exited and the rollback induced in lines 125–128.

6. Repeat. Lines 131–138 loop over the preceding steps.

Perhaps a more straightforward recap of the script itself would be

1. Lines 25–30 connect.

2. Lines 32–45 define the tables we will be replicating.

3. Lines 47–80 define methods to generate all the SQL we will need to do our job.

4. Lines 82–95 prepare all the SQL for all the tables on the appropriate database handle (master or slave).

5. Lines 97–129 apply the process of fetching changes from the master, applying them to the slave, recording the application with the master, and committing (or rolling back on failure).

6. Lines 131–138 continually do this work on a defined interval.

All in all, it is simple. To start, we run the script (and leave it running); then we export the master table and import it manually. From that point on, the script will keep the replica up-to-date (within $interval seconds).

One nuance that was not addressed in this example is that the DMLProcessed tables will grow unbounded. There should be periodic, automated administrative action taken to remove old records from the DML logs on the master.

Snapshot Replication for Small Datasets

Now is a perfect time to take a detour. We have one table that is rather small. AdminUsers is only roughly 5,000 rows. The act of pulling that data from the database is tiny, and the act of creating a new table of that size is hardly worthy of mention.

Tables like these often do not merit the complexity of tracking changes, shipping them over, and reapplying them to slave nodes. Instead, each slave node can simply truncate its copy, pull a new one, insert it, and commit. On some databases this has unappealing, locking behavior and can affect read-only queries referencing the target table. We see this in PostgreSQL sometimes, so we will implement something called *flipping snapshots*.

The concept is simple. We have two copies of the table, and we alternate between them, applying the snapshot procedure. At the end of each procedure, we replace a publicly used view to reference the table that we just finished populating.

The first thing we need, as in the DML replay examples, is a table to hold our AdminUsers information. Unlike the DML replay example, we will not use the name of the table directly because we want to alternate between two snapshots. We do this by creating two identical snapshot tables and a view against one of them:

```
CREATE TABLE AdminUsers_snap1 (
  UserID INTEGER PRIMARY KEY,
  UserName VARCHAR(32) NOT NULL UNIQUE,
  Password VARCHAR(80) NOT NULL,
  EmailAddress VARCHAR(255) NOT NULL
);
CREATE TABLE AdminUsers_snap2 (
  UserID INTEGER PRIMARY KEY,
```

```
  UserName VARCHAR(32) NOT NULL UNIQUE,
  Password VARCHAR(80) NOT NULL,
  EmailAddress VARCHAR(255) NOT NULL
);
CREATE VIEW AdminUsers AS SELECT * FROM AdminUsers_snap1;
```

Now our tables and view are there, but they are empty. Populating a snapshot table is much more straightforward than the previous examples because it is not fine-grained. Although the process is clearly less efficient, for small tables that change infrequently it is a simple and easy solution because it requires no instrumentation on the master node.

The process of populating tables is simple:

1. Truncate the local, unused snapshot table (the one to which the view is not pointing).

2. Pull all rows from the master table and insert them into the now empty snapshot table.

3. Alter the view to point to the snapshot table we just populated.

4. Commit.

As you can imagine, there are several ways to do this. In most databases, performing bulk data loads efficiently requires using a separate API: Oracle has sqlldr, PostgreSQL has COPY, and MySQL has LOAD DATA INFILE. Additionally, many databases support the concept of *dblinks*, which are direct connections to other databases usually over some connection such as ODBC. Using a direct dblink or a native bulk loading method is the correct implementation of this, but we will use a generic (yet less efficient) approach here so that the code is less baroque and more generally applicable. The code for `snapshot.pl` follows:

```
01: #!/usr/bin/perl
02:
03: use strict;
04: use DBI;
05:
06: my $master = DBI->connect("dbi:Oracle:MASTER", "user", "pw",
07:                           { AutoCommit => 0, RaiseError => 1 } ) ||
08:   die "Could not connect to master";
09: my $slave  = DBI->connect("dbi:Pg:database=slave", "user", "pw",
10:                           { AutoCommit => 0, RaiseError => 1 } ) ||
11:   die "Could not connect to slave";
12:
13: # This is how we will find out the view's current source table
14: my $whichsnap = $slave->prepare(q{
15:     SELECT substring(definition from '%_snap#"_#"%' for '#')
16:       FROM pg_views
17:      WHERE viewname = lower(?)
18:   }) || die "Cannot prepare snapshot detector\n";
19:
```

```
20: while(my $table = shift) {
21:   eval {
22:       # Which snapshot is the view pointint to? (1 or 2)
23:       $whichsnap->execute($table);
24:       my($snap) = $whichsnap->fetchrow();
25:       $whichsnap->finish();
26:
27:       # Choose the non-active snapshot for population
28:       my $newsnap;
29:       $newsnap = "${table}_snap2" if($snap eq '1');
30:       $newsnap = "${table}_snap1" if($snap eq '2');
31:       $newsnap || die "[$table] which snapshot to use?\n";
32:
33:       # Empty the snapshot table
34:       $slave->do(qq{TRUNCATE TABLE $newsnap}) ||
35:         die "[$table] could not truncate $newsnap\n";
36:
37:       # Pull all the rows from the master and put them
38:       # in the slave table
39:       my $src = $master->prepare(qq{SELECT * FROM $table});
40:       $src->execute();
41:       # Our column names are @{$src->{NAME}}
42:       my $dst = $slave->prepare(qq{
43:         INSERT INTO $newsnap (}. join(',', @{$src->{NAME}}).q{)
44:             VALUES (}.join(',', map { "?" } @{$src->{NAME}}).')');
45:       while(my $row = $src->fetchrow_hashref()) {
46:         $dst->execute(map { $row->{$_} } @{$src->{NAME}});
47:       }
48:       $src->finish();
49:
50:       # Replace the view with a view onto the new snapshot
51:       $slave->do(qq{CREATE OR REPLACE VIEW $table AS
52:                     SELECT * FROM $newsnap}) ||
53:         die "[$table] cannot replace view\n";
54:
55:       $slave->commit();
56:   };
57:   # Rollback on any sort of error
58:   if($@) { eval { $slave->rollback(); }; }
59: }
60: $master->disconnect();
61: $slave->disconnect();
```

The preceding code sample is much simpler than the DML replay script. In this script we simply connect to the database (lines 6–11), determine which snapshot the current view references (lines 13–18 and 22–31), truncate the "other" snapshot (lines 33–35), pull the rows from the master and stick them into our empty table (lines 37–48), flip the view to look at our fresh snapshot (lines 50–53), and commit (line 55). The script takes the tables to snapshot as additional arguments to the script itself.

Again, although this script is functional, a production version should leverage the database vendor-specific extensions for bulk data loading to reduce overall load on the slave node. In my personal experience doing this from Oracle to MySQL, we used the LOAD DATA INFILE with success, and when performing snapshots from Oracle to PostgreSQL we used the pl/perl procedural language in combination with dbi-link to perform all aspects of the snapshot procedure from within PostgreSQL itself.

Same Vendor Database Replication Is Easy

Anyone who has set up Oracle to Oracle or MySQL to MySQL master-slave replication will know that it is a well-documented and straightforward process. So, why go through a laborious example of how to replicate from one vendor to another? There is a good reason—thanks for hanging in there!

When an architecture relies on a specific vendor at the core, people tend to narrow their vision. This isn't limited to developers alone, but developers in particular always attempt to solve problems with the tools they best understand—regardless of the tools' suitability for the job at hand.

We should make it very clear that if you are using Product X at the core of the architecture and you are in the position of needing similar or related functionality elsewhere in the architecture, it makes the most sense to use the same Product X. The reasons for this should be obvious, but here are just a few:

- Limiting the number of different products in the architecture reduces the overall set of expertise needed by staff.
- Each product has its own bugs, release cycles, and life cycles, all of which must be accounted for in operational planning.
- You'd be out of your mind to manage and maintain two separate tools to do the exact same job.

With that said, similar or related functionality is often poorly assessed. Often, the reason for needing a database replica is due to a performance concern or a different usage pattern on the existing database that would negatively impact existing operations. If the new task at hand causes a performance issue or demonstrates a different usage pattern, clearly the functionality will not be the same on the new slave nodes as on the current master.

It takes some experience, but the ultimate goal is to evaluate how different the demands on the new database architecture will be from the current ones. If they are indeed different, it is worth the time to step back from the architecture for some serious deliberation. You should be asking yourself several questions. Why doesn't my current database serve this new purpose well? Are there specific features of functions that are missing from this product that exist in a different RDBMS? Could I solve my problem without a database at all?

After answering these questions (without specific products in mind!), you may find that it makes the most sense to have the new portions of your architecture built on the same database (and go buy a replication book for Product X), have a different vendor's database (this chapter should make that a little less intimidating), or don't have a database at all (which is why there is Chapter 10, "The Right Tool for the Job," in this book).

9

Juggling Logs
and Other Circus Tricks

Production architectures are generally busy places. Things are happening all the time: Customers are being served, reports are being run, and things are breaking and getting fixed. How do we know this? Logs.

The logs that are written throughout the architecture are of vital importance for monitoring, auditing, and troubleshooting. However, despite their being crucial, the infrastructure to journal and analyze logs is often one of the most neglected components in a large architecture.

There are two types of logs: those needed to provide reporting and those needed to troubleshoot problems. Because reports serve a purpose and are expected and reviewed, the logs that feed them must be correctly processed. Logs used to troubleshoot problems are often needed only when disaster strikes and nearly as often, those logs are inefficient to adequately address the troubleshooting needs.

This leads to the obvious question: "What is so difficult about logging?" Writing the logs from 20, 50, or 100 web servers into a centralized location is not rocket science. There are bad ways, good ways, and great ways to go about logging. Amazingly, a vast majority of the enterprise architectures that I have reviewed go about it completely wrong.

In this chapter, we will cover several methods of log aggregation and discuss how logging infrastructures have evolved to address the needs of today's large architectures.

Why Is Logging a Challenge?

Logging is a challenge for two reasons: volume and aggregation. Let's take a large website as an example. In Chapter 6, "Static Content Serving for Speed and Glory," we had a goal to serve 11,750 requests per second at 70% capacity. To handle 11,750 requests per second at 70% we need an actual capacity of 16,786 requests per second, so we will round up and assume that our logging system must handle journaling and analyzing 17,000 log lines per second. Although this is peak traffic during our peak time (constituting 15% of the day's traffic), this still winds up being 360 million log events per day. That is quite a few log messages to write. Additionally, no single source is generating these events; they are streaming in from at least 20 different web servers.

If you compare the logs from your web server, database server, switch, workstation, and even your mobile phone, you will find one thing in common: time stamps. Every logging event occurred at a particular point in time, and knowing when it occurred is fundamental to its usefulness. This may seem obvious, but the importance of it is multifaceted, and the classic "solution" to the problem may not be sufficient to solve the larger problem at hand.

Knowing when a logging event occurred allows us to quantize information for general consumption. A typical example of this is a report detailing the quantity of web request services broken out by HTTP code on 1-hour intervals, 30-minute intervals, and 5-minute intervals. This type of report is common because it is useful for determining overall traffic trends. Although this type of reporting requires all log events to have time stamps, the relative accuracy of those time stamps does not affect the outcome of the report. In other words, a time skew of 5, 10, or even 30 seconds across the web servers would not dramatically skew the results of such a report where the time granularity of the report is significantly larger than the time skew on machines.

Let's look at a misconfiguration in this situation. Perhaps a single machine is not configured to observe daylight savings time, but the others are. This would clearly damage the report, but how much? From a signal analysis perspective it would be as if the signal had 5% loss and an echo with one-hour latency with around 5.3% signal strength. This type of mild signal "damage" is easy for a human to tune out and otherwise compensate for. It does not give a perfect representation of what is going on at any given time, but the ability to understand overall trends is not compromised.

This may lead us to believe that, although time stamps are crucial, their accuracy is highly overrated. This might be true in the specific case of quantized reports; however, there are other uses for log events where the relative accuracy of time stamps is paramount—enter the land of distributed system troubleshooting.

By definition, troubleshooting occurs only when there is trouble. Trouble in a deterministic system is simple cause and effect. The *cause* is your problem, and the *effect* is the trouble. On a single system, troubleshooting is at its most basic. You are looking for an event on the system that induced failure directly or destabilized the environment in a fashion that allowed a failure to be noticed. All the components playing a part are running on a single system, with a single clock, and thus all logs generated are written "in order" and allude to a cause and effect stream of occurrences.

Because this book is all about scalable systems, we don't deal much with how to solve problems that involve a single machine. When troubleshooting problems whose ill effects are the product of a set of actions that occur across a cluster of machines, we have a troubleshooting environment that is far from "basic."

For example, let's look at a flow through our website that results in the purchase of a paid service subscription. If we are alerted to the fact that the arrival-to-conversion rate has dropped by some non-nominal amount, we must look for a cause for that effect. To effectively troubleshoot this problem, we must have a view into each purchasing "session" and all the events that happen during that session. We must have them all in the order they occurred to be relevant to our troubleshooting task. In this situation, it is imperative that we log all events that happen—clusterwide—in an order that represents their relative transactional timing. In other words, events that comprise a "transaction" must be logged in the order they were executed. This is a difficult problem.

Classic Solutions

Before we discuss a powerful solution that provides the underlying mechanics to solve the previously proposed problems, we will visit a few of the traditional logging approaches. We will discuss their strong and weak points, and attempt to demonstrate their inadequacies in large mission-critical environments.

Periodic "Batch" Aggregation

Perhaps the oldest trick in the book when managing the logging of a multinode cluster is the simple aggregation of their local logs.

This configuration of log storage and eventual aggregation (shown in Figure 9.1) is probably the most commonly deployed architecture. In this configuration, web servers (or other log-producing application servers) write their logs to disk in a standard way. Periodically, a dedicated log management server connects to each log-producing server and "pulls" the logs. This typically happens on multihour or daily intervals. Although this configuration is simple and well tested, it leaves a bit to be desired.

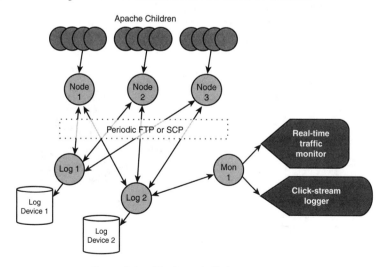

Figure 9.1 Classic periodic log aggregation.

The first major problem is that when a server crashes, we possibly could have a large segment of logs (those journaled between the last fetch and the time of the crash) that are unavailable for analysis and incorporation. When the server returns to service, a decision must be made to dispose of the logs, archive the logs, or even go so far as pull the logs and retroactively incorporate the data found into the statistics for the time period in question. This has serious implications because the data is important and by incorporating it into historic data, previously calculated statistics and summarizations will be altered. It isn't intuitive (and I argue it is entirely unacceptable) to have statistics for a past period of time change.

Another serious shortcoming of this methodology is the lack of real-time exposure to the data. It is impossible to do passive, real-time analysis on logs because the aggregated data on which you can perform analysis is stale (and possibly incomplete). Real-time analysis is often not considered in architectures because the configuration simply does not afford the opportunity to perform it. As we will see later, real-time access to log data can offer tremendous benefits to systems engineering tasks, as well as enhance business knowledge.

Real-time Unicast Aggregation

The main disadvantages of batch aggregation revolve around the fact that there is significant latency. This can be addressed simply by pushing logs from the web servers in real-time. One such "push" implementation is logging via Syslog.

If you reconfigure your applications to write logs by the Syslog API, you can configure Syslog to use a foreign log host. In this configuration (shown in Figure 9.2), logs are effectively written in real-time to the log aggregation host.

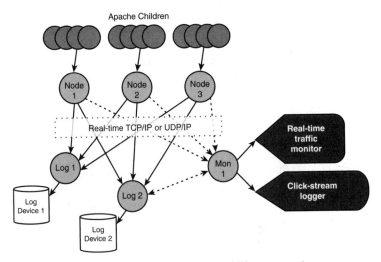

Figure 9.2 Real-time unicast "push" log aggregation.

One serious shortcoming of a naive Syslog implementation is that Syslog uses UDP as a transport protocol. UDP is unreliable, and logging should be reliable—so we have a fundamental mismatch. Conveniently, logging in real-time in unicast is a paradigm not tied to a specific implementation. Syslog-NG is a Syslog replacement that will use TCP to reliably log to a remote log host. mod_log_mysql is an Apache module that will insert Apache logs directly into a MySQL database. Both of these approaches follow this basic paradigm.

This technique eliminates the major disadvantage of periodic aggregation. We can now look at the log files on our aggregation host and watch them grow in real-time. This also means that by processing the new data added to log files, we can calculate real-time metrics and monitor for anomalies—this is powerful!

Additionally, if we want to add a second logging host for redundancy, it will require reconfiguration of each log publishing server—because it is a "push" technology, the servers must know where to push. This is a legitimate approach, but because more advanced and flexible techniques exist, we won't dig into implementing this.

Passive "Sniffing" Log Aggregation

Due to the inherent difficulty of configuring both batch aggregation and push-style unicast aggregation, the concept of passive sniffing aggregation was conceived. Using this approach, we "monitor" the network to see what web traffic (or other protocol) is actually transiting, and we manufacture logs based on what we see. This technique compensates for needing to reconfigure web servers when the logging host changes and allows for a secondary failover instance to be run with no significant modification of network topology or reconfiguration of servers.

The beauty of this implementation is that you will manufacture logs for all the traffic you see, not just what hits the web servers you intended. In other words, it is more "Big Brother" in its nature. It uses the same tried-and-true techniques that exist in network intrusion detection systems. In a simple sense, the technique is similar to the traditional promiscuous network sniffing provided by tools such as tcpdump, snoop, ethereal, and snort. The log aggregator is designed to be able to passively reconstruct the protocol streams (which can be rather expensive in high throughput environments) so that it can introspect the stream and generate a standard-looking log for traffic seen on that protocol (for example, an Apache common log format file). I welcome you to pause at this point to ponder why this solution is imperfect.

In Figure 9.3, we see that the passive log aggregation unit is placed in front of the architecture so that it can witness all client-originating traffic. Although it can be deployed in other parts of the network, this is the best position to attempt to reproduce the logs we would expect from our batched aggregation and/or unicast push aggregation.

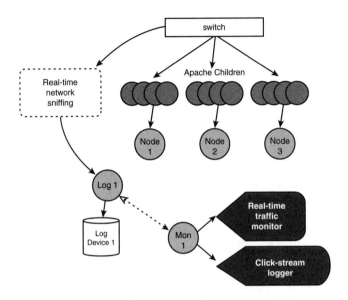

Figure 9.3   Passive "sniffing" log aggregation.

This approach is inadequate in several ways, however. First, it requires a network topology where a single point can monitor all incoming network traffic—effectively, one egress point. The larger your network, the less likely your topology will be conducive to this restriction. Not only does your topology have to lend itself to this approach, by implementing this, you add some inflexibility to the architecture. For instance, referring back to Chapter 6, we have several web serving clusters serving traffic from around the world, and, as such, there is no single egress point that we could monitor to "catch" all the web requests for logging. This becomes a matter of the technology fitting well into your architecture, and, often, these issues aren't showstoppers.

What else is wrong? Many protocols are specifically designed to prevent passive listening. HTTP over Secure Socket Layer (SSL) is one such protocol. SSL traffic is designed to be secure from eavesdropping and injections (man-in-the-middle attacks). As such, there is no good way that a passive log aggregator can determine the data payload of the HTTP sessions performed over SSL. A security expert can argue that if the passive listener has access to the secure key used by the web server (which would be simple in this case), you could effectively eavesdrop. However, there is no way to efficiently eavesdrop, and we are talking about scalable systems here. This shortcoming is a showstopping obstacle in almost every production architecture.

Let's think about what would happen if we tried to passively decrypt SSL sessions and reconstruct the payload and log the traffic. What happens when we don't have enough horsepower to get the job done? In any networked system, when too much is going on, you start dropping packets. As these packets are not destined to the aggregator, it cannot request a retransmission. (It would cause the TCP/IP session to break.) If the packets are dropped, there is no way to reconstruct the session, and you end up discarding the incomplete session and with it the logs that should have been generated. There will be countless "legitimate" TCP/IP sessions that will not be complete enough to log (for example, when a client disconnects or there is a sustained routing issue). As such, these passive aggregators typically log no errors, or if they do, they are mixed in with countless "errors" that don't represent an error due to resource saturation induced packet loss. Basically, you'll be losing logs without knowing it. Although this is an almost certainty if you were to attempt to tackle SSL traffic, you could also just be logging HTTP and somehow saturate your resources and lose logs and not really now it.

The bottom line here is that if your logs are vital to your business, this type of solution is prone to problems and generally a bad idea.

Logging Done Right

We want a few simple things to make our logs more reliable and the data inside them work for us on an operational level. When something goes wrong, we all turn to logs to attempt to backtrack from the symptom to the cause. If the cause is in the logs, why should we have to look for it? Why not simply be told about it?

From a reliability standpoint, we want our logs—all of them. If a server crashes, we need to know what transpired up to the point of failure. It is much less useful to bring the machine back online (if possible) at a later point and attempt to retrieve and integrate the old as-of-yet unseen logs. Additionally, if our logs are important, we may want to write them to more than one location at a time—redundant logging servers.

Making logs work for your architecture on an operational level is something you may have never thought of, but you should. Logs hold invaluable data about events that have immediately transpired, and, in a simple way, they can provide a great deal of evidence that something has gone wrong. By aggregating logs in real-time, we can analyze them to determine whether they meet our expectations. Some common expectations that can be transformed into monitors are an upper bound on 500 errors from the servers (perhaps 0), an upper bound on 404 errors, an expected number of requests served per second either in raw numbers or a reasonable proximity to some historical trend. The goal is to construct business-level monitors that can trigger in real-time rather than the typical approach of looking at 24-hour statistical roll-ups and realizing problems exist after they have already had a significant impact on your business.

Although the real-time delivery of logs is a critical requirement not found in other logging methodologies, there are other advantages to be had. Particularly, an efficient substrate for multiple log subscribers is key to the overall usability of the solution. This means that if we are going to start using our logs in an operational sense and have fault tolerant log journaling in place, we will have many different processes subscribing to the log stream. This may not sound like a big deal, but logging incurs a not-insignificant cost. Writing logs to multiple locations can increase that cost linearly unless the right approach is taken. Here we want reliable multicast.

We need to be able to allow many subscribers to the log streams without the potential of bringing the system to its knees. A reliable protocol that uses IP multicast will allow us to scale up the number of subscribers without scaling up the network infrastructure to support it. Spread is one such tool that provides reliable messaging over IP multicast.

The Architecture (Servers, Software, and Roles)

In traditional logging configurations, the server software and roles involved are somewhat minimal. It is expensive to juggle logs and, as such, servers tend to have multiple roles so there are as few moving parts as possible. Alongside your cluster of web servers, you'll see one "logging server" that is responsible for a great many things: collection, archival, analysis, and so on.

In a configuration where logs are published and subscriptions are inexpensive, the opportunity for delegating responsibility and adding redundancy increases as the challenge decreases. This makes our current tasks easier and affords us the opportunity to be innovative with our logs, which we will discuss in Chapter 10, "The Right Tool for the Job."

The previously discussed logging architectures change shape and form as depicted in Figure 9.4.

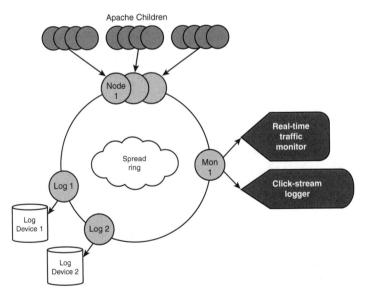

Figure 9.4 Logging based on group communication.

First, let's get some nomenclature in place so that we are all talking about the same thing. The word *cluster* is too generic, and in this case it is ambiguous. Instead we will refer to the servers according to their roles:

- Web servers—Servers responsible for serving web pages and publishing logs or the operations that they perform.

- Log servers—Servers responsible for journaling (to permanent storage) logs of the events published by web servers. They are responsible for abiding by the retention and archival policies the business dictates for this data.

- Log monitors—Servers that subscribe to the log stream and perform some form of analysis on the stream. These monitors feed back into the overall enterprise monitoring solution implemented for the architecture and supply passive metrics and alerts to be acted on appropriately.

- Casual monitors—Servers that subscribe to the log stream occasionally but serve no core infrastructure purpose. Subscribers of this fashion would typically be systems administrators attempting to troubleshoot a problem or developers attempting to retrieve logs (errors and access) during development, staging, and occasionally production.

In systems administrator terms, think of the web servers as the system, the log servers as `sar` or some system accounting and auditing service, the log monitors as SNMP and SNMP traps, and the casual monitors as tools such as `top`, `vmstat`, `iostat`, `ps`, and so on. All these services and tools are vital to running a healthy system—now you have something comparable for web logs.

The irony is that when someone asks a systems admin what is going on or what happened at a certain point in time on his system, he can answer the question quickly and easily. Typically, no such answer can be had quickly or easily in large web environments. It is imperative that we rectify this situation.

By separating the roles, we allow them to be fulfilled by different servers. This has the obvious advantage of allowing each server to have separately defined uptime requirements, service levels, mission criticality, and management responsibility.

Building It

Building such a beast may sound intimidating, but in truth it is actually much simpler and more elegant than the traditional logging approaches. You only need to put in place three components: a mechanism for publication, a subscriber that can satisfy on-disk log aggregation needs, and a substrate over which they will operate.

We've already discussed Spread briefly in previous chapters, and we will put it to good use again here. Spread is a fast and efficient messaging bus that can provide exactly the publish/subscribe substrate we are looking for to solve the problem at hand.

We will install Spread on each web server, log host, and monitor server in our architecture; launch it; and verify that it works. This is the first step of using any underlying framework, networking system, or messaging substrate. Because several chapters in this book refer to using Spread, the configuration and installation is described in detail in Appendix A, "Spread."

Subscribers—`spreadlogd`

Before we jump into how to publish logs into a substrate on which no one will be listening, it seems reasonable to first tackle the issue of journaling said logs to storage. You might think that the tool to accomplish such a task would be simple because it is responsible only for reading such messages from Spread and writing those messages to disk. If you thought that, you were right; the tool is brain-dead simple, and it is called `spreadlogd`.

`spreadlogd` is a simple C program that uses the Spread C API to connect to Spread, subscribe to a predefined set of groups, and journal the messages it reads from those groups to a set of files. It is amazingly simple.

Listing 9.1 `spreadlogd.conf`—**A Simple** `spreadlogd` **Configuration**

```
Buffer = 65535
Spread 4803 {
    Group logdomain1 {
        File = /data/logs/logdomain1/debug_log
    }
    Group logdomain2 {
        File = /data/logs/logdomain2/common_log
        RewriteTimestamp = CommonLogFormat
    }
}
```

The sample configuration detailed in Listing 9.1 and presented in diagram form in Figure 9.4 is short and simple. Effectively, we'd like to read messages up to 64 kilobytes in length from the Spread daemon listening on port 4803. We want to subscribe to the groups named `logdomain1` and `logdomain2` and write them to the files `/data/logs/logdomain1/debug_log` and `/data/logs/logdomain2/common_log`, respectively. As an extra, added feature we want the `spreadlogd` instance to recognize the logs it reads from `logdomain2` as Apache common log format, find the time stamp therein, and rewrite it with the current local time stamp on the machine. `spreadlogd` is a simple program and as such is reliable and fast.

You can test the operation now (after running `spreadlogd` on your logging host) by running `spuser` (a tool that comes with Spread) from any machine in your cluster (logger, monitor, or web server). The following output presents a `spuser` publishing session:

```
# /opt/spread/bin/spuser -s 4803
Spread library version is 3.17.3
User: connected to 4803 with private group #user#admin-va-1

==========
User Menu:
----------
```

```
        j <group> -- join a group
        l <group> -- leave a group

        s <group> -- send a message
        b <group> -- send a burst of messages

        r -- receive a message (stuck)
        p -- poll for a message
        e -- enable asynchonous read (default)
        d -- disable asynchronous read

        q -- quit

User> s logdomain1
enter message: This is a test message. Walla walla bing bang.

User> q

Bye.
```

We should see that log line immediately (sub second) appear in /data/logs/ logdomain1/debug_log on our logging server. If we are running two logging servers, it will appear in both places, and if we were running spuser on another machine subscribed to the logdaemon1 group (j logdaemon1), we would also see it appear on our spuser console. It's like magic.

Now, we have something in place to write the logs published to our groups to disk and thus it is safe to explore methods to actually publishing them.

Publishers—mod_log_spread

Before I jump into explaining how to configure Apache to log web logs through our new Spread infrastructure, I'd like to rant a bit about the danger of inertia.

Spread has a C, Perl, Python, PHP, Ruby, Java, and OCaml API—just for starters. It is trivial to write support into any application to publish messages into Spread. Although there is no good reason to fear code modification, it is a common fear nonetheless. Ironically, most systems engineers and developers are comfortable using a modification (patch) written by someone else. I suppose it is a lack of self-confidence or a misplaced faith in the long-term support interests the author has for the changeset. Whatever it is, I suggest we get past that—it hinders thinking out of the box and causes the wrong technologies to be used despite the simplicity of adopting new ones.

A specific example of this is that a few large enterprises I've worked with simply would not consider this logging option, despite the advantages it offered, because it didn't expose a log4j (a popular Java logging specification) implementation. They did not want to invest in the effort to switch from log4j to something new. If you don't know what log4j is, you should be confused by now. log4j is an API more than anything else, and below that API there is an implementation that knows how to write to a disk, or to JMS, or to a database, and so on. There is no good reason why some engineer couldn't spend an hour building a log4j implementation that published to Spread. The fear of new technology was irrational in this case, and the company was prepared to forfeit an extreme advantage due to its fear of having to write code. This is ridiculous—end of rant.

mod_log_spread, available at http://www.backhand.org/, is a version of mod_log_config (a core Apache module for logging) that has been patched to allow publishing logs to a Spread daemon; as such, you have all the features of mod_log_config. mod_log_config allows you to specify the log destination as the path to a file to which it will append or, alternatively, a program to which it will pipe the logs—this is accomplished by preceding the name of the program with a | character as is conventional on UNIX systems. To this, mod_log_spread adds the capability to publish to a group by specifying the log destination as the group name prepended by a $ character. In our case, instead of specifying the target of the CustomLog statement as a path to a local file or a pipe to Apache's rotatelogs program, we specify $logdomain2. This can be seen in the following httpd.conf excerpt:

```
LoadModule log_spread_module libexec/mod_log_spread.so
AddModule mod_log_spread.c
SpreadDaemon 4803
CommonLog $logdomain2
```

The preceding configuration loads the mod_log_spread module into Apache (1.3), configures it to talk to Spread locally on port 4803 (actually through /tmp/4803 on UNIX), and writes logs in Common Log Format (CLF) to the Spread group logdomain2. Start up your server with that, and you should immediately see log lines (in CLF) written as prescribed by your spreadlogd configuration whenever a page is loaded.

Understanding the Beauty of the Beast

You may not realize it, but you've just created a monster. You have just instrumented your web architecture for performance assessment, debugging, monitoring, and auditing—and it was really easy.

Now, you can take my word for it that this stuff is cool, but we will present a few examples of things we can now see that were painful, if not impossible, in a previous logging architecture (whatever it may have been).

The most obvious is that you now have one or more log hosts running spreadlogd journaling your logs to disk. This isn't very glamorous, so instead of staring at those for a long time (but by all means, do so if it makes you happy), we'll spend the next few sections looking at live streams.

Real-time Analysis

First, let's look at a stream going by. In previous examples we used the group
`logdomain2`, so we should be able to connect to Spread using its cantankerous
command-line tool `spuser` and see some logs. The following output presents a `spuser`
real-time observation session:

```
# /opt/spread/bin/spuser -s 4803
Spread library version is 3.17.3
User: connected to 4803 with private group #user#admin-va-1


==========
User Menu:
----------


        j <group> -- join a group
        l <group> -- leave a group

        s <group> -- send a message
        b <group> -- send a burst of messages

        r -- receive a message (stuck)
        p -- poll for a message
        e -- enable asynchonous read (default)
        d -- disable asynchronous read


        q -- quit

User> j logdomain2
=============================
Received REGULAR membership for group lethargy with 2 members,
where I am member 1:
        #sld-05988#gollum
        #user#admin-va-1
grp id is 182571332 1118158447 4
Due to the JOIN of #user#admin-va-1

User>
=============================
received RELIABLE message from #ap26194#www-va-2, of type 1,
(endian 0) to 1 groups
(216 bytes): 85.192.40.13 - - [12/Aug/2005:15:21:30 -0400]
"GET /~jesus/archives/29-isaexec-and-magical-builds.html HTTP/1.0"
200 12502 "http://order-carisoprodol.9k.com" "Mozilla/4.0
(compatible; MSIE 6.0; Windows NT 5.1; SV1)"
```

```
User>
============================
received RELIABLE message from #ap26590#www-va-1, of type 1,
(endian 0) to 1 groups
(210 bytes): 85.192.40.13 - - [12/Aug/2005:15:21:36 -0400]
"GET /~jesus/archives/29-isaexec-and-magical-builds.html HTTP/1.0"
200 12502 "http://order-cialis.9k.com" "Mozilla/4.0 (compatible;
MSIE 6.0; Windows NT 5.1; SV1)"


User>
============================
received RELIABLE message from #ap26196#www-va-3, of type 1,
(endian 0) to 1 groups
(202 bytes): 216.86.156.205 - - [12/Aug/2005:15:21:40 -0400]
"GET /~jesus/archives/1970/01.html HTTP/1.1" 200 12493
"http://buy---adipex.at.tut.by" "Mozilla/4.0 (compatible;
MSIE 6.0; Windows NT 5.1; en) Opera 8.0"


User>
============================
received RELIABLE message from #ap26192#www-va-2, of type 1,
(endian 0) to 1 groups
(209 bytes): 85.192.40.13 - - [12/Aug/2005:15:21:47 -0400]
"GET /~jesus/archives/29-isaexec-and-magical-builds.html HTTP/1.0"
200 12502 "http://1st-levitra.9k.com" "Mozilla/4.0 (compatible;
MSIE 6.0; Windows NT 5.1; SV1)"


User>
Bye.
```

The first message is one indicating a group membership change. The new users are
#sld-05988#gollum and #user#admin-va-1. Well, we're logged in to admin-va-1, so
we are the #user#admin-va-1, and on the machine named gollum we are running a
spreadlogd daemon (gollum is running Linux):

```
# ssh gollum "ps auxwww | awk '/spreadlogd/{print "'$2" "$11'";}'"
5988 /usr/local/sbin/spreadlogd
```

Lo and behold! A spreadlogd process is running at process ID 5988, hence the private
member name #sld-05988#gollum. I no longer feel alone.

Now, what are all those other lines? Well, aside from the Apache log line that we see,
we have some other useful information:

- RELIABLE is a word describing the semantics with which the message was published; mod_log_spread uses RELIABLE messaging by default.

- `from #ap26192#www-va-2` indicates the sender of the message, which is informative. It means that the Apache child at process ID 26192 on the machine www-va-2 just serviced the request and sent us that log line.

- `type 1` is an advanced Spread internal that can be ignored.

- `endian 0` is used to indicate whether the sending machine has a different byte ordering than the local Spread daemon to which we connected.

- `to 1 groups` indicates the cardinality of groups to which this message was sent. `mod_log_spread` only sends individual messages to a single group.

The rest of the message is the Apache Common Log Format line and shows us more interesting things. These hits happen to be against my personal blog, and we can see that they are all coming from the same IP address from different referrers all within a few seconds of one another. This is suspect. Why would someone be coming to my site four times (this is just a small clip of time, there are actually thousands of these) all from different places?

Well, blogs (at least mine) track the referrers and list the top referrers in a side bar on the page. So if you refer to my blog many times from a particular URL, you may get some exposure under the top referrers section. Looking at these URLs, this person clearly isn't interested in the information on my blog. He just wants his prescription drug website link on my page. I don't like this guy already.

I could write a script that listens to this Spread group to check for IP addresses that contain three non-blank, differing URL referrers within 60 seconds and add them to a suppression list that my blog would use to eliminate "the bad guys" from my top referrers. Just a thought.

A demonstration on my blog doesn't expose the challenges involved with doing real-time assessments on large sites. In those environments, the logs stream by so fast that automated tools are absolutely required to perform any useful analysis—unless something is catastrophically broken.

Real-time Monitoring

From the administrative point of view (systems, network, database), real-time monitoring is the capability to understand what is happening over some period of time. Specifically, it is the capability to correlate clearly realized effects with clearly reported occurrences. On the systems administration side, there are some age-old tools that allow administrators to understand system metrics in real-time. Two such tools are `iostat` and `vmstat`. These tools allow you to understand disk I/O activity, service times, virtual memory, and scheduling-related activity in near real-time. It is far out of the scope of this book to talk about how you would go about interpreting the output of such tools, but we can use them to draw a parallel into clustered systems.

Where are the tools that tell us what is going on in real-time in our web cluster? `iostat` and `vmstat` are fundamentally important to monitoring and troubleshooting

problems on production systems. They allow administrators to quickly pinpoint bottlenecks or points of resource contention. As such, they are available on every modern system. When you install your Apache web cluster, where are the analogous tools? Absent.

If you install a load-balancing device in front of your cluster, often that system will
provide real-time metrics—at least those that it uses to make its load-balancing decisions.
As we have learned, these load-balancing devices are not always the right tools for the
job, so there must be another way to ascertain these vital metrics in real-time.
Additionally, there very well may be metrics related to your web application that should
be monitored, and because these load-balancing devices operate above the web application, there is no feasible way they could report application specific metrics. Listing 9.2
shows an example of a real-time web traffic monitor.

Listing 9.2 `wwwstat`—**A Real-time Web Traffic Monitor**

```perl
 1: #!/usr/bin/perl
 2:
 3: use strict;
 4: use Spread;
 5: use Getopt::Long;
 6: use Time::HiRes qw/tv_interval gettimeofday/;
 7:
 8: # return the maximum of two inputs
 9: sub max { my($a,$b) = @_; ($a>$b)?$a:$b; }
10:
11: use vars qw /$daemon @group $interval $last $quit $banner $rows_since_banner
12:             %servers %hits %statuses/;
13:
14: GetOptions("d=s" => \$daemon,
15:            "g=s" => \@group,
16:            "i=i" => \$interval);
17:
18: $interval ||= 1;
19: my ($m, $g) = Spread::connect( { spread_name => "$daemon",
20:                                   private_name => "tt_$$" } );
21: die "Could not connect to Spread at $daemon" unless $m;
22: die "Could not join group" unless(grep {Spread::join($m, $_)} @group);
23:
24: sub pretty_hits {
25:   my ($servers, $statuses, $hitcnt, $banner) = @_;
26:   my @slist = sort keys %$servers;
27:   my @stlist = sort { $a <=> $b } keys %$statuses;
28:   my $minw = scalar(@stlist) * 4 - 1;
29:
30:   # If we were asked to print a banner or it has been over 19 rows
31:   if($banner || $rows_since_banner > 19) {
32:     # print out server names
```

```perl
33:    foreach (@slist) {
34:      printf "%".max($minw, length($_))."s ", $_;
35:    }
36:    print "\n";
37:    foreach (@slist) {
38:      # print out status codes
39:      my $str;
40:      foreach my $st (@stlist) { $str .= sprintf("%3d ", $st); }
41:      $str =~ s/\s*$//;
42:      printf "%".max($minw, length($_))."s ", $str;
43:    }
44:    print "\n" . ('-' x 72) . "\n";
45:    $rows_since_banner = 0;
46:  }
47:
48:  # Print out counts for each server/statuscode
49:  foreach (@slist) {
50:    my $str;
51:    foreach my $st (@stlist) { $str.=sprintf("%3d ",$hitcnt->{"$_/$st"}); }
52:    $str =~ s/\s*$//;
53:    printf("%".max($minw, length($_))."s ", $str);
54:  }
55:  $rows_since_banner++;
56:  print "\n";
57: }
58:
59: $SIG{'INT'} = sub { $quit = 1; };
60: $last = [gettimeofday];
61: while(!$quit and my @p = Spread::receive($m, 0.2)) {
62:   if(@p[0] & Spread::REGULAR_MESS()){
63:     # For each regular message, parse the common log
64:     if(@p[5] =~ /^(\S+)          # remote host address
65:                  \s(\S+)         # remote user
66:                  \s(\S+)         # local user
67:                  \s\[([^\]]+)\]  # date
68:                  \s"([^"]+)"     # request
69:                  \s(\d+)         # status
70:                  \s((?:\d+|-))   # size
71:                  \s"([^"]+)"     # referrer
72:                /x) {;
73:       my ($raddr, $ruser, $luser, $date, $req, $status, $size, $ref) =
74:         ($1,    $2,     $3,     $4,    $5,   $6,      $7,    $8);
75:       (my $lhost = @p[1]) =~ s/^#[^#]+#//;
76:
77:       # account for the server and status code, if either is "new" we
78:       # must issue a new header/banner
```

```
79:        $banner = 1 unless exists $servers{$lhost};
80:        $banner = 1 unless exists $statuses{$status};
81:        $servers{$lhost} = 1;
82:        $statuses{$status} = 1;
83:        # tally the server/status hit
84:        $hits{"$lhost/$status"}++;
85:      }
86:    }
87:    if(tv_interval($last) > $interval) {
88:      # if $interval has elapsed, print out our tallies and zero them
89:      pretty_hits(\%servers, \%statuses, \%hits, $banner);
90:      $banner = 0;
91:      undef %hits;
92:      $last = [gettimeofday];
93:    }
94: }
95:
96: Spread::disconnect($m);
```

The wwwstat program provides the insight we're missing. Let's take it for spin on a small web cluster of three nodes serving only dynamic page traffic. Output from wwwstat is as follows:

	www-va-1				www-va-2				www-va-3			
2:	200	302	404	500	200	302	404	500	200	302	404	500
3:	---	---	---	---	---	---	---	---	---	---	---	---
4:	51	3	0	0	69	2	0	0	54	2	0	0
5:	40	0	0	0	57	1	0	0	48	2	0	0
6:	68	2	0	0	70	4	0	0	55	2	0	0
7:	68	2	0	0	94	2	0	0	71	1	0	0
8:	54	2	0	0	60	0	0	0	53	1	1	0
9:	61	1	0	0	69	2	0	0	64	0	0	0
10:	99	4	0	0	92	5	0	0	101	1	0	0
11:	70	4	0	0	89	4	0	0	83	3	0	0
12:	65	2	0	0	57	1	0	0	49	1	0	0
13:	59	4	0	0	60	2	0	0	56	2	0	0
14:	48	3	0	0	50	2	0	0	46	4	0	0
15:	44	2	0	1	58	1	0	0	44	1	0	0
16:	49	0	0	0	64	3	0	0	54	3	0	0
17:	54	6	0	0	50	2	0	0	54	2	0	0
18:	94	1	0	0	84	0	0	0	76	4	0	0

Hey! There's an internal server error on www-va-1 (line 15)! Someone should take a look at that. Most importantly, however, we can see that the number of requests per time interval to each node in the cluster is distributed reasonably well (uniformly).

Now, the wwwstat tool certainly can be cleaned up a bit. The rendering could be prettier, and the information could be more thorough. However, it demonstrates that we can whip up a tool to suit our needs in short order as long as the information we need to analyze is at our fingertips. Getting the information here was cake (lines 19-22, 61, and 96).

This example was fun, but you may say, "I can look on my load balancer and see this information." You are absolutely right, if you (as a developer or sys admin) have access to that load balancer.

Demonstrating this passive analysis technique with web logs in common log format was simple and useful. That is certainly not the be-all, end-all of what can be accomplished. Spread is a simple communications medium, and publishers can publish anything they want. You could change the common log format to a custom one that includes the time it took to service each web request. With this modification, you could augment wwwstat to display average, minimum, and maximum service times (much like iostat does).

> **Note**
>
> Sadly, to get resolution finer than 1 second in Apache 1.3 (you'd want millisecond or microsecond granularity), you have to modify the mod_log_config source code. If you don't code C, or have never touched Apache source or Apache module source, this is a fabulous first project. It is short, simple, and amazingly useful. Apache 2.0 already provides sub-second timing granularity.

Aside from web logs, you could have your database abstraction layer log to a spread group on every statement execution and report the query being run and the time it took to execute it.

Outside the monitoring space (in a manner of speaking) is the capability to track user click-streams in real-time, regardless of the servers they access.

Passive Log Aggregation for Metrics

When you spend a lot of time in a large architecture you begin to realize that looking up at the system from the ground floor is a great way to troubleshoot problems. It also happens to be one of the worst ways to find problems. Your vision is shortsighted, and your view on the system as a whole is poor. So, the best architects and engineers have a healthy respect for the down-and-dirty details, as well as a macroscopic view of the business.

When I say "macroscopic view of the business" I don't mean accounting, HR, cleanliness of the office space—we haven't left the technical landscape. I'm referring to technical business metrics. The marketing initiatives, the new registrations, the number of orders placed, and so on. These elements make the business money and, in the end, pay your salary, so *you* better be monitoring them. Somebody has to see the big picture, and if you are the CTO or the director of operations, that is your job. If you aren't and you report to someone, there is no excuse for you to not see the big picture—that's the path to the D and C levels.

The key here is not to lose your analytical *engineering-focused* thinking. So, you might ask (though I hope not) what I hear from developers and administrators when I speak on this subject. "What good does it do me to see how many orders were placed yesterday or last hour?" "Who cares how many new customers we have as long as the number is positive?" "No one tells me when a new marketing initiative starts, that's handled by another department; besides, what does it have to do with my job?"

There are many answers to these questions. Usually they are delivered after a smack in the head of the person who asked them in the first place. The most obvious reason is because you should care what is going on. The other reason is because you are in the unique position to see an even bigger picture.

On the nontechnical side of the business, you better believe they have reports on every single business related metric. Chances are good that the data for those reports mostly comes from the logs and databases in your architecture. So...you can see those reports, too. However, the business side doesn't see all the technical reports such as bandwidth utilization, database query volume, and cache hit rates on your static content servers.

By seeing all of this data at a high level, you can learn what to expect. You see normal trends and correlations between metrics that fall more on the business side to metrics that fall more on the technical side. Understanding the relationship between these things can lead to profound insights.

So, where are we going with this? Am I saying that you should have daily reports of all the important business metrics and technical metrics in one place so that you can see the picture? Well, obviously, but that's the tip of the iceberg. With centralized real-time logging you can get reports by the minute and see trends as they form. Although understanding a trend that is just forming is pretty much impossible, if you have familiarized yourself with all the big picture data and understand what the relationships between all the metrics look like in a healthy system, you can spot an unhealthy situation as it is gestating.

Visualizing Data with RRDtool

If you have ever worked with large number sets, the first thing you learned was that visualization tools are priceless. I can look at the number of octets sent every minute of the day from each of our 10 web servers (1440 times 10) or I can look at a simple graph. Both are useful, but I certainly want to start with the graph—if everything looks okay, I have no need to look deeper. Graphs, specifically those that share a common axis (such as time), make it easy to correlate cause and effect, which can be difficult when there are multiple causes and effects spanning several systems.

Let's stay with our news site as an example. Most operations groups use graphing as an invaluable data correlation tool. Typical graph sources are bandwidth and errors on each switch port, as well as CPU, memory, load, and disk utilization on each server. These graphs are an invaluable resource when attempting to diagnose performance issues and the effects that new strains (new pushed services or code) have caused.

Suppose that we launch a new service that offers users a listing of the most popular "next page visited" list based on the site-local page loaded by all people who were viewing the page in question directly prior. In other words, if 1,000 users viewed page A and then performed some action to deliver them to another page on the site, all those pages would be ranked by popularity and displayed on page A. Implementing this in a scalable manner will be left as an exercise to the reader (read the rest of the book first).

The service has been launched and metrics are down by 5%. Why and what metrics? These are questions posed to senior technologists, and having a firm grasp of how to arrive at a solution quickly is a valuable skill. New user registrations are following an expected trend, the bandwidth is up by 2%, as well as the number of hits on the site. However, the advertising click-through is down by 5%. This is the landscape for our puzzle. How can all these system metrics be up and the business be down?

To answer this question we need more data—or an aware operations team. However, we also can have data coming out our ears, and it all will be useless unless we find a good means of visualizing it…. Enter Tobias Oetiker and his useful RRDtool (http://people.ee.ethz.ch/~oetiker/webtools/rrdtool/).

A Bit About RRDtool

The more I work with RRDtool, the more I realize that it is utterly obtuse, and yet irreplaceable. RRDtool stands for *Round Robin Database tool*, and it allows streamlined data metric retention and visualization. Perhaps the most common use of this type of tool is for monitoring the activity on network interface cards on routers, switches, and even hosts. RRDtool will allow you to create a database of tracked metrics with a specific expected frequency and well-defined database retention policies, feed new metrics into the database, and then generate both ugly and stunning visualizations of the data therein.

Like many engineering tools, RRDtool provides an engineer with just enough options to require constant access to the manual page and defaults/samples that are designed to convince people that engineers don't know what really looks good. However, it is powerful and flexible and a tremendous asset to any monitoring suite.

The ins and outs of RRDtool could fill the pages of at least one book, and it simply isn't important to understand how to install, configure, and use RRDtool for me to illustrate its usefulness. Luckily, the documentation for RRDtool and the various open source products that use it are excellent starting points.

We will walk through a simple usage of RRDtool and show how the additional collected information can help us solve the "metrics are up and business is down" problem posed earlier.

Setting Up Our Databases

The first thing we'll do is set up some RRDs to track the metrics we're interested in. Note that you must be interested in these things before the problems occur; otherwise, you will see only the data representing the problematic situation and not historical data for comparison. In other words, we should set up the metric collection as part of launching the service, not as a part of troubleshooting.

We want to track the number of bytes in and out of our web environment and the number of page hits by server, error code, and user registration status. To make this example shorter, we'll set up traffic metrics and page hits by user registration status here and leave the rest as an exercise to the reader.

For all our information we want second to second accurate data. However, updating all these databases once a second for each metric can be expensive, and it really doesn't add much value. Basically, we want to be able to see spikes and anomalies better. For example, if something bad happens for one minute out of the hour, we don't want to see it averaged into 60 minutes worth of data. There is a trade-off here, and I'm giving you some insight into choosing a lower bound on the data collection period. If a graph or set of graphs is displayed, what is the amount of time that it will take to fully understand what we're seeing? This includes the big picture, trends, identifying anomalies, and correlating them across data sources. On a good day, it takes me about two minutes, so I collect data twice that often.

The next questions are "how long will this data be retained?" and "how far back must be it available on 60-second intervals?" These are much tougher questions. Typically, I retain information for two years when I set up RRD files. If I want data back farther than that, it is never needed on a granularity finer than a week, so archiving could actually be done by taking RRD-generated graphs and saving one a week forever.

To create the RRDs for the inbound byte counters and outbound byte counters to be used to measure overall traffic, we create one RRD for each (though multiple metrics can be stored in a single RRD, I find juggling them easier when they are one-to-one):

```
rrdtool create /var/rrds/web-inbytes.rrd --step 60 DS:bytes:COUNTER:60:0:U \
    RRA:AVERAGE:0.5:1:5760 RRA:MAX:0.5:1:5760 RRA:MIN:0.5:1:5760 \
    RRA:AVERAGE:0.5:10:4032 RRA:AVERAGE:0.5:60:5376 \
    RRA:AVERAGE:0.5:120:8064 RRA:MAX:0.5:120:8064 RRA:MIN:0.5:120:8064
rrdtool create /var/rrds/web-outbytes.rrd --step 60 DS:bytes:COUNTER:60:0:U \
    RRA:AVERAGE:0.5:1:5760 RRA:MAX:0.5:1:5760 RRA:MIN:0.5:1:5760 \
    RRA:AVERAGE:0.5:10:4032 RRA:AVERAGE:0.5:60:5376 \
    RRA:AVERAGE:0.5:120:8064 RRA:MAX:0.5:120:8064 RRA:MIN:0.5:120:8064
```

We will create RRD files for tracking hits by registered versus unregistered users similarly:

```
rrdtool create /var/rrds/web-visitorhits.rrd --step 60 DS:hits:COUNTER:60:0:U \
    RRA:AVERAGE:0.5:1:5760 RRA:MAX:0.5:1:5760 RRA:MIN:0.5:1:5760 \
    RRA:AVERAGE:0.5:10:4032 RRA:AVERAGE:0.5:60:5376 \
    RRA:AVERAGE:0.5:120:8064 RRA:MAX:0.5:120:8064 RRA:MIN:0.5:120:8064
rrdtool create /var/rrds/web-userhits.rrd --step 60 DS:hits:COUNTER:60:0:U \
    RRA:AVERAGE:0.5:1:5760 RRA:MAX:0.5:1:5760 RRA:MIN:0.5:1:5760 \
    RRA:AVERAGE:0.5:10:4032 RRA:AVERAGE:0.5:60:5376 \
    RRA:AVERAGE:0.5:120:8064 RRA:MAX:0.5:120:8064 RRA:MIN:0.5:120:8064
```

The preceding statements maintain single step (60 seconds) averages, minimums, and maximums for 5760 intervals (4 days), 10 step (10 minute) averages for 4032 intervals (28 days or 4 weeks), 60 step (60 minute) averages for 5376 intervals (224 days or 32 weeks), and lastly 120 step (2 hour) averages, minimums and maximums for 8064 intervals (2 years).

Collecting Metrics

Perhaps the most challenging aspect of managing stores of metrics is collecting the data in the first place. There are two categories of metrics in the world: those that can be queried via SNMP (Simple Network Management Protocol) and those that cannot. Many a tool sits on top of RRDtool that can collect SNMP-based metrics for you. Cacti (http://www.cacti.net/) is one such tool that manages to make its way into production a lot around here.

Querying data from SNMP is simple—there are supporting libraries or extensions for almost every common programming language. I highly recommend using one of the many prebuilt packages to do automated metric collection from all your SNMP-capable devices. Many of these packages even automate the creation and population of the RRD files. For now, we'll set up a simple cron job that updates the two byte counters from the router that sits in front of our web architecture (see Listing 9.3). (Its IP address is 10.10.10.1.)

Listing 9.3   `simple_out_rrdupdate.sh`—**Simplistic RRDtool Update Script**

```sh
#!/bin/sh
FILE=$1
AGENT=$2
OID=$3

if test ! -f "/var/rrds/$FILE.rrd"; then
  echo No such RRD file
  exit
fi


COMMUNITY=public
BYTES='snmpget -c $COMMUNITY -v 2c -Oqv $AGENT $OID'
if test "$BYTES" -le "0"; then
  echo Bad SNMP fetch;
  exit
fi
rrdtool update /var/rrds/$FILE.rrd -t bytes N:$BYTES
crontab entry:
* * * * * /usr/local/bin/simple_oid_rrdupdate.sh web-inbytes 10.10.10.1 \
        .1.3.6.1.2.1.2.2.1.10.1
* * * * * /usr/local/bin/simple_oid_rrdupdate.sh web-outbytes 10.10.10.1 \
.1.3.6.1.2.1.2.2.1.16.1
```

It should be clear that you would not want to run a cron job every minute for every single metric you monitor. This specific example is for brevity. Additionally, the SNMP OID `.1.3.6.1.2.1.2.2.1.10.1` is in no way intuitive. It represents the inbound octets (old networking lingo for bytes) on interface 1 of the specified device. Any SNMP collection tool worth its weight in electrons will make OIDs human readable and easy to find.

Now that we have statistics being collected (and we'll assume we have been collecting them all along), we can move on to something that is a bit more obtuse (if that's possible). Collecting SNMP metrics is easy because all the tools do all the complicated actions described previously for you, and you just point it at a device, or set of devices, and click Go. This can be done because SNMP is an established protocol, and the OIDs (the long dot-delimited numeric) are well established as either an industrywide standard or are well documented by the vendor of the device. Graphing other stuff is not so simple.

To graph the rate of page loads (hits) for visitors to the site, as well as for registered users, we need to know more than any vendor could generally know. Specifically, we need to know how we classify a loaded page as being loaded by a registered user (in our case a user with an account that is currently "signed in" while viewing the page) or a visitor (anyone else).

To do this, we can alter the `wwwstat` program we wrote before to track the hits and update the RRD files. In our web application we will use the second field of the common log format (remote user) to represent the current viewing user. It is in the form `V-{VISITORID}` for visitors and `U-{USERID}` for users. We place it in the remote user field of the log format because it will not change the format and thus will not break existing processes that read those logs. The remote user field is relatively useless these days because many clients don't support RFC1413, and most sites don't attempt to perform RFC1413 (ident) lookups. This means that we simply need to monitor the live log stream and tally logs with a remote user starting with 'V' in the `web-visitorhits` file and everything else in the `web-userhits` file. We do this in `userhits2rrd.pl` seen in Listing 9.4.

Listing 9.4 `userhits2rrd.pl`—**Updating RRD Files with External Data**

```perl
01: #!/usr/bin/perl
02:
03: use strict;
04: use Spread;
05: use Getopt::Long;
06: use Time::HiRes qw/tv_interval gettimeofday/;
07: use RRDs;
08:
09: use vars qw /$daemon @group $interval $last $quit %ahits/;
10:
11: GetOptions("d=s" => \$daemon,
12:            "g=s" => \@group,
13:            "i=i" => \$interval);
14:
15: $interval ||= 60;
16: my ($m, $g) = Spread::connect( { spread_name => "$daemon",
17:                                   private_name => "tt_$$" } );
18: die "Could not connect to Spread at $daemon" unless $m;
19: die "Could not join group" unless(grep {Spread::join($m, $_)} @group);
20:
```

```
21: $ahits{visitors} = $ahits{users} = 0;
22: sub tally {
23:    # This should be called every $interval seconds
24:    RRDs::update("/var/rrds/web-visitorhits.rrd",
25:                  "--template", "hits", "N:$ahits{visitors}");
26:    RRDs::update("/var/rrds/web-userhits.rrd",
27:                  "--template", "hits", "N:$ahits{users}");
28: }
29:
30: $SIG{'INT'} = sub { $quit = 1; };
31: $last = [gettimeofday];
32: while(!$quit and my @p = Spread::receive($m, 0.2)) {
33:    if(@p[0] & Spread::REGULAR_MESS()){
34:       # For each regular message, parse the common log
35:       if(@p[5] =~ /^(\S+)          # remote host address
36:                   \s(\S+)          # remote user
37:                   \s(\S+)          # local user
38:                   \s\[(([^\]]+)\]  # date
39:                   \s"([^"]+)"      # request
40:                   \s(\d+)          # status
41:                   \s((?:\d+|-))    # size
42:                   \s"([^"]+)"      # referrer
43:                   /x) {;
44:          my ($raddr, $ruser, $luser, $date, $req, $status, $size, $ref) =
45:             ($1,     $2,     $3,     $4,    $5,   $6,      $7,    $8);
46:
47:          if($ruser =~ /^V/) { $ahits{"visitors"}++; }
48:          } else             { $ahits{"users"}++;    }
49:       }
50:    }
51:    if(tv_interval($last) > $interval) {
52:       tally();
53:       $last = [gettimeofday];
54:    }
55: }
56:
57: Spread::disconnect($m);
```

Now we run the userhits2rrd.pl script, and data collection and storage into RRD is done. The reason this is substantially more complicated than SNMP is that there are no good generic tools to collect your custom business metrics. Each time you want to track a new data source that isn't SNMP capable, you either have to glue it into an SNMP agent or query via custom logic as we have done here. These metrics are absolutely useful and warrant maintaining one-off collection scripts for each of the business metrics you want to track. In the end, you'll find that your scripts aren't very complicated, aren't all that different from one another, and will yield substantial intra-organizational reuse.

Visualizing Data Through RRDtool

So, we're collecting metrics, but this doesn't help us solve our problem. We must be able to visualize it for it to prove useful. Like everything else with RRDtool, the visualization can do exactly what you want, but the user interface to do it is 100% engineer and 0% designer. We have a web wrapper around most of the RRD graphs we can generate, which makes them quite nice; but I'll show you the "under the hood" graph generation here so that you can have a healthy respect for why someone should wrap it with a simple web interface.

To generate a graph that is ugly, we can call `rrdtool` in its simple form:

```
rrdtool graph \
    ugly.png -title "web traffic" -a PNG \
    --vertical-label "bits/sec" -width 800 -height 500 \
    "DEF:inbytes=/var/rrds/web-inbytes.rrd:inbytes:AVERAGE" \
    "DEF:outbytes=/var/rrds/web-outbytes.rrd:inbytes:AVERAGE" \
    "CDEF:realinbits=inbytes,8,*" \
    "CDEF:realoutbits=outbytes,8,*" \
    "AREA:realinbits#0000ff:Inbound Traffic" \
    "LINE1:realoutbits#ff0000:Outbound Traffic" \
    --start -172800
```

Yes, that's the simple form. It pulls the in and out byte metrics over the last 172,800 seconds (two days) from their respective RRD files, multiplies them by 8 (to get bits), and graphs the inbound in a blue area curve and the outbound in a red line curve.

It produces something usable, but so ugly I refuse to grace this book with it. So, we will consult a visualization expert and show the traffic sent to the Internet on the positive y-axis and the traffic received from the Internet on the negative y-axis (the total hits being the area in between). Additionally, we will add some gradient pizzazz and end up with the following (utterly obtuse) command that produces Figure 9.5:

```
rrdtool graph webtraffic.png -title "web traffic" -a PNG
    --vertical-label "bits / sec"
    --width 450 --height 180
    DEF:outbytes=/var/rrds/web-outbytes.rrd:outbytes:AVERAGE
    DEF:inbytes=/var/rrds/web-inbytes.rrd:inbytes:AVERAGE
    "CDEF:realout=outbytes,8,*,-1,*" \
    "CDEF:realin=inbytes,8,*" \
    "CDEF:realout1=outbytes,8,*,-1,*,3,*,4,/" \
    "CDEF:realout_h=outbytes,8,*" \
    "CDEF:realout2=outbytes,8,*,-1,*,2,*,4,/" \
    "CDEF:realin3=inbytes,8,*,1,*,4,/" \
    "CDEF:realoutb=outbytes,8,*,-1,*" \
    "CDEF:realinb=inbytes,8,*" \
    "CDEF:realin_h=inbytes,8,*" \
    "CDEF:realin1=inbytes,8,*,3,*,4,/" \
    "CDEF:realin2=inbytes,8,*,2,*,4,/" \
    "CDEF:realout3=outbytes,8,*,-1,*,1,*,4,/" \
```

```
"AREA:realout#ffaa44:" \
"AREA:realin#ffaa44:" \
"AREA:realout1#ffcc55:" \
"AREA:realin1#ffcc55:" \
"AREA:realout2#ffee77:" \
"AREA:realin2#ffee77:" \
"AREA:realout3#ffff88:" \
"AREA:realin3#ffff88:" \
"LINE1:realoutb#888833:web outbound traffic" \
"LINE1:realinb#888833:web inbound traffic" \
--start -172800
```

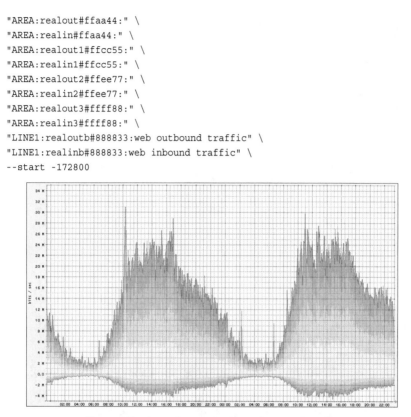

Figure 9.5 A graph representing web network traffic.

Now let's graph our user hit metrics using the same technique (shown in Figure 9.6):

```
rrdtool graph webhits.png --title "online users" -a PNG \
    --vertical-label "users" -width 800 -height 500 \
    DEF:uhits=/var/rrds/web-userhits.rrd:hits:AVERAGE \
    DEF:vhits=/var/rrds/web-visitorhits.rrd:hits:AVERAGE \
    "CDEF:realv=vhits" \
    "CDEF:realv3=vhits,1,*,4,/" \
    "CDEF:realvb=vhits" \
    "CDEF:realv_h=vhits" \
    "CDEF:realv1=vhits,3,*,4,/" \
    "CDEF:realv2=vhits,2,*,4,/" \
    "CDEF:realu=uhits,-1,*" \
    "CDEF:realu1=uhits,-1,*,3,*,4,/" \
    "CDEF:realu_h=uhits" \
    "CDEF:realu2=uhits,-1,*,2,*,4,/" \
    "CDEF:realub=uhits,-1,*" \
```

```
"CDEF:realu3=uhits,-1,*,1,*,4,/" \
"AREA:realu#ffaa44:" \
"AREA:realv#ffaa44:" \
"AREA:realu1#ffcc55:" \
"AREA:realv1#ffcc55:" \
"AREA:realu2#ffee77:" \
"AREA:realv2#ffee77:" \
"AREA:realu3#ffff88:" \
"AREA:realv3#ffff88:" \
"LINE1:realub#888833:Registered Users" \
"LINE1:realvb#888833:Visitors" \
--start -172800
```

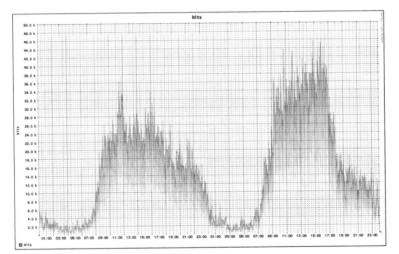

Figure 9.6 A graph representing web page-load traffic.

Being Hit in the Face with Data

Back to our problem, so that we don't wander aimlessly without purpose any longer: New user registrations are following an expected trend, the bandwidth is up by 2%, as is the number of hits on the site. However, the advertising click-through is down by 5%.

As our problem describes, we should see an increase in bandwidth by about 2% from the previous day. Figure 9.5 shows something that looks reasonably consistent with the problem description.

In Figure 9.6, however, we see something entirely unexpected. We were told that the hits on the site have increased by 2% as well, but the data for today (the right hump) is substantially more than 2% larger than yesterday (the left hump). So, either someone doesn't know what he is talking about, or that person's definition of "hit" doesn't match our definition of "hit."

Indeed this is the case. If we look at our script, it tallies all log lines it sees as a hit for either a registered user or a visitor. It does not limit the count to those requests serviced by a 200 HTTP response code (as is common in some reporting tools). Although this doesn't identify the problem, we clearly see that a problem of some type is occurring today that did not occur yesterday—progress.

If we believe that this graph shows dramatically different trends from what the problem report indicates because of the response codes, we should be looking at graphs of response codes.

Figure 9.7 shows a graph of pages served over time broken down by HTTP response code. The problem couldn't be more obvious now. We are throwing 404 (page not found errors) now, and we were not doing so yesterday. Looking at these graphs to come to this conclusion took only a few seconds. The data behind most problems, when visualized correctly, will hit you like a ton of bricks.

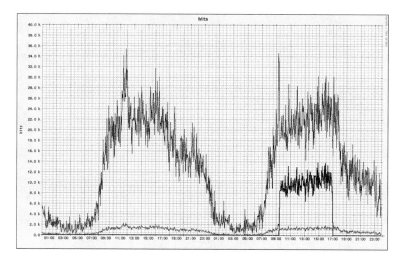

Figure 9.7   A graph representing web page-load traffic by HTTP response code.

Generic Uses

We've talked a lot about web logging. Web logs are important in their own way; however, a smoothly running architecture has a plethora of logs encompassing just about every possible aspect of the system.

If you log in to a server that you don't pay much attention to and spend about 15 minutes poring over the various logs on the machine, you are almost guaranteed to find something out of line. Modern UNIX and Windows deployments have so many moving parts that it is easy to lose track. Centralized logging can provide a single portal through which the normal day-to-day operations can be audited.

When a machine begins to exhibit unexpected behavior, the first thing that any systems engineer (developer, DBA, network admin, systems admin) will do is log in and look around. However, if the machine is truly misbehaving, we often find ourselves unable to access it; but, you could access the logs, if they were being written elsewhere.

To any seasoned systems admin, I'm describing all the benefits of using `syslog` to log events to a remote logging server. I hope that reading the previous sections of this chapter enlightened you regarding what can be accomplished when logging is performed via a multiple-subscriber communications medium such as Spread.

10

The Right Tool for the Job

THIS IS PERHAPS THE MOST IMPORTANT chapter of the book. This chapter goes into depth where we did not in previous chapters with the hope of lending insight into real problem solving as well as providing a useful base for a real implementation. Although we present a specific solution to a specific problem, this chapter illustrates some valuable architectural lessons and highlights mistakes often made in feature design.

Hopefully, this begs the first question. Why do I say "feature design" and not "web application design?" This has a simple answer: I have a web application. We've discussed various aspects of this web application in several of the preceding chapters—it has been designed. We are now challenged with adding something to it, hence feature design. This is the most common vector of development and as such the most common ground for mistakes.

Although some web applications have been redesigned several times from the ground up, that should never be a goal for anyone. Web applications ideally are designed once, and during that design you have the opportunity to screw everything up...once. It is fundamental that the initial design be a good one because it is the basis for all other development work. This leads into the rest of this web application's life. Every day, week, month, and year, there will be new business problems to solve that require the design and development of new features. And every time you will have opportunities to make mistakes.

This may sound intimidating, but remember that these design decisions are smaller and often easy to recover from. Feature redesign is much less intimidating than core application redesign. The trick is realizing when things are improperly designed and ensuring that they are refactored. Although these design decisions are significantly less important than the design of the core web application, bad design is still possible, and death by pin pricks is a bad way to die.

Who's Online?

Throughout this book we have used a news site as a basis for the examples. On this site there are articles and commentary, and presumably many people view the content. A recent popular trend in online services is the development of a social community where like-minded people can virtually "hang out." On some sites, the overall content is so focused that the simple fact that a user is visiting puts him in the same community as every other visitor. A news site is not like that.

News sites have a tremendous amount of content, and the reader communities are many and overlapping. The articles represent political opinions, ethnic and racial interests, as well as geographically focused information. As a white male who reads the technology section, you might imagine I am not in the same community as a Hispanic woman who only reads about the political activities in Washington D.C. However, she is my neighbor, so we do have tremendous commonalities.

How do we establish and represent a sense of community to the visitors of our news site? The approach is a basic one and a spectacular basis for many useful website features as well as market research opportunities. We will track who is viewing each page and expose to the visitor the other users who are viewing the same pages.

The premise is that when I view a page, I am considered to be actively viewing that page for the next 30 minutes or until I load another page. On each page there will be a buddy list that will dynamically update with the 30 most recent viewers of that page or (for more popular pages) there will be a count of current readers. Users will be allowed to expose their profiles publicly, and from the buddy list you can see information (if the user allows it) about your peer readers.

Technical Setup

Although we have discussed Oracle and PostgreSQL previously in this book, MySQL is an excellent and tremendously popular RDBMS solution for websites. Just for the sake of diversity (and as a reminder that this book is about techniques and approaches, not products), we will assume that our entire news site has been built atop MySQL.

We want to track the most recently loaded page of each user. This is a trivial exercise using mod_perl because it provides the capability to run code in the log-handling phase of the Apache request. Before we jump into the code, we should figure out what questions we must answer and of what subsystem we will ask them. We need to know the following:

- The total number of users viewing the site
- The total number of users viewing any given dynamic page
- The list of users who last viewed any given dynamic page—we will limit it to the 30 most recent views

To answer these questions, we store information (such as user ID or username) on each user who has loaded any dynamic page within the last 30 minutes. When a user loads a new object, her information is tracked on the new dynamic page and not on the previous dynamic page. This will tell us at any point in time who last viewed each object. After 30 minutes pass without the user loading a dynamic page, we will consider her offline, and her information should not contribute to the current viewers of the site.

Why do we want to do this? The first and foremost reason is because the business (and likely marketing) thought it would be a product differentiator and both attract and retain more users. Knowing the trend of online users can tell you (without deep log analysis) how you are growing and can allow you to relatively gauge the captivity of your site.

This seems like a rather simple problem. We use MySQL already to drive our site, and it does so with gusto. All we need to do is add a table to MySQL called recent_hits and stick users into that table as they load dynamic pages on the site; the SQL to achieve that follows:

```
CREATE TABLE recent_hits (
  SiteUserID INT NOT NULL PRIMARY KEY,
  URL VARCHAR(255) NOT NULL,
  Hitdate DATETIME NOT NULL
);
CREATE INDEX recent_hits_url_idx on recent_hits(URL,Hitdate);
CREATE INDEX recent_hits_hitdate_idx on recent_hits(Hitdate);
```

To track new page loads, we simply REPLACE INTO the table with all the columns filled in. Because this will track users forever, it may be in our best interest to have a periodic administrative task that performs a DELETE FROM recent_hits WHERE Hitdate < SUBDATE(NOW(), INTERVAL 30 MINUTE) to cull rows that are not important. However, because this table will always be strictly limited to the number of users in the database (primary keyed off SiteUserID), this isn't strictly necessary.

When attempting to answer the three questions we posed, we quickly derive simple SQL statements that do the job perfectly:

- Total users:
    ```
    SELECT COUNT(*)
      FROM recent_hits;
      WHERE HITDATE > SUBDATE(NOW(), INTERVAL 30 MINUTE)
    ```

- Total users on a page:
    ```
    SELECT COUNT(*)
      FROM recent_hits
      WHERE HITDATE > SUBDATE(NOW(), INTERVAL 30 MINUTE)
        AND URL = ?;
    ```

- Thirty most recent users on a page:
    ```
    SELECT SiteUserID, Hitdate
      FROM recent_hits
      WHERE HITDATE > SUBDATE(NOW(), INTERVAL 30 MINUTE)
        AND URL = ?
    ORDER BY Hitdate DESC
      LIMIT 30;
    ```

A Quick perl Example

Implementing the previous solution within our application should be an exercise devoid of intensity and challenge. Were our application a `mod_perl` application, we would (after authorizing the user) poke the `SiteUserID` into the Apache connection using `Apache->request->connection->user($SiteUserID)` and provide something like the following for the PerlLogHandler:

```
01: package NewSite::RealtimeExtensionToAppendRequestData;
02: use DBI;
03: use vars qw/$g_dbh $g_sth/;
04:
05: sub handler {
06:   my $r = shift;
07:   return unless($r->connection->user); # bail if no user information.
08:   for ( 1 .. 2 ) {  # Two tries (if the first errors)
09:     eval {
10:       if(!$g_dbh) {
11:         # If we are not connected, connect and prepare our statement.
12:         $g_dbh = DBI->connect("dbi:mysql:database=db;host=dbhost",
13:                               "user", "pw");
14:         $g_sth = $g_dbh->prepare(q{
15:             REPLACE INTO recent_hits
16:                     (SiteUserID, URL, Hitdate)
17:                 VALUES (?,?,NOW()) });
18:       }
19:       # Insert the user and the URI they loaded.
20:       $g_sth->execute($r->connection->user, $r->uri);
21:     };
22:     return unless($@); # No error, we are done.
23:     undef $g_sth;      # Error... drop our statement handle
24:     undef $g_dbh;      #     and our database connection.
25:   }
26: }
27: 1;
```

We can activate this handler by adding the following line to our Apache configuration file:

```
PerlLogHandler NewSite::RealtimeExtensionToAppendRequestData
```

After we do this, during the logging phase Apache/mod_perl will invoke the handler and replace that user's row in the `recent_hits` table with the page she just loaded.

That's Not Fair!

For all the PHP programmers out there screaming "That's not fair!"—relax. Although PHP does not have hooks in all the various phases of the Apache request serving process, if there is a will, there is a way. This should encourage you to not be intimidated by the prospect of bending the tools at hand to your will—after all, they are there to serve you.

The only two clever things in the previous example are

- Changing the apparent authorized user from the Apache perspective
- Performing some action (a database insertion) at the end of the request after the payload has been handed to the client

We will create a PHP extension that provides a `newssite_poke_user` function that updates the user information on the connection servicing the current Apache request. Also, we will hook the request shutdown phase to log to MySQL, which emulates the perl variant's behavior as closely as possible given that PHP lacks the capability to run code in Apache's log handler phase.

To build a PHP extension, you need to create a `config.m4` that indicates how the module should be named and linked and a source file that contains all intelligence. The `config.m4` file follows:

```
01: PHP_ARG_ENABLE(RealtimeExtensionToAppendRequestData,
02:                 NewsSite request logging,
03:   [ --enable-newssite   Enable NewsSite request logging ])
04:
05: if test "$PHP_REALTIMEEXTENSIONTOAPPENDREQUESTDATA" != "no"; then
06:   PHP_NEW_EXTENSION(RealtimeExtensionToAppendRequestData,
07:                 RealtimeExtensionToAppendRequestData.c,
08:                 $ext_shared)
09: fi
10:
11: PHP_ADD_INCLUDE(/opt/ecelerity/3rdParty/include)
12: PHP_ADD_INCLUDE(/opt/ecapache/include)
13:
14: PHP_SUBST(REALTIMEEXTENSIONTOAPPENDREQUESTDATA_SHARED_LIBADD)
15: PHP_ADD_LIBRARY_WITH_PATH(
16:   mysqlclient, /opt/ecelerity/3rdParty/lib/amd64,
17:   REALTIMEEXTENSIONTOAPPENDREQUESTDATA_SHARED_LIBADD)
```

As described in our `config.m4` file, the C source file is called `RealtimeExtensionToAppendRequestData.c`:

```
01: #include "config.h"
02: #include "php.h"
03: #include "SAPI.h"
04: #include <mysql.h>
05: #include <httpd.h>
06:
07: static int is_connected = 0;
08: static MYSQL dbh;
09:
```

```
10: static PHP_FUNCTION(newssite_poke_user) {
11:    long SiteUserID;
12:    char number[32];
13:    request_rec *r;
14:    if(FAILURE == zend_parse_parameters(ZEND_NUM_ARGS() TSRMLS_CC,
15:                                         "l", &SiteUserID))
16:      return;
17:    snprintf(number, sizeof(number), "%ld", SiteUserID);
18:    /* Stick our SiteUserID as a string into the */
19:    /* request->connection->user                 */
20:    r = (request_rec *)SG(server_context);
21:    if(r && r->connection)
22:      r->connection->user = ap_pstrdup(r->connection->pool, number);
23:    return;
24: }
25:
26: static function_entry newssite_functions[] = {
27:    PHP_FE(newssite_poke_user, NULL)
28:    { NULL, NULL, NULL },
29: };
30:
31: #define RECENT_HITS_REPLACE \
32:    "REPLACE INTO recent_hits (SiteUserID, URL, Hitdate) " \
33:    "                VALUES (\"%s\", \"%s\", NOW())"
34:
35: static PHP_RSHUTDOWN_FUNCTION(newssite) {
36:    request_rec *r;
37:    char *sql_buffer, *uri_buffer, *user_buffer;
38:    int sql_len, uri_len, user_len, err, should_reattempt = 1;
39:    r = (request_rec *)SG(server_context);
40:
41:    /* If we don't have information to log, leave now. */
42:    if(!r || !r->connection || !r->connection->user || !r->uri)
43:      goto bail;
44:
45:  reattempt:
46:    if(!is_connected) {
47:      if(!mysql_real_connect(&dbh, "dbhost", "user", "pw", "db",
48:                             3308, NULL, 0)) goto bail;
49:      is_connected = 1;
50:    }
51:    /* calculate room we need to escape args and construct SQL */
52:    user_len = strlen(r->connection->user)*2 + 1;
53:    uri_len = strlen(r->uri)*2 + 1;
54:    sql_len = strlen(RECENT_HITS_REPLACE) + user_len + uri_len;
55:    /* allocate space */
56:    user_buffer = emalloc(user_len);
```

```
57:    uri_buffer = emalloc(uri_len);
58:    sql_buffer = emalloc(sql_len);
59:    /* escape our arguments */
60:    user_len = mysql_real_escape_string(&dbh, user_buffer,
61:                                         r->connection->user,
62:                                         strlen(r->connection->user));
63:    uri_len = mysql_real_escape_string(&dbh, uri_buffer,
64:                                        r->uri, strlen(r->uri));
65:    /* Build our SQL */
66:    sql_len = snprintf(sql_buffer, sql_len, RECENT_HITS_REPLACE,
67:                       user_buffer, uri_buffer);
68:    /* Run the query and bail out if there are no errors */
69:    if((err = mysql_real_query(&dbh, sql_buffer, sql_len)) == 0) goto bail;
70:    /* There was a error close down the connection */
71:    mysql_close(&dbh);
72:    is_connected = 0;
73:    if(should_reattempt--) goto reattempt;
74:  bail:
75:    /* We always return success.          */
76:    /* Our failures aren't interesting to others. */
77:    return SUCCESS;
78: }
79:
80: zend_module_entry newssite_module_entry = {
81:    STANDARD_MODULE_HEADER,
82:    "RealtimeExtensionToAppendRequestData",
83:    newssite_functions,
84:    NULL, NULL, NULL,
85:    PHP_RSHUTDOWN(newssite),
86:    NULL,
87:    "1.0",
88:    STANDARD_MODULE_PROPERTIES,
89: };
90:
91: #ifdef COMPILE_DL_REALTIMEEXTENSIONTOAPPENDREQUESTDATA
92: ZEND_GET_MODULE(newssite)
93: #endif
```

This PHP example is longer than the perl one. This is due to current versions of PHP not supporting hooks outside of Apache's actual content handler. This will likely be addressed formally in future versions of PHP because it can be useful. The reason we wrote a module in C for PHP (a PHP extension) is so that we could stick our fingers into parts of the Apache runtime that we cannot do via PHP scripting.

Lines 10–24 illustrate the newssite_poke_user function that will take the SiteUserID argument and place it in the user field of the Apache connection record. This will allow it to be logged via other logging systems already in Apache.

The RSHUTDOWN function (lines 35–78) does all the heavy lifting of performing the REPLACE INTO SQL statements against MySQL.

Lines 80 and on describe the module to PHP when it is loaded from the php.ini file, and the config.m4 file is used by phpize to aide in compiling the extension.

As with all PHP extensions, you place these two files in a directory and run the following:

```
phpize && ./configure && make && make install
```

Then you add to your php.ini:

```
extension=RealtimeExtensionToAppendRequestData.so
```

In the authentication code that drives the website, we will take the resultant SiteUserID of the visiting user and "poke" it into the right spot in Apache's data structures:

```
<?php newssite_poke_user($SiteUserID); ?>
```

Now on any page, users who are logged in will be journaled to the recent_hits table with the URI they are visiting and the time stamp of the request.

Although this may seem intimidating at first, it took me about an hour to write the previous code, set up a MySQL database, create the tables, configure Apache, and test it end-to-end. It is reasonable to expect any C programmer (without knowledge of Apache, PHP, or MySQL) to produce these 94 lines within a day.

Defining Scope

Now that we have an implementation that can track the data we need, we can define the size and scope of the problem. Wait a minute! Perhaps we should have defined the size and scope of the problem before we built a solution!

Based on the results of Chapter 6, "Static Content Serving for Speed and Glory," we are aiming to service 500 new arrivals per second and 2,000 subsequent page views per second. This was an expected average, and we had projected, based off empirical data, needing to support 15% of the overall traffic in the peak hour. This turns out to be a peak of 9,000 dynamic page loads per second in our peak hour.

Each of the pages served will display information about the total number of users online, the number of users viewing the served page, and the last 30 users who viewed that page.

Let's see whether we can get MySQL to do the things we want it to do. With 500 new arrivals per second and a 30-minute window on our user activity, we see an average of 900,000 users online at any given time. However, we must account for the 15% over-all traffic peak hour. That brings this number to 3.24 million users considered to be online at once.

So, we have 9,000 insert/updates per second against the recent_hits table and 9,000 of each of the three previously described SQL queries. Each insert/update will completely invalidate MySQL's query cache. So, the test of the total users online will effectively induce a full table scan over a three million row table. And the other two queries will involve index range scans (one with a sort). You might think at first that the latter queries that are limited by URLs will be efficient; however, popular URLs will have many rows in the range scan, and, obviously, the same URLs will be queried more often for results. In other words, popular URLs will induce a greater number of insert/updates and queries and as such will perform worse because more data must be digested to answer the queries.

In my tests, by pushing on this implementation I was able to achieve around 800 operations per second. An operation in this case consists of the three queries used to display information on the page followed by the insert/update query used to track the page view. Eight hundred is a far cry from 9,000. Clearly this was not well thought out.

Stepping Back

Clearly, we need to step back from our proposed solution and revisit the problem. The problem was clearly stated and mentioned no requirement that we use an RDBMS to solve it. Why did we choose to use MySQL? Simply put, because it was there. MySQL drives our site; we use it for retrieving information about users and the page content, so it only seemed natural to leverage the existing infrastructure for this task.

The questions being asked are acutely painful for a relational database. Why? ACID. Quite frankly, these semantics are of little importance in providing this specific feature. Specifically, durability is not required. The information being used to compose the "who's online" display is only relevant for a 30-minute window of time. Isolation has no importance either as the operations are effectively single-row manipulations of a single table. Consistency and atomicity are the same thing in this situation because there are no views on the data, and all the data modifications are the result of single-statement transactions. Basically, there is no need to use SQL for this.

There are several fundamental problems with the previously offered solution:

- Most databases do not keep an accurate cardinality for tables or index ranges. This means (even ignoring the `Hitdate` limitation) that `SELECT COUNT(*) FROM RECENT_HITS` and `SELECT COUNT(*) FROM RECENT_HITS WHERE URL=?` require a significant amount of work.

- A statement such as `SELECT SiteUserID FROM RECENT_HITS WHERE URL=? ORDER BY Hitdate DESC LIMIT 30` will perform a full sort of the resultset despite the index on `Hitdate` and the `LIMIT`.

- The method in which logging was instrumented happens serially with the delivery of content. This means that if, for some reason, the `REPLACE INTO` statements were to slow down, the whole site would come screeching to a halt when the desired behavior would be to instead display slightly outdated information while the system catches up.

It is important to note that these requirements are in addition to the already demanding requirements of the site. The previous tests were performed against idle hardware in the best of conditions. If I was to repeat the tests and actually push a MySQL-based solution into production, I predict the end of the website moments later.

Thinking Outside the Box

The only information we really need to solve this problem is who is viewing which page—in real-time. Note that the slow part of the application before was the direct logging to a database. There was nothing egregiously bad about poking the SiteUserID into the logs. In fact, it means that all the information we need is in the logs.

Glancing back at Chapter 9, "Juggling Logs and Other Circus Tricks," note that all these logs flying across our network and subscribing to the log stream are effectively free. This is a crucially important mental step in the problem solving.

One of the serious bottlenecks in the previously posed solution was that the logging of the page view to the recent_hits table was synchronous with the serving of the page. Even though we made a specific point to engineer the logging of that information after the page was served to the end-user, the fact that the Apache resource used to serve the page will not be available to service another request until the SQL command is processed is a recipe for disaster. By processing the page views from the log stream passively, we still achieve near real-time accuracy while ensuring that no slowness in the logging of such data can ever slow down the application. In the event of an unexpected surge of traffic, the only possible negative effect is that the information lags "reality" by a small margin until the back-end layer can catch up.

This, of course, does not solve the issue that MySQL is simply "too slow" to provide this service to your application. I put "too slow" in quotation marks because that is the type of speak you would hear from someone casually describing the problem. The truth of the matter is that MySQL is not at all too slow; it is inappropriate. MySQL is simply the wrong tool for this job.

We need something that is less expensive than a database. Preferably something that doesn't touch storage and has data structures that make it easy (computationally inexpensive) to answer the exact questions we are asking.

Choosing a Platform

The first step to implementing a solution is to choose the platform on which it will be built. We chose MySQL unsuccessfully, but now we have revised the approach to be driven by passive log analysis. We already have a system called spreadlogd that is passively collecting all of our logs via Spread. It seems natural that because spreadlogd is privy to all the information necessary it be considered as a platform for supporting this new service.

Spreadlogd already has the infrastructure for subscribing to mod_log_spread log channels as well as supporting loadable modules (extensible in C and perl). Because this needs to perform rather well (9,000 requests/second), we'll approach this problem in C so that we have better control over the data structures that will manage our 3.24 million "online" users.

Spreadlogd's module API provides three hook points: initialization, logline, and shutdown. Initialization and shutdown are each called once in rather obvious places, and logline is called for each log entry seen. Additionally, spreadlogd has a multi-indexed skiplist data structure that will allow us to store hit information in an ideal form.

Let's start by setting up an online.h header that will house some defaults and simple structures to hold the information we need to track:

```
01: #ifndef _ONLINE_H_
02: #define _ONLINE_H_
03:
04: #include "sld_config.h"
05: #include "module.h"
06: #include "echash.h"
07: #include "nethelp.h"
08: #include "skip_heap.h"
09:
10: #define MAX_AGE 30*60
11: #define MAX_USER_INFO 30
12: #define DEFAULT_PORT 8989
13: #define DEFAULT_ADDRESS "*"
14:
15: typedef struct urlcount {
16:   char *URL;                /* The URL, so we only store one copy  */
17:   unsigned int cnt;         /* count of users who last viewed this */
18: } urlcount_t;
19:
20: typedef struct hit {
21:   unsigned long long SiteUserID;  /* The viewer's ID */
22:   char *URL;                      /* The URL, refs urls */
23:   time_t Hitdate;                 /* the time of the hit */
24: } hit_t;
25:
26: void online_service(int fd, short event, void *vnl);
27: urlcount_t *get_url(const char *url, int len);
28: void cull_old_hits();
29: struct skiplistnode *get_first_hit_for_url(const char *url);
30: unsigned int get_current_online_count();
31:
32: #endif
```

Although C is always a bit more lengthy than we'd like it to be, it certainly won't do anything we don't tell it to. Outside the run-of-the-mill C header stuff, in lines 10–13 we can see declarations for the 30-minute timeout, the interest in only the last 30 users, and a default listing address for the "who's online" service we will be exposing. Lines 15–18 describe the urlcount_t type that will hold a URL and the number of users (just a count) whose last viewed page was this URL. Lines 20–24 describe the `hit_t` structure that tracks the time of the last URL loaded by a given user (identified by `SiteUserID`). Lines 26–30 just expose some functions that will be used to drive the service portion of the module. All these functions' roles should be obvious except for `get_first_hit_for_url`, which we will cover later.

Although we haven't yet discussed tracking the information, we have an API for accessing the information we need to answer our three service questions: total users online globally, total users on a specific URL, and the last 30 users on a URL.

Spreadlogd uses libevent to drive its network-level aspects such as receiving data from Spread. We, too, can leverage the libevent API to drive our "who's online" service.

The Service Provider

We want this to be fast and efficient (and easy to write), so we will use a simple binary format for the client-server communications. The client will connect and send an unsigned 16-bit integer in network byte order describing the length in bytes of the URL it would like information on followed by the URL. The server will respond to this request by passing back the results as three unsigned 32-bit integers in network endian describing the total users online, the total users on the specified URL, and the number of detailed user records that will follow, respectively. It will follow this with the detailed user records each of which consists of a 64-bit network endian SiteUserID, a 32-bit network endian age in seconds, and 32 bits of padding (because I'm lazy and the example is shorter if we can assume 64-bit alignment). Figure 10.1 illustrates the client-server communication.

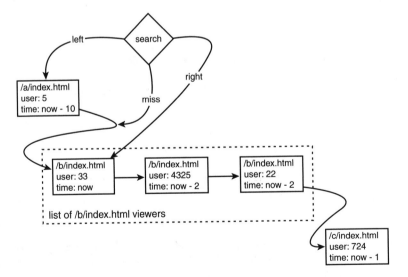

Figure 10.1 A sample client-server "who's online" session.

The code listing for `online-server.c` follows:

```
01: #include "online.h"
02: typedef struct user_hit_info {
03:    unsigned long long SiteUserID;  /* This viewer's ID */
04:    int age;                        /* Seconds since view */
05:    int pad;                        /* 4-byte alignment pad */
06: } user_hit_info_t;
```

The `user_hit_info_t` structure sends back the requesting client for each of the (up to 30) more recent viewers of the subject URL.

```
07: static void get_hit_info(const char *url, unsigned int *total,
08:                          unsigned int *url_total,
09:                          user_hit_info_t *uinfo,
10:                          unsigned int *nusers) {
11:    struct skiplistnode *first;
12:    urlcount_t *uc;
13:    time_t now;
14:    int max_users = *nusers;
15:
16:    /* Clean up any hits that are too old */
17:    cull_old_hits();
18:    *total = get_current_online_count();
19:    if((uc = get_url(url, strlen(url))) == NULL) {
20:      *nusers = *url_total = 0;
21:      return;
22:    }
23:    now = time(NULL);
24:    *url_total = uc->cnt;
25:    first = get_first_hit_for_url(uc->URL);
26:    *nusers = 0;
27:    if(!first) return; /* something is very wrong */
28:    while(*nusers < max_users && first) {
29:      hit_t *hit = (hit_t *)first->data;
30:      /* keep going until we see a new URL */
31:      if(!hit || strcmp(hit->URL,uc->URL)) break;
32:      uinfo[*nusers].SiteUserID = hit->SiteUserID;
33:      uinfo[*nusers].age = now - hit->Hitdate;
34:      (*nusers)++;
35:      sl_next(&first);
36:    }
37:    return;
38: }
```

The `get_hit_info` function takes a URL and fills out all the information we need to send back the requesting client. The first step in the function (line 17) removes any users from the tallies whose last access is considered too old. Lines 18–22 set the totals, fetch specific information about the URL, and return early if no users are currently viewing that URL. The rest of the function finds the "first" view of the specified URL and populates the `uinfo` list with *nusers of the most recent viewers.

Next comes the tricky network programming part. We need to read the request from the client, format the information retrieved in `get_hit_info` function into an on-wire format, and send it the client.

```
39: void online_service(int fd, short event, void *vnl) {
40:    netlisten_t *nl = (netlisten_t *)vnl;
41:    int expected_write, actual_write, i;
42:    struct iovec io[4];
43:    unsigned int total, url_total, nusers = MAX_USER_INFO;
44:    user_hit_info_t uinfo[MAX_USER_INFO];
45:    struct {
46:      unsigned short sofar;
47:      unsigned short ulen;
48:      char *url;
49:    } *req;
50:
51:    if(NULL == (req = nl->userdata))
52:      nl->userdata = req = calloc(1, sizeof(*req));
53:
```

The `userdata` member of `nl` lives for the life of the client connection. The first time we enter the function, it is `NULL`, and we allocate it to represent `req` that describes the progress of reading the request from the client. We need to track the process because we are non-blocking and we may read only a portion of the request and then be re-entered later to finish reading the rest of the socket. This is a nuance of non-blocking network socket programming.

```
54:    if(!req->ulen) {
55:      /* Read the length the URL to be passed (network short) */
56:      if(read(nl->fd, &req->ulen, sizeof(req->ulen)) !=
57:        sizeof(req->ulen)) goto bail;
58:      req->ulen = ntohs(req->ulen);
59:      /* Allocate our read length plus a terminator */
60:      req->url = malloc(req->ulen + 1);
61:      req->url[req->ulen] = '\0';
62:    }
```

The `ulen` member of `req` describes the length of the URL we expect to read from the client. If it is zero, we haven't read the expected URL length from the client yet and proceed to do so. In this implementation we expect to read all two bytes that we are expecting at once (and fail if we do not). The two bytes we read are the 16-bit network endian length of the URL to follow. We turn the datum into host-endian form and allocate enough room to read the URL.

```
63: while(req->sofar < req->ulen) {
64:    int len = read(nl->fd, req->url, req->ulen - req->sofar);
```

```
65:        if(len == -1 && errno == EAGAIN) return; /* incomplete read */
66:        if(len <= 0) goto bail;                   /* error */
67:        req->sofar += len;
68:    }
69:
```

Although we have not read as many bytes as we expect to see in the URL, we will read it into our URL buffer. By returning when we see an EAGAIN error, we will be called later to finish the job when more data is available.

```
70:    /* Get the answer */
71:    get_hit_info(req->url, &total, &url_total, uinfo, &nusers);
72:
73:    /* Pack it on the network */
74:    expected_write = sizeof(total) * 3 + nusers * sizeof(*uinfo);
75:    io[0].iov_base = &total;     io[0].iov_len = sizeof(total);
76:    io[1].iov_base = &url_total; io[1].iov_len = sizeof(url_total);
77:    io[2].iov_base = &nusers;    io[2].iov_len = sizeof(nusers);
78:    io[3].iov_base = uinfo;
79:    io[3].iov_len = nusers * sizeof(*uinfo);
80:
81:    total = htonl(total);
82:    url_total = htonl(url_total);
83:    for(i=0;i<nusers;i++) {
84:      uinfo[i].SiteUserID = bswap64(uinfo[i].SiteUserID);
85:      uinfo[i].age = htonl(uinfo[i].age);
86:    }
87:    nusers = htonl(nusers);
88:
```

After calling the get_hit_info function (line 71) we must fill out the I/O vector (lines 74–79) with the results and make sure that they are in network endian (lines 81–87).

```
89:    /* We should be able to write it all at once. We don't support */
90:    /* command pipelining, so the total contents of the outbound   */
91:    /* buffer will only ever be this large.                         */
92:    actual_write = writev(nl->fd, io, 4);
93:    if(actual_write != expected_write) goto bail;
94:
95:    free(req->url);
96:    memset(req, 0, sizeof(*req));
97:    return;
```

On line 92 we write out the response to the client. We expect to write the whole response in one call to writev. This is a reasonable assumption because we will write out only one response at a time because the client doesn't issue multiple questions without reading the answer to the first. Once written, we free the memory we allocated and zero out the progress tracking structure in preparation for a subsequent request.

```
098: bail:
099:   if(req) {
100:     if(req->url) free(req->url);
101:     free(req);
102:   }
103:   close(nl->fd);
104:   event_del(&nl->e);
105:   return;
106: }
```

The last bit of code is the path to execute if there is an error servicing the request. It
frees memory, closes down the socket, and removes itself from the libevent system.

The Information Collector

Now that our structures are defined, we need to populate them with the log information. We'll do this by storing the URLs (unique with counts) in a hash table and the last
hit by user in a multi-indexed skiplist. The multiple indexes on the skiplist will be (you
guessed it) same as those on our original database table: unique on SiteUserID,
ordered on Hitdate, and ordered on URL-Hitdate. The code listing for online.c follows:

```
01: #include "online.h"
02:
03: static Skiplist hits;     /* Tracks each users's last hit */
04: static ec_hash_table urls; /* Tracks the count on each URL */
05:
06: void urlcount_free(void *vuc) {
07:   if(((urlcount_t *)vuc)->URL) free(((urlcount_t *)vuc)->URL);
08:   free(vuc);
09: }
10: urlcount_t *get_url(const char *url, int len) {
11:   void *uc;
12:   if(echash_retrieve(&urls, url, len, &uc)) return uc;
13:   return NULL;
14: }
15: static void urlcount_decrement(const char *url) {
16:   urlcount_t *uc;
17:   if((uc = get_url(url, strlen(url))) != NULL) {
18:     if(!(--uc->cnt))
19:       echash_delete(&urls, url, strlen(url), NULL, urlcount_free);
20:   }
21: }
22: void hit_free(void *vhit) {
23:   urlcount_decrement(((hit_t *)vhit)->URL);
24:   free(vhit);
25: }
```

As can be seen with this leading code snippet, C is not a terse or compact language. As discussed earlier, we place the URL view counts in a hash table (line 4) and the actual per-user view information in a multi-indexed skiplist (line 3). Lines 6–9 and 22–25 are resource deallocation functions (free). When a user's hit information is freed from the system, we must decrement the count of current views on that URL (line 23 and implemented during 15–21).

More C verbosity is evident when we go to implement the comparison functions that drive each skiplist index.

```
26: /* comparator for the URL,Hitdate index */
27: static int url_hitdate_comp(const void *a, const void *b) {
28:    int ret = strcmp(((hit_t *)a)->URL, ((hit_t *)b)->URL);
29:    if(ret) return ret;
30:    /* Newest (greatest) in front */
31:    return (((hit_t *)a)->Hitdate < ((hit_t *)b)->Hitdate)?1:-1;
32: }
33: /* comparator for the Hitdate */
34: static int hitdate_comp(const void *a, const void *b) {
35:    /* Oldest in front... so we can pop off expired ones */
36:    return (((hit_t *)a)->Hitdate < ((hit_t *)b)->Hitdate)?-1:1;
37: }
38: /* comparator for the SiteUserID */
39: static int SiteUserID_comp(const void *a, const void *b) {
40:    if(((hit_t *)a)->SiteUserID == ((hit_t *)b)->SiteUserID) return 0;
41:    if(((hit_t *)a)->SiteUserID < ((hit_t *)b)->SiteUserID) return -1;
42:    return 1;
43: }
44: static int SiteUserID_comp_key(const void *a, const void *b) {
45:    if(*((unsigned long long *)a) == ((hit_t *)b)->SiteUserID) return 0;
46:    if(*((unsigned long long *)a) < ((hit_t *)b)->SiteUserID) return -1;
47:    return 1;
48: }
```

Lines 26–32 implement our URL-Hitdate index, lines 33–37 implement our Hitdate index, and lines 38–48 implement the unique SiteUserID index.

Now we have the tools to implement the API that powers the service offered in `online-server.c`.

```
49: unsigned int get_current_online_count() {
50:    return hits.size;
51: }
52:
53: void cull_old_hits() {
54:    hit_t *hit;
55:    time_t oldest;
56:    oldest = time(NULL) - MAX_AGE;
57:    while((hit = sl_peek(&hits)) != NULL && (hit->Hitdate < oldest))
58:       sl_pop(&hits, hit_free);
```

```
59: }
60:
61: struct skiplistnode *get_first_hit_for_url(const char *url) {
62:    struct skiplistnode *match, *left, *right;
63:    hit_t target;
64:    target.URL = (char *)url;
65:    /* ask for the node one second in the future.  We'll miss and */
66:    /* 'right' will point to the newest node for that URL.        */
67:    target.Hitdate = time(NULL) + 1;
68:    sl_find_compare_neighbors(&hits, &target, &match, &left, &right,
69:                              url_hitdate_comp);
70:    return right;
71: }
```

The get_current_online_count function returns the total number of online users that is simply the size of the skiplist holding unique online users.

One of the things that we had to do in the SQL version of this service was limit our queries to hits that had occurred within the last 30 minutes. In this approach, instead of counting only hits that occurred within the last 30 minutes, we actually just eliminate them from the system before they answer any such questions; the cull_old_hits function (lines 53–59) performs this. It's good to note that because one of the indexes on the hits skiplist is on Hitdate in ascending order, the first element on that index is the oldest. This means that we can just pop items off the front of the list until we see one that is not too old; popping off a skiplist is O(1) (that is, really inexpensive computationally).

Lines 61–71 are likely the most complicated lines of code in this entire example because the approach for finding the 30 most recent viewers of a URL may not be intuitive. The sl_find_compare_neighbors function attempts to find a node in a skiplist with the side effect of noting the element to the left and right of the node. If the node is not in the skiplist, it will note the nodes that would be on the left and right if it were to exist.

The index we are using for this lookup is URL-Hitdate index. This means that all the viewers for a given URL are grouped together in the list and are ordered from newest (largest time stamp) to oldest (smallest time stamp). Because this list is used to track the hits that have happened, it stands to reason that the largest time stamp possible would be the current time. On line 67, we set the "target" time stamp to be one second in the future (guaranteeing no match) and then look up the target URL in the hits table. We anticipate that the node we are looking for will be absent, but we also count on the fact that the "right neighbor" returned will be the most recent viewer of the URL in question. This is depicted in Figure 10.2.

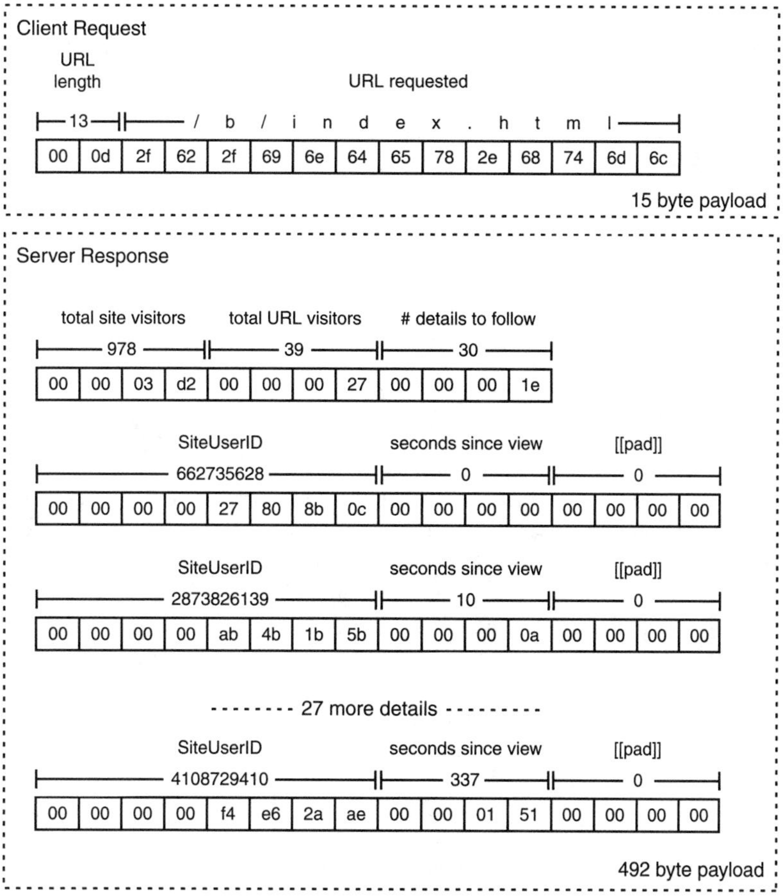

Figure 10.2 Finding the most recent viewer for a URL.

Now we have done everything but take log data and populate our system.

```
72: static int online_init(const char *config) {
73:   char *host = NULL, *sport = NULL;
74:   unsigned int port;
75:   echash_init(&urls);
76:   sl_init(&hits);
77:   sl_set_compare(&hits, hitdate_comp, hitdate_comp);
78:   sl_add_index(&hits, SiteUserID_comp, SiteUserID_comp_key);
79:   sl_add_index(&hits, url_hitdate_comp, url_hitdate_comp);
80:
81:   if(config) host = strdup(config);
82:   if(host) sport = strchr(host, ':');
83:   if(sport) {
```

```
84:     *sport++ = '\0';
85:     port = atoi(sport);
86:   } else
87:     port = DEFAULT_PORT;
88:   if(!host) host = DEFAULT_ADDRESS;
89:   if(tcp_dispatch(host, port, 100, EV_READ|EV_PERSIST, online_service,
90:                     NULL) < 0) {
91:     fprintf(stderr, "Could not start service on %s\n", config);
92:     return -1;
93:   }
94:   return 0;
95: }
96:
97: static void online_shutdown() {
98:   fprintf(stderr, "Stopping online module.\n");
99: }
```

The `online_init` function is invoked during the configuration phase of spreadlogd's startup sequence when the `LoadModule` directive is seen. Lines 75–79 initialize our hash table and create our skiplist with the three indexes we need. Lines 81–88 parse an option argument (passed from the `spreadlogd.conf`), and lines 89–90 register the "who's online" service we built in `online-server.c` with libevent (via the spreadlogd helper function `tcp_dispatch`). Lines 98–99 just implement an `online_shutdown` function that says goodbye.

```
100: #define SET_FROM_TOKEN(a,b) do { \
101:   a ## _len = tokens[(b)+1]-tokens[(b)]-1; \
102:   a = tokens[(b)]; \
103: } while(0)
104:
105: static void online_logline(SpreadConfiguration *sc,
106:       const char *sender, const char *group, const char *message) {
107:   const char *tokens[8];
108:   const char *user, *url;
109:   unsigned long long SiteUserID;
110:   int user_len, url_len;
111:   urlcount_t *uc;
112:   hit_t *hit;
113:   int i;
114:
115:   tokens[0] = message;
116:   for(i=1; i<8; i++) {
117:     tokens[i] = strchr(tokens[i-1], ' ');
118:     if(!tokens[i]++) return;  /* couldn't find token */
119:   }
120:   /* the userid is field 3 and the URI is field 7 based on white space */
121:   SET_FROM_TOKEN(user, 2);
122:   SET_FROM_TOKEN(url, 6);
```

Lines 100–103 and 115–122 perform tokenization of the logline (passed to us by spread-logd) based on white space. We know that in the Apache common log format the user is field 3, and the URL is field 7 (which are array index offsets 2 and 6, respectively).

```
123:    SiteUserID = strtoul(user, NULL, 10);
124:    /* Find the URL in the URL counts, creating if necessary */
125:    if((uc = get_url(url, url_len)) == NULL) {
126:      uc = calloc(1, sizeof(*uc));
127:      uc->URL = malloc(url_len+1);
128:      memcpy(uc->URL, url, url_len);
129:      uc->URL[url_len] = '\0';
130:      echash_store(&urls, uc->URL, url_len, uc);
131:    }
132:    /* Increment the counter on the URL */
133:    uc->cnt++;
134:
```

We translate the user to an unsigned long (because our user IDs are numeric), and we look up the URL in our URL hash table. If we don't find a copy, this is the only user viewing this URL in the system, so we create a new urlcount_t object with this URL and insert it. We also increment the count of current viewers on this URL.

```
135:    /* Fetch this users's last hit */
136:    hit = sl_find_compare(&hits, &SiteUserID, NULL, SiteUserID_comp);
137:    if(!hit) {
138:      /* No hit for this user, allocate one */
139:      hit = calloc(1, sizeof(*hit));
140:    }
141:    else {
142:      /* We have an old hit.  We must reduce the count on the old URL.
143:       * it is not our string, so we don't free it. */
144:      sl_remove_compare(&hits, &SiteUserID, NULL, SiteUserID_comp);
145:      urlcount_decrement(hit->URL);
146:    }
147:    hit->URL = uc->URL;
148:    hit->SiteUserID = SiteUserID;
149:    hit->Hitdate = time(NULL);
150:    sl_insert(&hits, hit);
151:    cull_old_hits();
152: }
```

Finally, we pull a switch. We attempt to find the URL the user was viewing immediately before this hit was logged and remove it if successful. Then we insert the new hit information marking the user, time, and URL. Finally, we preemptively remove any hit information that is no longer pertinent.

```
sld_module_abi_t online = {
 "online",
 online_init,
```

```
online_logline,
online_shutdown,
};
```

The last bit of code required is used to provide spreadlogd's module loader a handle to our logging implementation. The `sld_module_abi_t` is a structure that contains the name of the module and function pointers to our initialization, logging, and shutdown routines.

C, as you know by now, is not a wonderful example language to be used in a book that isn't about C. However, because we are building a performance-centric solution here, it simply makes sense to use a language that won't blink at 9,000 queries per second. The particular features we need to achieve such performance are cheap data management and extremely granular control over the data structures we use. This is possible in other languages as well, but I know C—so sue me.

Loading the Module

Now that we have a module, we will compile it, link it, and install it as `/opt/spreadlogd/modules/online.so` on a server called sldhost running spreadlogd installed in `/opt/spreadlogd/`. Then we tailor a `spreadlogd.conf` file to log our news site logs through our new module:

```
BufferSize = 65536
ModuleDir = /opt/spreadlogd/libexec
LoadModule online *:8989
Spread {
  Port = 4803
  Log {
    Group newssite
    ModuleLog online
  }
}
```

This connects to Spread on port 4803 and listens for `mod_log_spread` published logs to the group `newssite`, pumping all the messages it sees though our new module.

After this is up and running, we have a fully usable "who's online" service running on port 8989. But how do we pull data from it?

Writing a Client

We have a service running that presumably has all the data we need to meet the goals for our new feature. Our website is written in perl, so we can scratch together the following modules to implement the client-server protocol written earlier from the client side. `NewsSite/WhosOnline.pm` contains our client base class:

```
01: package NewsSite::WhosOnline;
02:
03: use Net::WhosOnline::INET;
04: use vars qw/$VERSION/;
```

```
05: use strict;
06: use bigint;
07:
08: $VERSION = "1.0";
09:
10: sub new {
11:   my $class = shift;
12:   return NewsSite::WhosOnline::INET->new(@_);
13: }
```

This is the class perl package preamble that declares a version number and provides a new class method. In this method, we just hand our arguments to the new method of one of our subclasses NewsSite::WhosOnline::INET to build a TCP/IP client. This is good practice because perhaps in the future we will provide some other method of connecting to the service.

```
14: sub query {
15:   my($self, $url) = @_;
16:   $url = pack('n', length($url)) . $url;
17:   # Binary net-strings-style request
18:   my $wlen = $self->syswrite($url, length($url));
19:   die if(!defined($wlen) || ($wlen != length($url)));
20:   return $self->read_response;
21: }
```

The query method takes a URL as it writes it to the server preceded by the length as a 16-bit network-endian unsigned integer.

```
22: sub getcounts {
23:   my $self = shift;
24:   my $pss;
25:   # 4 bytes x (total, url_total, nusers)
26:   die if($self->sysread($pss, 12) != 12);
27:   return unpack('NNN', $pss);
28: }
29: sub getuserinfo {
30:   my ($self, $count) = @_;
31:   my ($pss, @hits);
32:   # The structure handed back to us is (for each user)
33:   # 8 bytes of SiteUserID, 4 bytes of age in seconds
34:   # and 4 bytes of padding.
35:   die if($self->sysread($pss, 16 * $count) != (16 * $count));
36:   my @part = unpack('NNNN' x $count, $pss);
37:   while(@part) {
38:     # this little trick will allow bigint to kick in without
39:     # rolling an int on 32bit systems.
40:     my $rv = $part[0];
41:     $rv *= 0xffffffff;
42:     $rv += $part[0] + $part[1];
```

```
43:     push @hits, [ "$rv", $part[2] ];
44:     # We don't do anything with $part[3], it's padding.
45:     splice(@part, 0, 4); # eat these 4, and onto the next
46:   }
47:   return \@hits;
48: }
49: sub read_response {
50:   my $self = shift;
51:   my $response;
52:   eval {
53:     my ($total, $url_total, $nusers) = $self->getcounts;
54:     $response = { total       => $total,
55:                   url_total   => $url_total,
56:                   recent_hits => $self->getuserinfo($nusers) };
57:   };
58:   return $@?undef:$response;
59: }
60: 1;
```

The read_response method (lines 49–59) simply calls the getcounts and getuserinfo methods to populate a hash and return it to the caller. The getcounts method reads and unpacks our three 32-bit unsigned integers in network endian (lines 26–27). In getuserinfo we read and unpack all the user hit information on lines 35 and 36 and spend lines 37–46 processing them and compensating for the fact that the SiteUserID is a 64-bit integer. We want to support large integers, so we used the bigint package on line 6—this allows perl to handle that "magically." The NewsSite/WhosOnline/Inet.pm code listing follows:

```
01: package NewsSite::WhosOnline::INET;
02:
03: use NewsSite::WhosOnline;
04: use IO::Socket::INET;
05: use vars qw/$VERSION @ISA/;
06: use strict;
07:
08: $VERSION = "1.0";
09: @ISA = (qw/Net::WhosOnline IO::Socket::INET/);
10:
11: sub new {
12:   my ($class, $hostname, %args) = @_;
13:   $args{Port} ||= 8989;  # set the default port
14:   return $class->IO::Socket::INET::new(PeerAddr => $hostname,
15:                                        PeerPort => $args{Port},
16:                                        Proto => 'tcp',
17:                                        Timeout => $args{Timeout});
18: }
19: 1;
```

The `NewsSite::WhosOnline::INET` implements the TCP/IP specific details of the client by subclassing `IO::Socket::INET`. On line 13, we default the remote port to 8989 to keep it in line with our server implementation.

It's important to note that the "who's online" client implementation is only 79 lines of code. Were our application written in PHP, Java, or just about any other language, the client code would be similarly simple.

Running Some Tests

Now that we have a working client we can ping our service and see who is currently visiting `/index.html`:

```
# perl -MNewsSite::WhosOnline -MData::Dumper \
  -e 'print Dumper(NewsSite::WhosOnline->new("sldhost")
                                    ->query("/b/index.html"))'
$VAR1 = {
          'url_total' => 39,
          'recent_hits' => [
                             [
                               '662735628',
                               0
                             ],
                             [
                               '2873826139',
                               10
                             ],
                             # 27 more detail here
                             [
                               '4108724910',
                               337
                             ],
                           ],
          'total' => 978
        };
```

Now that we have everything working, did we solve our problem? Of course, we think we did. We are confident that our design doesn't suffer from the acute performance issues identified in the SQL-based implementation. But was it enough?

Testing the Solution

How do you go about testing a solution like this? Our goal was to sustain 9,000 queries per second. Although it is easy to write a simple test that runs and requests information on 9,000 URLs as rapidly as possible, that is only useful if the service is populated with a dataset that fairly represents what we expect to see in production.

One of the truly beautiful aspects of this solution is that the tracking side of it does not sit in the critical path. If it is not being queried for URL information there is no way it can disrupt our architecture. This allows us to do performance tests without investing a tremendous amount in test-harness design. We can run our test queries against a new, unused spreadlogd instance feeding on real production logs.

So, we crank up a new box running spreadlogd and our "who's online" service module, and we wait. It tracks users' clickstreams up to 30 minutes old. The instance will only have usable data (realistic size, quantity, and diversity) after 30 minutes of operation.

After the system is warmed up with some real data, we run a really simple test that requests a frequently viewed page 100,000 times in a loop and calculates the actual queries per second. This isn't a bad test in general because we know a bit about our data structures. Every URL looked up costs the same, and there is limit of 30 records handed back; as long as the URL in our test has many users associated with it, it will be a "worst case" and a thus a fairly good test. We can script this test case as `whosonline-test.pl`:

```
use strict;
use NewsSite::WhosOnline;
use Time::HiRes qw/gettimeofday tv_interval/;

my $cnt = shift || 100000;
my $nw = NewsSite::WhosOnline->new("sldhost");
my $start = [gettimeofday];
for(my $i=0; $i<$cnt; $i++) {
  $nw->query("/b/index.html");
}
printf "$cnt queries [%0.2f q/s]\n", $cnt/tv_interval($start);
```

We can run our test and find out how fast our spectacular new service is.
```
; perl whosonline-test.pl
100000 queries [43.29 q/s]
```

Oh, dear! Forty-three queries per second, that's just not right! How could that possibly be? Is it the test script or is it the server?
```
; time perl -d:DProf whosonline-test.pl
100000 queries [43.29 q/s]
1911.386u 132.212s 38:30.46 88.4%       0+0k 0+0io 390pf+0w
```

The preceding line shows 1911 seconds of CPU time to run the script! The script isn't doing anything but asking questions. What is taking so much horsepower?
```
; perl -d:DProf whosonline-test.pl
100000 queries [43.29 q/s]
; dprofpp tmon.out
Total Elapsed Time = 1314.906 Seconds
  User+System Time = 1203.177 Seconds
Exclusive Times
%Time ExclSec CumulS #Calls sec/call Csec/c  Name
 20.7   249.0 407.63 640001  0.0000 0.0001  Math::BigInt::new
 19.4   233.4 257.00 182000  0.0000 0.0000  Math::BigInt::numify
 14.4   173.2 164.10 920000  0.0000 0.0000  Math::BigInt::round
 13.0   156.4 1355.1 276000  0.0000 0.0000  Math::BigInt::__ANON__
```

```
9.48   114.0 392.31 300000   0.0000 0.0001   Math::BigInt::badd
9.19   110.6 1424.2 100000   0.0011 0.0142   NewsSite::WhosOnline::getuserinfo
8.95   107.6 236.65 340000   0.0000 0.0001   Math::BigInt::objectify
8.90   107.1 207.33 320000   0.0000 0.0001   Math::BigInt::bmul
6.50   78.15 59.958 182000   0.0000 0.0000   Math::BigInt::Calc::_num
5.48   65.88 62.890 300000   0.0000 0.0000   Math::BigInt::_split
5.28   63.50 57.109 640001   0.0000 0.0000   Math::BigInt::Calc::_new
3.76   45.26 72.699 300000   0.0000 0.0000   Math::BigInt::bstr
3.03   36.42 33.430 300000   0.0000 0.0000   Math::BigInt::Calc::_str
2.70   32.50 29.310 320000   0.0000 0.0000   Math::BigInt::Calc::_mul_use_div
2.64   31.77 28.780 300000   0.0000 0.0000   Math::BigInt::Calc::_add
```

It should be clear that we spend pretty much all of our time dealing with Math::BigInt, which is the way that 32-bit perl can deal transparently with 64-bit integers. This is not what we bargained for, so let's eliminate this by passing the SiteUserID back to the perl caller as an array of a high and low part (that is, the 32 most significant bits as a 32-bit integer and the 32 least significant bits as a 32-bit integer). By doing this we will avoid the majority of the expense highlighted in our profiling output, and, hopefully, our solution will perform adequately.

We will comment out line 6 of the NewsSite/WhosOnline.pm file and change the getuserinfo method as follows:

```
29: sub getuserinfo {
30:    my ($self, $count) = @_;
31:    my ($pss, @hits);
32:    # The structure handed back to us is (for each user)
33:    # 8 bytes of SiteUserID, 4 bytes of age in seconds
34:    # and 4 bytes of padding.
35:    die if($self->sysread($pss, 16 * $count) != (16 * $count));
36:    my @part = unpack('NNNN' x $count, $pss);
37:    while(@part) {
38:       # this little trick will allow bigint to kick in without
39:       # rolling an int on 32bit systems... TOO EXPENSIVE
40:       # my $rv = $part[0];
41:       # $rv *= 0xffffffff;
42:       # $rv += $part[0] + $part[1];
43:       push @hits, [ [ $part[0], $part[1] ], $part[2] ];
44:       # We don't do anything with $part[3], it's padding.
45:       splice(@part, 0, 4); # eat these 4, and onto the next
46:    }
```

We comment out lines 40–42, which was our "clever" bigint helper. Then we change line 43 to pass the SiteUserID back as an array of $part[0] and $part[1]. Then, we rerun our test.

```
; time perl -d:DProf whosonline-test.pl
100000 queries [2858.75 q/s]
27.208u 4.078s 0:35.11 89.0%   0+0k 0+0io 388pf+0w
```

This is much more reasonable. The example is still not where we want to be, but we also don't want to be running test cases in the end. Our goal is to have our web application be a client to this service and be able to perform 9,000 queries per second against it.

To better emulate this, we take the previous test and run it from a number of our web servers. We're no longer interested in how long the test takes or what the perl profiling looks like, we just want the "q/s" results. Starting tests across all the various servers involves an element of human error. The tests will not start at the same time, and they won't end at the same time. The goal is to gain an understanding of what performance we can achieve with them all running in parallel. The easiest way to do this is to understand the human error and make sure that its effect on the outcome is minimal. Going overboard in the testing process here can be a waste of time as well. The purpose of this exercise is to build confidence in the performance of our solution. We'll bump the iterations up to 10,000,000 and let the test run on eight nodes. It takes just over two hours, and the results are excellent:

```
www-0-1:   1534 q/s
www-0-2:   1496 q/s
www-0-3:   1521 q/s
www-0-4:   1501 q/s
www-0-5:   1524 q/s
www-0-6:   1462 q/s
www-0-7:   1511 q/s
www-0-8:   1488 q/s
```

That should do just fine. Across all the nodes, we are seeing 12,037 queries per second.

This chapter contains a lot of complicated code and as such the "who's online" module discussed is included in the spreadlogd source distribution for your convenience.

Who's Online Reviewed

The "who's online" solution we've built scales. However, we focused only briefly on the real reason the solution scales well. Is it because it can serve more than 10,000 requests per second on a single box? Although impressive, that is performance, not scalability.

Scalability means that the general implementation and use of this system will not change if the scope of the problem changes. If the site shrinks, our system becomes less used. If the problem scope increases, to say 100,000 hits per second, we have a solution.

The "who's online" server collects information outside the critical service path. It is passive, and because it uses log streams from mod_log_spread, more can be added without significant overhead. This means that it can scale horizontally. The fact that we could run a "who's online"-enabled spreadlogd instance on every web server without introducing load on any other architectural component is the ultimate testament to its scalability.

A

Spread

A KEY RULE IN SOLVING ANY PROBLEM, no matter how challenging, is "know your tools!" As you have learned from several of the previous chapters, one such tool is the Spread Group Communication Toolkit. Spread may very well be the Swiss army knife of the distributed systems world, but there are several aspects to consider when choosing to use such a tool. First, you need to properly understand the principles behind the features that the tool provides to pick the appropriate ones to solve a problem. Second, you must evaluate the price that you pay for having features that you don't really need—you don't want to be the hero of the classic tale of squashing a mosquito by using a cannon. Finally, you need to learn how to properly use the tool, to understand its quirks and caveats.

This appendix covers these aspects for Spread, providing a minimal theoretical background, installation instructions, and configuration and usage examples.

Group Communication

Every distributed architecture has one inherently fundamental component that is also critical to its overall effectiveness: communication between the various participants. Communication between only two nodes in the Internet may occasionally pose some problems as well, but the methods and caveats are well understood and are the object of any Introduction to Networking class. Basically, using UDP/IP for unreliable communication and TCP/IP for reliable communication covers 99% of point-to-point communication needs. What happens, though, when communication is needed between several participants—especially if they are not all part of the same LAN?

Point-to-point communication between all participants without any additional logic is obviously both expensive and chaotic. Reliable IP-multicast can be employed in certain situations, but it is more adequate in scenarios that involve a single sender and a large number of receivers, whose identities are not necessarily important to the sender. In contrast, the problems that we want to tackle usually involve a relatively small number of participants, whose identities are important to be known at all times, and who may act simultaneously both as senders and receivers. This points us toward another possible communication paradigm: group communication.

The group communication paradigm provides a framework meant to ease the process of managing the communication aspect of distributed applications. The paradigm provides an intuitive abstraction and a set of communication primitives with meaningful and well-defined properties that are not trivial to satisfy in an asynchronous, unreliable network.

First, we identify the participants (or processes) in a distributed application as members of a *group*. Any member of a group can send messages to the entire group and also receive all the messages sent by the other members. Groups may also be *open*, in which case processes that are not part of the group are allowed to send messages to the entire group.

The second important abstraction, directly related to the notion of group, is the *group membership*. A group communication system provides the process with primitives that identify all the members of a group that the process is part of at any given moment time. This may include notifications when new members join the group or when current members leave the group, either voluntarily or due to intermittent network communication issues or process crashes.

Finally, group communication systems provide primitives that enable and govern the communication between the participating processes. These primitives are basically group broadcast primitives whose properties are defined from two perspectives:

- Reliability
- Ordering

Messages sent to a group may be unreliable or reliable. *Unreliable messages* may be lost and are not recovered by the group communication system. *Reliable messages* are received by all members of a group, as long as they do not crash or become otherwise disconnected from the group.

The ordering guarantees define the order in which messages are delivered by the group communication system to each recipient. Several common ordering guarantees are identified here:

- **FIFO ordering**—If process X sends messages A and B, in this order, all members of the group who receive A and B will receive them in the order in which they were sent.

- **Causal ordering**—If messages A and B are sent by process X in this order, or if process X sends message B subsequent to receiving message A sent by another member, all members of the group will receive message A before receiving message B (B is potentially causally dependent on A). Causal order is an extension of FIFO ordering.

- **Total ordering**—If process X receives messages A and B in this order, any process Y that receives messages A and B will receive them in the same order. Total ordering is not necessarily consistent with FIFO or causal ordering, although in practice it is particularly useful when combined with causal or at least FIFO guarantees.

Introducing...Spread

Spread is a group communication toolkit developed at the Center for Networking and Distributed Systems at Johns Hopkins University and distributed as source and binary under a BSD-style license with an advertisement clause.

Spread uses a tiered architecture, which it leverages to optimize communication between a larger set of participants, spanning multiple groups. This architecture may prove confusing, however, for those not used to this paradigm. An application/process that wants to use Spread must connect, using primitives provided as library calls, to a Spread *daemon*. The Spread daemon may reside on the same machine as the application, but it may be on any machine that the application can access in the Internet or the local network. The ideal image of a Spread network consists of several Spread daemons "spread" across the Internet, each with many applications connected to it locally (LAN or "closer" network-wise). Most of the uses of Spread in this book revolve around strictly local area use. We'll touch a bit on the aspects of wide area operation but stick to examples that pertain mainly to previous discussions. Figure A.1 depicts a typical local area Spread configuration.

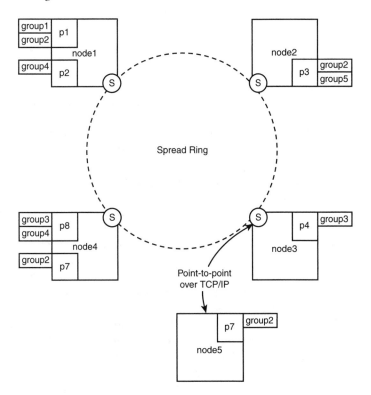

Figure A.1 Typical local area Spread topology and usage.

After connecting to a Spread daemon, the application may request to join one or more groups and can start sending/receiving messages to/from these groups. The Spread daemons connect to each other automatically, forming the *Spread network*, and act as brokers for the applications, managing multiple groups, enforcing the requested delivery and ordering guarantees within each group, and providing notifications of membership changes to the application for the groups that they belong to.

All Spread daemons in a Spread network (or configuration) know each other's identities and maintain a strict knowledge of their ability to communicate with each other. In effect they establish and maintain a *daemon membership*. The daemon membership is transparent to the applications, but a change in the daemon membership, either due to a daemon crash or to temporary network partitioning, may induce changes in the application group membership. The application group membership may also change due to applications voluntarily joining/leaving the group or due to an application crashing.

Spread supports all the standard group communication delivery properties mentioned previously. When a process sends a message to a group, it can specify the level of service requested for the delivery of that message:

- Unreliable
- Reliable
- FIFO (also reliable)
- Causal (also FIFO)
- Agreed (provides Total Order and Causal guarantees)
- Safe (provides Total Order with additional safety delivery guarantee)

The safe delivery is the most powerful delivery guarantee offered by Spread. A safe message is delivered to a receiving application only if the Spread daemon that the application is connected to knows that all the other Spread daemons have the message and will therefore deliver it to their respective receiving applications unless they or the applications crash. It is possible that a Spread daemon detects a change in the daemon membership before it can determine whether all daemons that were part of the old membership have the message. In this case, the daemon will deliver the safe message to the applications interested in receiving it, only after signaling them that a membership change is about to occur. This is done using a transitional membership change notification.

The safe delivery mechanism is part of the Extended Virtual Synchrony (EVS) paradigm mentioned in Chapter 8, "Distributed Databases Are Easy, Just Read the Fine Print," and can be used to build powerful and delicate distributed applications that require a high degree of synchronization between the participating processes. However, safe delivery is significantly slower than agreed or FIFO delivery, and therefore it should not be employed casually if the application does not require the additional guarantees.

Installation and Configuration

Spread is licensed as Open Source. The license is similar to a BSD license with the addition of an advertisement requirement clause.

Spread can be downloaded either as a collection of binaries or as source tarball from http://www.spread.org/. Although the binaries may do the trick for some systems, we recommend compiling from source. Because Spread uses `autoconf`, for most users the installation is as simple as `./configure; make; make install`.

At the time of publishing, in addition to the stable 3.17.3 release, RC2 of the new Spread 4.0 is also available for download. If you're using Spread for the first time, you may consider trying this version because it presents several significant improvements, including support for dynamic configuration of sets of daemons without requiring a restart and enforcing identical configuration files at all nodes. However, because Spread 4.0 is still in release candidate status and we have not had the chance to test this release thoroughly yet, we will base the instructions and examples in the remainder of this appendix on the 3.17 release.

Each Spread daemon relies on a configuration file (`spread.conf`) to define some of the runtime parameters and, more importantly, to specify the list of all other potential Spread daemons in the network.

There are two common ways to configure Spread. In the first situation as seen in Listing A.1, we establish a LAN Spread configuration.

Listing A.1 `spread.conf`—**A Simple Local Area Spread Configuration**

```
Spread_Segment 192.168.221.255:4803 {
        ifog2               192.168.221.102
        ifog3               192.168.221.103
        ifog4               192.168.221.104
        ifog5               192.168.221.105
        ifog6               192.168.221.106
        ifog7               192.168.221.107
        ifog8               192.168.221.108
        ifog9               192.168.221.109
        ifog10              192.168.221.110
        ifog11              192.168.221.111
        ifog13              192.168.221.113
        ifog14              192.168.221.114
        ifog15              192.168.221.115
        ifog16              192.168.221.116
}
```

In the second situation, as seen in Listing A.2, the Spread daemons are distributed in several sites connected by the Internet.

Listing A.2 `spread.conf`—**A Simple Wide Area Spread Configuration**

```
Spread_Segment x.220.221.255:4803 {
        machine1             x.220.221.21
        machine2             x.220.221.206
}


Spread_Segment x.44.222.255:4913 {
        machine1             x.44.222.31
        machine4             x.44.222.35
        machine5             x.44.222.201
        machine              x.44.222.12
}


Spread_Segment x.22.33.255:4893 {
        m1                   x.22.33.31
        m2                   x.22.33.111
}
```

The key aspect about the Spread configuration files is that they need to be identical on all servers. If by chance you end up with configurations that are slightly different, you may end up with daemons that act as if nothing is wrong, yet cannot talk to each other.

Several other options can be set in the configuration file. `DebugFlags` specifies the level that debug information will be displayed during the daemon's run. By default, these messages are displayed either to standard error or to the log file specified by `EventLogFile` in the configuration. The amount of logged information is highly configurable. You may specify which levels to include and which to exclude. For example:

```
DebugFlags = {PRINT EXIT}
DebugFlags = {ALL !EVENTS !MEMORY}
```

Getting Started

Let's try to set up a Spread network with just two daemons:

```
# cat spread.conf
DebugFlags = { PRINT EXIT }
EventTimeStamp
DangerousMonitor = true


Spread_Segment 10.0.0.255:4913 {
        www-0-1                  10.0.0.132
        www-0-2                  10.0.0.133
}
#./spread
/=======================================================================\
| The Spread Toolkit.                                                    |
| Copyright (c) 1993-2002 Spread Concepts LLC                           |
```

```
...
| All rights reserved.                                                    |
| Version 3.17.03 Built 15/October/2004                                   |
\========================================================================/
Conf_init: using file: spread.conf
[Mon 08 May 2006 07:32:19] ENABLING Dangerous Monitor Commands! Make sure Spread
network is secured
[Mon 08 May 2006 07:32:19] Conf_init: My proc id (192.168.221.22) is not in
configuration
Exit caused by Alarm(EXIT)
```

It looks like we were unable to start. This is the first hurdle that you may encounter when trying to start up Spread. Notice that the error we get even refers to a different IP address from any of the ones in our config file. In fact, Spread by default does something that you might not expect: It determines the name of the hostname, resolves that to an IP address, and looks for that in the configuration file. However, we can tell Spread which named entry from the configuration file it should use to start up:

```
$ ./spread -n www-0-1
| Version 3.17.03 Built 15/October/2004                                   |
\========================================================================/
Conf_init: using file: spread.conf
[Mon 08 May 2006 08:15:54] ENABLING Dangerous Monitor Commands! Make sure Spread
network is secured
```

Looks like the daemon was able to start! Well, we don't have a message saying that, but at least it is not exiting like before. From this point on, we basically have a couple of options: Start up another daemon and see whether the two can communicate, or start the spuser application that comes with Spread and try to join a group and send a message to show that we have a functioning daemon. Let's go the second route:

```
# ./spuser
Spread library version is 3.17.3
SP_error: (-2) Could not connect. Is Spread running?

Bye.
# ./spuser usage
Usage: spuser
        [-u <user name>]   : unique (in this machine) user name
        [-s <address>]     : either port or port@machine
        [-n <username>]    : username for authentication
        [-p <password>]    : users password
        [-r ]     : use random user name
# ./spuser -s 4913
Spread library version is 3.17.3
User: connected to 4913 with private group #user#fog1

==========
```

```
User Menu:
----------

        j <group> -- join a group
        l <group> -- leave a group

        s <group> -- send a message
        b <group> -- send a burst of messages

        r -- receive a message (stuck)
        p -- poll for a message
        e -- enable asynchonous read (default)
        d -- disable asynchronous read

        q -- quit

User> j test

User> s test
enter message: weee
User> q

Bye.
```

I may be paranoid, but all's too quiet on the western front as the saying goes. We did find out that we have to specify the port that Spread is running on for spuser to be able to connect, but after that I am a bit disappointed that the message I sent to a group that I joined does not seem to be received. At this point we need to find out more about what is going on, so let's enable a few more DebugFlag options in the spread.conf file and start over:

```
# grep DebugFlags spread.conf
DebugFlags = { PRINT EXIT SESSION MEMBERSHIP GROUPS }
# ./spread -n www-0-2
[Mon 08 May 2006 07:58:57] Sess_init: ended ok
[Mon 08 May 2006 07:58:57] Scast_alive: State is 2
[Mon 08 May 2006 07:58:58] Scast_alive: State is 2
[Mon 08 May 2006 07:58:59] Send_join: State is 4
[Mon 08 May 2006 07:59:00] Send_join: State is 4
[Mon 08 May 2006 07:59:01] Send_join: State is 4
[Mon 08 May 2006 07:59:02] Send_join: State is 4
[Mon 08 May 2006 07:59:03] Send_join: State is 4
[Mon 08 May 2006 07:59:09] Memb_token_loss: I lost my token, state is 5
[Mon 08 May 2006 07:59:09] Scast_alive: State is 2
[Mon 08 May 2006 07:59:10] Scast_alive: State is 2
[Mon 08 May 2006 07:59:11] Send_join: State is 4
[Mon 08 May 2006 07:59:12] Send_join: State is 4
```

```
[Mon 08 May 2006 07:59:13] Send_join: State is 4
[Mon 08 May 2006 07:59:14] Send_join: State is 4
[Mon 08 May 2006 07:59:15] Send_join: State is 4
[Mon 08 May 2006 07:59:21] Memb_token_loss: I lost my token, state is 5
[Mon 08 May 2006 07:59:21] Scast_alive: State is 2
[Mon 08 May 2006 07:59:22] Scast_alive: State is 2
[Mon 08 May 2006 07:59:23] Send_join: State is 4
[Mon 08 May 2006 07:59:24] Send_join: State is 4
[Mon 08 May 2006 07:59:25] Send_join: State is 4
[Mon 08 May 2006 07:59:26] Send_join: State is 4
[Mon 08 May 2006 07:59:27] Send_join: State is 4
[Mon 08 May 2006 07:59:33] Memb_token_loss: I lost my token, state is 5
[Mon 08 May 2006 07:59:33] Scast_alive: State is 2
[Mon 08 May 2006 07:59:34] Scast_alive: State is 2
[Mon 08 May 2006 07:59:35] Send_join: State is 4
```

Aha! Although it may not be obvious what each of the preceding messages means, something seems not right about the fact that the token gets lost all the time and the states seem to be changing periodically in a loop that doesn't seem to finish. Let's go back to the basics. The good news is that the Spread configuration is simple, so there are not many places that we could have gone wrong. In fact, let's check the nodes definitions again. We are telling Spread to start on the node called www-0-2, which has the IP address 10.0.0.133. Let's make sure just in case:

```
# /sbin/ifconfig
fxp0: flags=8843<UP,BROADCAST,RUNNING,SIMPLEX,MULTICAST> mtu 1500
        options=8<VLAN_MTU>
        inet 10.0.0.132 netmask 0xffffff00 broadcast 10.0.0.255
        inet6 fe80::290:27ff:fef6:3a0e%fxp0 prefixlen 64 scopeid 0x2
        ether 00:90:27:f6:3a:0e
        media: Ethernet autoselect (100baseTX <full-duplex>)
        status: active
```

Oops! It looks like we got confused about the machine we're running on, and we're trying to start up Spread on www-0-1, telling it that it is www-0-2 instead! That's our mistake, although you would expect to see a more alarming message when Spread cannot bind to the network interface. Let's see whether this is our only problem:

```
#./spread -n www-0-1
Conf_init: using file: spread.conf
[Mon 08 May 2006 07:48:21] ENABLING Dangerous Monitor Commands! Make sure Spread
network is secured
[Mon 08 May 2006 07:48:21] Memb_token_loss: I lost my token, state is 1
[Mon 08 May 2006 07:48:21] Sess_init: INET bind for port 4913 interface 0.0.0.0 ok
[Mon 08 May 2006 07:48:21] Sess_init: INET went ok on mailbox 6
[Mon 08 May 2006 07:48:21] Sess_init: UNIX bind for name /tmp/4913 ok
[Mon 08 May 2006 07:48:21] Sess_init: UNIX went ok on mailbox 7
[Mon 08 May 2006 07:48:21] G_init:
```

```
[Mon 08 May 2006 07:48:21] Sess_init: ended ok
[Mon 08 May 2006 07:48:21] Scast_alive: State is 2
[Mon 08 May 2006 07:48:22] Scast_alive: State is 2
[Mon 08 May 2006 07:48:23] Send_join: State is 4
[Mon 08 May 2006 07:48:24] Send_join: State is 4
[Mon 08 May 2006 07:48:25] Send_join: State is 4
[Mon 08 May 2006 07:48:26] Send_join: State is 4
[Mon 08 May 2006 07:48:27] Send_join: State is 4
[Mon 08 May 2006 07:48:28] Memb_handle_token: handling form2 token
[Mon 08 May 2006 07:48:28] Handle_form2 in FORM
[Mon 08 May 2006 07:48:28] Memb_transitional
[Mon 08 May 2006 07:48:28] G_handle_trans_memb:
[Mon 08 May 2006 07:48:28] G_handle_trans_memb in GOP
[Mon 08 May 2006 07:48:28] G_handle_trans_memb: Received trans memb id of:
{proc_id: -1062675178 time:    1147088908}
[Mon 08 May 2006 07:48:28] Memb_regular
Membership id is ( -1062675178, 1147088909)
[Mon 08 May 2006 07:48:28] --------------------
[Mon 08 May 2006 07:48:28] Configuration at www-0-1 is:
[Mon 08 May 2006 07:48:28] Num Segments 1
[Mon 08 May 2006 07:48:28]    1      10.0.0.255    4913
[Mon 08 May 2006 07:48:28]               www-0-1                 10.0.0.132
[Mon 08 May 2006 07:48:28] ====================
[Mon 08 May 2006 07:48:28] G_handle_reg_memb:  with (10.0.0.132, 1147088909) id
[Mon 08 May 2006 07:48:28] G_handle_reg_memb in GTRANS
```

This time it looks like we were successful! In fact, if we now go back to the minimal set of `DebugFlags`, we will be able to tell that we started successfully:

```
# grep Debug spread.conf
DebugFlags = { PRINT EXIT }
# ./spread -n relay-0-1
Conf_init: using file: spread.conf
[Mon 08 May 2006 08:12:52] ENABLING Dangerous Monitor Commands! Make sure Spread
network is secured
Membership id is ( -1062675178, 1147090380)
[Mon 08 May 2006 08:12:59] --------------------
[Mon 08 May 2006 08:12:59] Configuration at www-0-1 is:
[Mon 08 May 2006 08:12:59] Num Segments 1
[Mon 08 May 2006 08:12:59]    1      10.0.0.255    4913
[Mon 08 May 2006 08:12:59]               www-0-1                 10.0.0.132
[Mon 08 May 2006 08:12:59] ====================
```

Keep in mind that the preceding output is something we want to see after we start Spread because it shows that the daemon that we just started was able to successfully establish a membership. Let's see now whether we can get more satisfying results out of playing with the `spuser` application:

```
# ./spuser -s 4913
```

```
Spread library version is 3.17.3
User: connected to 4913 with private group #user#www-0-1


==========
User Menu:
----------


        j <group> -- join a group
        l <group> -- leave a group

        s <group> -- send a message
        b <group> -- send a burst of messages

        r -- receive a message (stuck)
        p -- poll for a message
        e -- enable asynchonous read (default)
        d -- disable asynchronous read

        q -- quit

User> j test

User>
============================
Received REGULAR membership for group test with 1 members, where I am member 0:
        #user#www-0-1
grp id is -1062675178 1147091682 1
Due to the JOIN of #user#www-0-1

User> s test
enter message: weee

User>
============================
received SAFE message from #user#www-0-1, of type 1, (endian 0) to 1 groups
(5 bytes): weee
```

Indeed, this looks much more like what we would expect to see. We joined a group that we called test and sent a message that was actually received. Let's attempt to bring the second server up as well:

```
# ./spread -n www-0-2
Conf_init: using file: spread.conf
[Mon 08 May 2006 08:44:41] ENABLING Dangerous Monitor Commands! Make sure Spread
network is secured
Membership id is ( -1062675179, 1147092289)
[Mon 08 May 2006 08:44:48] --------------------
[Mon 08 May 2006 08:44:48] Configuration at www-0-2 is:
```

```
[Mon 08 May 2006 08:44:48] Num Segments 1
[Mon 08 May 2006 08:44:48]    2      10.0.0.255    4913
[Mon 08 May 2006 08:44:48]           www-0-1                        10.0.0.132
[Mon 08 May 2006 08:44:48]           www-0-2                        10.0.0.133
[Mon 08 May 2006 08:44:48] ====================
++++++++++++++++++++++
Num of groups: 1
[1] group test with 1 members:
        [1] #user#www-0-1
----------------------
```

In the output generated by www-0-1, we can see the exact same membership—a good sign. We also notice that both daemons are aware of the existence of a group called `test` and an application that is a member of that group because we did not quit the `spuser` connection.

In this case, we probably passed most of the typical hurdles that you would encounter when starting and setting up Spread for the first time. It is possible, however, that when we start up the second Spread daemon, it will not be able to communicate with the first one. On www-0-2, you might see something like this:

```
Membership id is ( -1062675178, 1147092289)
[Mon 08 May 2006 08:44:48] --------------------
[Mon 08 May 2006 08:44:48] Configuration at www-0-2 is:
[Mon 08 May 2006 08:44:48] Num Segments 1
[Mon 08 May 2006 08:44:48]    2      10.0.0.255    4913
[Mon 08 May 2006 08:44:48]           www-0-2                         10.0.0.133
[Mon 08 May 2006 08:44:48] ====================
```

On www-0-1, the output might look like this:

```
Membership id is ( -1062675179, 1147092272)
[Mon 08 May 2006 08:44:48] --------------------
[Mon 08 May 2006 08:44:48] Configuration at www-0-1 is:
[Mon 08 May 2006 08:44:48] Num Segments 1
[Mon 08 May 2006 08:44:48]    2      10.0.0.255    4913
[Mon 08 May 2006 08:44:48]           www-0-1                         10.0.0.132
[Mon 08 May 2006 08:44:48] ====================
```

The two daemons cannot communicate with each other. Most commonly this behavior is caused by firewall restrictions. Spread needs to communicate via UDP/IP and TCP/IP on the port specified in the configuration file, as well as the port immediately above that! In the preceding example, these would be ports 4913 and 4914. By default, Spread comes configured to run on port 4803.

Alternatively, Spread may be configured to run using IP multicast by specifying a multicast address in the Spread segment. If you run into trouble while attempting to use multicast with Spread, the first step should be to independently check the multicast setup of the network. Often problems with multicast setups have nothing to do with Spread and require separate troubleshooting. Another common situation is that Spread seems to work in a setup with two daemons, but it stops working when a third daemon is added. Spread tacitly falls back from using multicast or broadcast, when they don't work, to using unicast if the configuration allows it. However, when three or more nodes are in a segment, unicast is not an option, and the network problem becomes apparent by causing Spread to stop working.

Spread comes with two other tools that are useful for troubleshooting network problems without using Spread itself at all—spsend and sprecv:

```
# make spsend
gcc -g -O2 -Wall -I. -I.   -DHAVE_CONFIG_H -c s.c
gcc -o spsend s.o alarm.o data_link.o events.o memory.o  -lnsl
fog2:~/spread-src-3.17.3 $ make sprecv
gcc -g -O2 -Wall -I. -I.   -DHAVE_CONFIG_H -c r.c
gcc -o sprecv r.o alarm.o data_link.o  -lnsl
$ ./spsend
Checking (127.0.0.1, 4444). Each burst has 100 packets, 1024 bytes each with
10 msec delay in between, for a total of 10000 packets
sent 1000 packets of 1024 bytes
sent 2000 packets of 1024 bytes
sent 3000 packets of 1024 bytes
sent 4000 packets of 1024 bytes
sent 5000 packets of 1024 bytes
sent 6000 packets of 1024 bytes
sent 7000 packets of 1024 bytes
sent 8000 packets of 1024 bytes
sent 9000 packets of 1024 bytes
sent 10000 packets of 1024 bytes
total time is (1,300054), with 0 problems
# ./spsend usage
Usage:
        [-p <port number>] : to send on, default is 4444
        [-b <burst>]       : number of packets in each burst, default is 100
        [-t <delay>]       : time (mili-secs) to wait between bursts, default 10
        [-n <num packets>] : total number of packets to send, default is 10000
        [-s <num bytes>]   : size of each packet, default is 1024
        [-a <IP address>]  : default is 127.0.0.1
# ./sprecv usage
Usage: r
        [-p <port number>] : to receive on, default is 4444
        [-a <multicast class D address>] : if receiving multicast is desirable,
                                        default is 0
        [-i <IP interface>] : set interface, default is 0
        [-d ]               : print a detailed report whenever messages are missed
```

The usage of the preceding programs is straightforward and orthogonal to Spread itself, so we will not go into details about them. However, Spread comes with another tool that is useful for both basic and advanced troubleshooting of problems: spmonitor. With

spmonitor we can view information about the current state of the Spread daemons, and
we can also cause artificial network partitions to test the robustness of our applications in
the presence of network faults:

```
#./spmonitor -n 'hostname'
=============
Monitor Menu:
-------------

        0. Activate/Deactivate Status {all, none, Proc, CR}

        1. Define Partition
        2. Send   Partition
        3. Review Partition
        4. Cancel Partition Effects

        5. Define Flow Control
        6. Send   Flow Control
        7. Review Flow Control

        8. Terminate Spread Daemons {all, none, Proc, CR}

        9. Exit

Monitor> 0


=============
Activate Status
-------------


        Enter Proc Name: www-0-1
        Enter Proc Name:
Monitor: send status query


Monitor>
============================
============================
Status at www-0-1 V 3.17. 3 (state 1, gstate 1) after 718730 seconds :
Membership : 9  procs in 1 segments, leader is www-0-1
rounds    : 18742726     tok_hurry : 3874314     memb change:      33
sent pack: 930924 recv pack : 6136167  retrans    : 1270737
u retrans: 1219986 s retrans :   50751  b retrans  :        0
My_aru   : 2560710 Aru       : 2560710  Highest seq: 2560710
Sessions :       2 Groups    :       5  Window     :      60
Deliver M: 12011390    Deliver Pk: 12479141    Pers Window:      15
Delta Mes:    146 Delta Pack:    146  Delta sec  :      10
=================================
```

Inspecting the state of a Spread daemon may provide good insight into the health of the Spread setup. The status message is sent at regular intervals until we turn it off; therefore, we can follow how the various figures change. On the first status line we notice the version of Spread that we are running and the uptime of the instance that we are looking at. The `state` and `gstate` variables should be "1" if the daemon membership is stable. We can see that we are looking at a membership that now has nine daemons in one segment (this is from a live configuration that has seven more nodes listed in its configuration). The number of rounds in the third line indicates the number of times the token has rotated around the Spread ring. The number of membership changes on the same line indicates how often we had daemons joining/leaving the system either due to crashes, restarts, or network issues. A large value there may indicate instability of the network setup. In the fourth and fifth lines of the status message we can see how many total packets were sent, received, and retransmitted, as well as a breakdown of the types of retransmissions (unicast, segment, broadcast). A high number of retransmissions may also indicate problems—a congested network, for example. Segment retransmissions (`s_retrans`) may indicate problems in the case of multisegment setups, when there are connectivity issues between two segments. The number of sessions represents the number of applications locally connected to this daemon instance; `Groups` refers to the number of groups that exist in the system, whereas the `Window` and `Pers Window` parameters define the flow control characteristics of the system—how many messages can be sent per token revolution and how many messages can each sender send when it holds the token. We can see the number of delivered messages and packets (a message may be split into multiple packets) from the start of this instance, as well as the number of messages/packets delivered in the `Delta` interval since the previous status message was sent.

We now have a Spread network running and can move on to look at the programming API used to build on our own applications.

A Practical Example

Spread provides a unified programming API available in several programming languages: C, C++, Java, Perl, Python, PHP, Ruby, and others. Detailed documentation about the C API comes distributed with Spread as man pages and is available online for the various other languages. To keep the code short, we will use the Perl interface for our example.

The application that we will use as an example of simple yet efficient usage of Spread is a distributed file cache purging daemon. Consider a file cache that is distributed across several servers. It is a common scenario that we want to either completely remove a file from the cache or replace it with a different version. In both scenarios, we first need to remove the existing version from all caches to force the caching system to refresh its local copy next time the data is needed.

To support this feature we will deploy a cache purging daemon on every cache. The daemon just waits for messages from clients requesting the purge of files that are no longer needed. Of course, we could implement this by having a client that connects to each of the cache servers and requests the purging. However, this method is cumbersome because it requires the client to know the identity of every cache server and to connect to each one of them, one by one.

Our proposed solution has all the cache purging daemons connected through Spread and joining the same group. A client that wants to request the removal of a file needs only to connect to Spread and send a message to the group that the daemons are listening to. Spread takes care of reliably passing the request along to all daemons connected to the group.

To exemplify, we present a sample implementation of the cache purging system written in Perl. First, let's have a look at the daemon outlined in Listing A.3, which we call sppurgecached.

Listing A.3 sppurgecached—**A Spread-Based Cache Purging Daemon**

```
01: #!/usr/bin/perl
02:
03: use strict;
04: use Spread;
05: use Getopt::Long;
06: use POSIX qw/setsid/;
07: use File::Find qw/finddepth/;
08: use IO::File;
09:
10: use vars qw /$daemon @group $cachedir $logfile/;
11:
12: GetOptions("d=s" => \$daemon,
13:            "g=s" => \@group,
14:            "l=s" => \$logfile,
15:            "c=s" => \$cachedir);
16: $daemon ||= '4803@127.0.0.1';
17: push(@group, 'cachepurge') unless(@group);
18:
19: close(STDIN);
20: if($logfile) {
21:   open LOGFILE, ">>$logfile" || die "Cannot open $logfile";
22: }
23: sub __log { syswrite(LOGFILE, shift) if($logfile); }
24:
25: die "You must be root, as I need to chroot" if($>);
26: die "Could not chroot" unless(chroot($cachedir) && chdir('/'));
27: # daemonize
28: close(STDOUT); close(STDERR);
29: fork && exit; setsid; fork && exit;
30:
31: sub removenode {
```

```
32:    return if /^\.{1,2}$/;
33:    -d $_ ? rmdir($_) : unlink($_);
34: }
35:
36: while(1) {
37:    my ($m, $g);
38:    eval {  # We eval so we can catch errors and reconnect.
39:       ($m, $g) = Spread::connect( { spread_name => "$daemon",
40:                                    private_name => "scpd_$$" } );
41:       die "Could not connect to Spread at $daemon" unless $m;
42:       die "Could not join" unless(grep {Spread::join($m, $_)} @group);
43:       __log("Connected to spread: $daemon\n");
44:       while(my @p = Spread::receive($m)) {
45:          if(@p[0] & Spread::REGULAR_MESS()){
46:             chomp(my $victim = @p[5]);
47:             __log("[@p[1]] purges $victim\n");
48:             if(-d $victim) {
49:                # For directories, we recursively delete
50:                finddepth( { postprocess => \&removenode,
51:                             wanted => \&removenode,
52:                             no_chdir => 1 }, $victim);
53:             } else {
54:                unlink($victim);
55:             }
56:          }
57:       }
58:    };
59:    __log($@) if($@);
60:    Spread::disconnect($m) if($m);
61:    sleep(1);
62: }
```

The cache purging daemon connects to a Spread daemon and then joins the designated group (lines 39–43). The Spread::connect call specifies the address of the daemon that the application connects to as well as a private name by which the application will be identified. The private name must be unique per the Spread daemon. By default, our application assumes that the Spread daemon runs on the standard Spread port on the local host. The group that the spcachepurged daemons listen to is cachepurge, but another group name can be specified using the -g command-line option (lines 16–17). Because our program is supposed to remove files at request, we also make sure that it can only do so within the designated cache directory (lines 25–26).

The daemon then starts listening for messages by calling the blocking Spread::receive call. The receive call reads both regular messages and membership change notifications, but for the current application we are only interested in REGULAR (data) messages (lines 44–45). After a message is received, we check its payload and attempt to remove the file whose name was sent (lines 46–55). The daemon then goes back to listening for another request.

Now let's have a look at the sample client on Listing A.4 that connects to the daemon and requests the purge of a file from the distributed cache.

Listing A.4 `spcachepurge`—**A Simple Local Area Spread Configuration**

```perl
01: #!/usr/bin/perl
02:
03: use strict;
04: use Spread;
05: use Getopt::Long;
06: use vars qw /$daemon $group/;
07:
08: GetOptions("d=s" => \$daemon,
09:           "g=s" => \$group);
10: $daemon ||= 4803;
11: $group  ||= 'cachepurge';
12:
13: my ($m, $g) = Spread::connect( { spread_name => "$daemon",
14:                                  private_name => "scp_$$" } );
15: die "Could not connect to Spread at $daemon\n" unless($m);
16:
17: if(!@ARGV) {
18:   print STDERR "$0 [-d spread] [-g group] file1 ...\n";
19:   exit;
20: }
21: while(my $file = shift) {
22:   Spread::multicast($m, RELIABLE_MESS, $group, 0, $file);
23: }
24: Spread::disconnect($m);
```

The client's sole purpose is to inform the cache daemons about the files that it needs deleted. Because we want to avoid cache inconsistencies, the request needs to be reliably delivered to all cache daemons. The client needs to be able to communicate to the spcachepurged daemons that are listening on a dedicated Spread group; therefore, we provide the clients with the option of specifying the Spread daemon that they need to connect to and the name of the group that the daemons are listening on. In a standard configuration the spcachepurge client is being run on one machine in the cluster. Therefore, by default, we set the $daemon variable to connect to the standard Spread port 4803 (line 10). The syntax used for specifying the Spread daemon is the same as the one used to start a Spread daemon. If the client is running on a machine without a Spread daemon, we can specify the proper daemon address: ./sppurgecache -d port@ip. The default communication group can also be overruled by using the -g parameter.

First the client connects to the Spread daemon (lines 13–15); then, for each file passed as an argument, it broadcasts a reliable message to the cache group. Because the message is broadcast using the RELIABLE delivery guarantee, all daemons listening to the group will remove the requested file.

This example shows the convenience and efficiency of using the right tool. However, the solution is not as perfect as it appears. Even though we send the purge request as a RELIABLE message, it is possible that one of the purge cache daemons, or its corresponding Spread daemon, was crashed at the time the purge request was made or was disconnected from the rest of the servers due to a temporary network partition. In both cases, when the cache server becomes operational, it will still have the file that was removed on the other servers. Attempting to deal with this scenario in our application is a much more difficult problem and would require both the use of the more expensive SAFE messages as well as adding additional logic into the cache purging daemons. However, this level of precaution is not necessary for an application such as the one we are describing. Instead, given the notion of a cache, we can clear the entire cache upon a restart, thereby making sure that we will serve the correct documents, paying the small price of repopulating the cache on demand.

Understanding the requirements and trade-offs of the distributed problem you are trying to solve and choosing the appropriate tool and approach for the solution is, as mentioned at the beginning of this appendix, essential for developing smart distributed applications.

Index

C

K–L

Q–R

How can we make this index more useful? Email us at indexes@samspublishing.com

T

BOOKS ONLINE
ENABLED

THIS BOOK IS SAFARI ENABLED

INCLUDES FREE 45-DAY ACCESS TO THE ONLINE EDITION

The Safari® Enabled icon on the cover of your favorite technology book means the book is available through Safari Bookshelf. When you buy this book, you get free access to the online edition for 45 days.

Safari Bookshelf is an electronic reference library that lets you easily search thousands of technical books, find code samples, download chapters, and access technical information whenever and wherever you need it.

TO GAIN 45-DAY SAFARI ENABLED ACCESS TO THIS BOOK:

- Go to **http://www.sampublishing.com/safarienabled**

- Complete the brief registration form

- Enter the coupon code found in the front of this book on the "Copyright" page

If you have difficulty registering on Safari Bookshelf or accessing the online edition, please e-mail customer-service@safaribooksonline.com.